Mothers on American television

Manchester University Press

Mothers on American television

From here to maternity

Kim Akass

MANCHESTER UNIVERSITY PRESS

Copyright © Kim Akass 2023

The right of Kim Akass to be identified as the author of this work has been asserted in accordance with the Copyright, Designs and Patents Act 1988.

Published by Manchester University Press
Oxford Road, Manchester M13 9PL

www.manchesteruniversitypress.co.uk

British Library Cataloguing-in-Publication Data
A catalogue record for this book is available from the British Library

ISBN 978 1 5261 6940 2 hardback
ISBN 978 1 5261 9118 2 paperback

First published 2023
Paperback published 2025

The publisher has no responsibility for the persistence or accuracy of URLs for any external or third-party internet websites referred to in this book, and does not guarantee that any content on such websites is, or will remain, accurate or appropriate.

EU authorised representative for GPSR:
Easy Access System Europe – Mustamäe tee 50, 10621 Tallinn, Estonia
gpsr.requests@easproject.com

Typeset by Newgen Publishing UK

*This book is dedicated to my family.
And to mothers everywhere.*

A primary role of feminism throughout history has been to challenge taken-for-granted assumptions that direct our lives. This is difficult because people don't usually notice the assumptions that underpin our everyday lives. So challenging basic assumptions is often met with resistance, partly because it makes people uncomfortable.

Amber E. Kinser, *Motherhood and Feminism* (2010)

Contents

List of figures	*page* viii
Preface	ix
Acknowledgements	xiv
Introduction	1

Part I Mothers on network television

1 Motherhood, culture and society	19
2 Motherhood on network television, 1940s to 1980s	30
3 Motherhood on network television, 1980s onwards	43

Part II Original dramas

4 *Sex and the City* (HBO, 1998–2004)	59
5 *The Sopranos* (HBO, 1999–2007)	77
6 *Six Feet Under* (HBO, 2001–5)	90
7 *Deadwood* (HBO, 2004–6)	102

Part III Adaptations

8 *The Killing* (AMC/Fox/Netflix, 2011–14)	117
9 *Game of Thrones* (HBO, 2011–19)	127
10 *The Handmaid's Tale* (Hulu, 2017–)	141
11 *Big Little Lies* (HBO, 2017–19)	154
Conclusion	166
Select bibliography	173
Index	187

Figures

4.1 'I Heart NY', *Sex and the City*, season 4, episode 18 (HBO, 2002) *page* 63
4.2 'Anchors Away', *Sex and the City*, season 5, episode 1 (HBO, 2002) 64
4.3 *Sex and the City 2* (directed by Michael Patrick King, Warner Bros Pictures, 2010) 71
4.4 Advertisement for *And Just Like That …* (HBO, 2021) 73
9.1 'The Climb', *Game of Thrones*, season 3, episode 6 (HBO, 2013) 134
9.2 'Mhysa', *Game of Thrones*, season 3, episode 10 (HBO, 2013) 136

Preface

This book was initially born out of my obsessive and fruitless search for mothers in Disney films. As I took my children to sit in darkened cinemas, I was only too aware of the dearth of mothers onscreen. Who was I to identify with while motherless heroes and heroines entertained my children? What were my children to make of a world bereft of maternal care? The brutal death of Bambi's mother, ineffectual mothering of Dumbo and Cinderella's treatment at the hands of her wicked stepmother had already scarred my childhood and I was shocked to find that the lack of motherly love was alive and well onscreen. Laura Mulvey's theory of looking within mainstream Hollywood cinema was ringing in my ears,[1] particularly her formulation of Hollywood cinema functioning as a projection of the male (patriarchal) unconscious.[2] It seemed to me that generations of children were growing up with an agenda that excluded any positive references to maternity and, in my eyes at least, demonstrated a distinct aversion to all things female. If fairy tales traditionally hinge upon the absence of any strong parent, a state of affairs that compels the young hero or heroine to embark on the (often risky) narrative journey in the first place, it does not explain why mothers are often removed from the picture altogether when they are alive and well in the original stories.[3] When maternal figures *are* allowed into the story, they are more often than not wicked stepmothers, malevolent witches or scorned and vindictive matrons. Running through a list of the matriarchs featured in Disney films, it is surprising that any mother ever allows her children to witness such vile feminine behaviour.

Disney films are only part of the story, though, if childhood fairy tales, films and books portray our mothers variously as nincompoops or monsters, leaving them out of the story or killing them off altogether, it is hardly surprising that we do not question the textual maltreatment of mothers as we grow older. Staying with film for a while, it is possible to see how this attitude towards women and motherhood has become acceptable, lauded even, with films such as Judd Apatow's *Knocked Up*, which won rave reviews and was hailed as one of the funniest comedies to come out of Hollywood in 2007.[4] To be sure, I am not part of the target young male audience, but it is still shocking that so little attention was paid to its unashamed and virulent misogyny. A kind of 'boys will be boys' approach underlies most of the reviews, with apologies all round if the critic misses the joke.[5] And even when critics do negatively review the film, little mention is made of its reprehensible attitude towards pregnancy and childbirth, a fact that led me to wonder whether there is another, more worrying kind of repression taking place here? One that is not only blind to the misogyny of Hollywood films but also oblivious to their rampant hostility towards mothers and motherhood.

If film shows little attempt to address the representation of motherhood on our screens, then surely television, as a domestic medium and targeting a female audience, should be different, particularly considering the long tradition of series featuring mothers. Thanks to soap operas, sitcoms, primetime soaps and quality American television, we have enjoyed a range of mothers in all their complex glory and television screens have become home to some of the most compelling representations of motherhood ever seen. A brief list of these women include: Carmela Soprano, whose mid-life yearning for hunky henchman Furio near-fatally undermined her maternal authority; *Weeds*' (Showtime, 2005–12) widow Nancy Botwin who supported her children by dealing drugs; *Nurse Jackie*'s (Showtime, 2009–15) Jackie Peyton snorting painkillers to get her through the day and *Desperate Housewives*' (ABC, 2004–12) Lynette Scavo who stole her son's Ritalin for an all-night costume-making frenzy. Who can forget *Mad Men*'s (AMC, 2007–15) Betty Draper, whose mothering techniques included berating her daughter for putting a plastic dry cleaning bag over her head – not for fear of suffocation, you understand, but for fear of the freshly laundered contents being spoiled? Quite a line up, and emblematic of the complex and contradictory issues that plague mothers into the twenty-first century.

Like motherhood itself, the mums on our television screens are everywhere and nowhere, centre screen and yet relegated to the margins, seen through children's and partner's eyes and rarely through their own. At the same time, and as if to reinforce negative attitudes towards motherhood, the print media has turned our mothers into maternal simulacra. It is not only the way they write about the mothers in these series that is revealing but how newspapers and magazines trade in stories of how women *should* behave once they have children, continually monitoring and criticizing them, exploiting the guilt of mothers to bolster political agendas and boost sales. As you will see in the pages that follow, mothers in a patriarchal, neoliberal, consumerist society are valued for their offspring and little else. While US birth rates remain at an all-time low, fears over women's fertility have reached an all-time high, as can be seen by the overturning of *Roe* v. *Wade* on 24 June 2022 and women's rights in general. With more women putting careers before childbirth, America is facing the consequences and looking at Japan as an example of a country whose economy is shrinking year on year along with its ageing population.[6] In 2022, the post-pandemic global recession is hitting women and families where it hurts, in their pockets, and there is less and less incentive for women to stop work and have children.

This is a very personal book for me. Having returned to study after having my first child I realized that, in society's terms, I was on my own. Without free childcare provided by parents, friends and family, I would never have been able to crawl my way back into the workplace, and even then, it has been a long and hard struggle. Having been a working, single, married and stay-at-home mother I can personally attest to the fact that women do dip in and out of these roles, adapting to the demands of various stages of life, and this despite the parlous nature of childcare and the inequality in wages that continue to this day. If I sound angry it is because

I am. It is because I believe that society should support mothers, make it easier for them to stay in work and, if they don't, pay a living wage to women, like myself, who have desperately tried to stay on the career track while bringing up two children. As far as I can see, unless we address the link between the way mothers are portrayed (whether in film or on television), how that links to their treatment in society and how that informs our economic and political positioning, we will find ourselves in a situation where women simply refuse to procreate. Without societal and representational respect mothers are being driven into a corner. I really hope that this book goes some way towards making people think about this subject, change their attitudes towards mothers, redress the imbalance that exists in society and start treating motherhood as vital to its health. It really is time to 'make people uncomfortable' and uncover the unconscious biases that control our representation. In so doing we can look to a future where, having overcome resistance, we can challenge the basic assumptions that have ruled mothers' everyday lives.[7]

Kim Akass
10 June 2022

Notes

1 Laura Mulvey, *Visual and Other Pleasures* (London and New York: Palgrave Macmillan, 1989), pp. 14–28.
2 Women in film function solely to serve the male hero as well as being sexual objects for the contemplation of the male hero and the male in the audience.
3 *Snow White* and *Aladdin* are just two examples of this.
4 'A hilarious, poignant and refreshing look at the rigors of courtship and child-rearing, with a sometimes raunchy, yet savvy script that is ably acted and directed' – see *Rotten Tomatoes*, which gave it a 90 per cent overall rating: https://tinyurl.com/3kcwsvma (accessed 10 June 2022).
5 Indeed the worst criticism levelled at the film is its use of the 'emotionally truncated language' of television sitcom. Thomas Peyser, 'Father-On Dude', *Style Weekly*, 6 June 2007, https://tinyurl.com/36xecx2z (accessed 10 June 2022).

6 Steven Malanga, 'Our Vanishing Ultimate Resource', *City Journal*, 20:1 (2010), https://tinyurl.com/rhctefs5 and, for an update, Claire Parker, 'Japan Records its Largest Natural Population Decline as Births Fall', *Washington Post*, 3 June 2022, https://tinyurl.com/yp22we6t (both accessed 10 June 2022).
7 Amber E. Kinser, *Motherhood and Feminism* (California: Seal Press, 2010), p. 9.

Acknowledgements

The first person to thank is the lovely Philippa Brewster who originally had faith in me to write this book. It's a pity that I didn't finish it before Philippa went to pastures new, but a full-time teaching job, two young children and the constant demands of higher education all got in the way. Without Philippa I would never have had the courage. Big thanks are also due to Janet McCabe who, as a partner-in-crime, made writing about American television so much fun as well as a respectable pastime. Thanks to various friends and work colleagues who have listened to me rant about the terrible way mothers are treated in the past thirty-odd years – you all know who you are. Lyndsay Duthie and Laura Mee for holding me up in the last few years we worked together. Special thanks go to Cathy Johnson and Sian Barber – from work colleagues and conference buddies to writing coaches, they have given me the support that I so desperately needed. A really big thank you goes to Dara Wittenberg for reading the first and second drafts and putting her head in the lion's mouth with editing suggestions. Lynne Omenson for keeping my writing juices going and treating my writer's block and back issues. David Bianculli also deserves a mention for encouraging me through this final write-up as well as supporting me through the past three years since my move Stateside. Douglas L. Howard has always been an enthusiastic champion. Last, but not least, I thank Matthew Frost from Manchester University Press for agreeing to publish this book after so many setbacks and Rachel Moseley whose enthusiasm for the validity of this subject gave me the energy and faith to take it over the finish line.

Acknowledgements

I am indebted to fellow travellers. Mothers that, along with me, have been on the long road of child-raising. No one could have ever told me how hard this path would be. All of the mums that have stood alongside me at the school gates have been inspirational in their approaches to mothering. Thanks to all of you. I would also like to extend my gratitude to all the other film, television and motherhood scholars that have inspired me to write about a subject that has been so under-researched. There are too many to mention here. Most of them are quoted and all of them have given me the courage to follow my obsession.

My biggest thanks are reserved for my family. The irony that I did not have time to write this book while I was mothering young children is not lost on me. Thanks to my son Daryl and daughter Caitlin for being the best children a mother could want and thanks to my daughter-in-law, Roisin, for joining our family. My most special thanks go to my husband, Jon, without him I would never have had the self-belief to make this journey – thank you for pushing me across the threshold of the Polytechnic of North London all those years ago, coaching me through my first essay while I sobbed over the keyboard, and believing in me all the way.

Introduction

We are currently living in a golden age of television: the digital explosion, streaming, time-shifting and multi-screening are all terms familiar to television viewers in the twenty-first century. In 2019 Netflix averaged 'just over one new original TV program or movie for every day' of the year,[1] HBO was slated for 20 returning and new shows in 2020,[2] and Amazon promised 17 new/returning original series.[3] Predictions that streaming services would soon overtake cinema box office spending[4] have come true with SVoD[5] subscriptions growing 'by around six billion US dollars between 2019 and 2020'.[6] The COVID-19 pandemic and enforced cinema closures sent people to streaming sites in their droves and temporarily assuaged Netflix's long-term debt issues, even though 2022 saw the streaming service under ever greater financial pressure after a loss of subscribers 'for the first time in more than 10 years'.[7] Even with the inevitable halt in television production during the global pandemic, there were still 493 series on our screens in 2020[8] and 550 in 2022.[9] Far too many for even the most die-hard television fan to watch while retaining any semblance of a normal life.

We are also living in a post-Weinstein, #MeToo, #TimesUp era, and, for many, 2017 will be remembered as the year that black was 'de rigueur' for red carpet attire of both the Oscars and the BAFTAs and where women from both sides of the screen stood up to demand equal pay and representation with their male counterparts. And yet, inequality persists in the worlds of film, television and beyond, with women's skills routinely disregarded.[10] It may be twenty-five years since *Sex and the City* first hit our screens but there is little to suggest that, in the intervening years, the glass ceiling has got any higher for women, particularly once they have children, beginning the long road of juggling childcare with a career and attempting to scale that ubiquitous maternal wall.

While this book is about the representation of motherhood in quality American television series,[11] the story starts long before and has its roots in a protracted and circuitous history. From philosopher Jean-Jacques Rousseau's philosophies about women's duties as wives and mothers,[12] through theorizations of feminist film and television scholars, to a possible reinvigorated future for feminist television theory, this book examines how motherhood has been theorized, how it has historically been culturally positioned and how this history informs the representations of maternity, motherhood and mothering in quality American television drama. In the pages that follow, and mindful of the work of Laura Mulvey who, in the mid-1970s, used psychoanalytic theory as a 'political weapon' to expose the workings of the 'patriarchal unconscious',[13] I will argue that an analysis of the representation of mothers in a selection of American television series can teach us much about the ingrained attitudes of a neoliberal western patriarchal society, how it views motherhood and the impact that has on mothers in society more broadly. The label 'postfeminist' is often used to describe the modern feminist movement (and even then, it is a hotly contested term) but, as I will argue, mothers remain in the trough of the feminist waves, waiting for economic and social equality, poised for action but left holding the baby.

Crucial to my reading of maternal representation on our television screens, and what it reveals about the inequality of women's lives, is the work that emerged from the Centre for Contemporary Cultural Studies at the University of Birmingham in the late 1960s, which focused on popular culture as central to society's struggle over meaning. For scholars such as Stuart Hall, cultural hegemony was understood not necessarily as a direct stimulation of thought or action, but dependent upon the way '[t]he dominant class sets the limits – mental and structural – within which subordinate classes "live"'.[14] Cultural hegemony's success, in Hall's formulation, is dependent upon how the subordinate class makes 'sense of their subordination in such a way as to sustain the dominance of those ruling over them'.[15] Marxist theories of class struggle, updated through the work of the Birmingham Centre and informed by Antonio Gramsci and Louis Althusser, are particularly useful in unlocking how the small, but powerfully dominant, ruling class maintains power over the masses through a mesh of ideological carriers. In this schema, class is not the only signifier and it is impossible to privilege one form of media over another or to contemplate one without considering its connection with other forms, like newspapers, magazines and films, as well as messages emanating from 'schools, businesses, political organizations, religious groups, the military' and how they and the mass media 'all dovetail together ideologically'.[16]

For feminist television scholars Charlotte Brunsdon, Julie D'Acci and Lynn Spigel, early feminist interest in television, and working within the consensus emerging from the Birmingham Centre, was a call 'to action growing out of the conviction that women's oppression was very much related to mass media representations and that change was not only urgent, but possible'.[17] Their mission was to raise awareness about 'how patriarchal ideology excluded, silenced and oppressed women'[18] and their initial investigations focused on the previously neglected and disparaged genre of soap opera and how it constructed the female viewer. While feminist theory had been marked by the work of theorists like Judith Butler who argued that gender is nothing more than a socially constructed phenomenon, early feminist television scholars looked to the audience to interrogate the social contexts within which television was viewed not only as a 'logical focus for studies on the relationship of viewers and televisual texts'[19] but also as a way of talking about how the viewing experience 'gets determined by, but also determines, a gendered sense of self'.[20]

Into the 1980s, and primetime soaps like *Dallas* and *Dynasty* (1981–9) became the focus of feminist theorists like Ian Ang whose ethnographic work studied the way women in the Netherlands viewed soaps;[21] Jane Feuer's Marxist feminist approach studied primetime soaps because of what they revealed about the 'ideological complexity and contradictory politics of US television';[22] and Christine Geraghty's work[23] was interested in the way soap operas were gradually becoming masculinized by combining 'narratives of personal relationships with "plot lines which deal more regularly with the public sphere and emphasise the male grip on themes of business and work"'.[24] The primetime soaps form a bridge between the daytime soaps and the quality television series under discussion, as they adopted 'serial narratives in traditional seasons, inflation of budgets and filmic production values' and were 'also predecessors of the current glut of must-see, "complex" (Mittel, 2015) or "quality television" (McCabe and Akass, 2007) which continue – perhaps to the extreme – the masculinisation of television'.[25]

It is worth pausing for a moment to think about this increasing masculinization of television and how the critical community has seized a primarily 'feminine' medium and re-packaged it for a male audience. A good example of this is Brett Martin's book, *Difficult Men*, which not only reduces the success of *Sex and the City* to a few lines but also describes the 'Third Golden Age of TV' as characterized by antiheroes and the complex male showrunners that created them. His hyperbolic claim that the HBO quality series have become 'the signature American art form of the first decade of the 21st century, the equivalent of what the films of Scorsese, Altman, Coppola and others had been to the 1970s or the novels of Updike, Roth and Mailer had been to the 1960s'[26] reveals much about the way women are elided from the history of film and literature as well as the quality television series under consideration. In addition, it shows us just how the male showrunner is privileged as, for Martin, these series focus on 'middle-aged men ... because middle-aged men had the power to create them'.[27]

To counter this increasing masculinization of the genre, and in order to understand the positioning of the mother within the series under consideration, I am going to focus on quality television's soap opera roots. Often described as 'high end', 'filmic' or 'complex TV', at the heart of these series is their long-standing debt to the soap opera, one of television and radio's oldest genres. What is particularly useful for my analysis is Tania Modleski's work on the centrality of the mother to the genre. Drawing on Laura Mulvey's theories on male spectatorship in cinema,[28] Modleski suggests that even the illusion of power offered to the film spectator is not available to soap opera viewers. Unable to assume a singular active identification with the 'main male protagonist' of film, soaps 'continually insist on the insignificance of the individual life' and 'present us with numerous limited egos' that deny the spectator even the illusion of power imagined by the film spectator.[29] While American television drama obviously caters to a different audience than the soaps under discussion, Modleski's formulation of the spectator of soaps as 'a sort of ideal mother'[30] is useful here. The ensemble casting that is so characteristic of these series not only offers the spectator multiple identification points, but also gives us insight into the motivations of each of the characters. Like the soap spectator, the quality television viewer is forced to tolerate characters' misdemeanours and has to extend their 'sympathy to both the sinner and victim'.[31] Being privy to such intimate knowledge of the characters' lives allows us, however powerless, to understand the motivation behind their actions as they confront obstacles and work their way towards often unpredictable outcomes. Like both the soap opera and primetime soap before it, the narrative of quality television is driven by an open-endedness that demands disruptions and inevitable suffering, and consolidates the strength of family by portraying one 'in constant turmoil and appealing to the spectator to be understanding and tolerant of the many evils which go on within that family'.[32]

If the spectator is imagined as the 'good' mother whose 'primary function' is to be sympathetic, to tolerate the foibles and errors of others' and to be forever forgiving – 'to know all is to forgive all'[33] – what about the 'bad' mother? Modleski argues that the repressed anger inevitably felt by the spectator doomed to 'sit helplessly by as her children's lives disintegrate'[34] does have an outlet. Thrust centre stage as the creator of 'surplus suffering' in the narrative is the 'bad' mother who constantly tries to control her children's lives and becomes the person that we are allowed to hate 'unreservedly: the villainess, the negative image of the spectator's ideal self'.[35] Even while we are not allowed to condemn any of the characters within the narratives 'until all the evidence is in', the disruption provoked by the villainess evokes memories of the 'bad' mother who 'tries to interfere with her children's lives' and provides the spectator with an outlet for their anger.[36] Modleski warns us that dismissing this character is a big mistake: 'The extreme delight viewers apparently take in despising the villainess testifies to the enormous amount of energy involved in the spectator's repression and to her (albeit unconscious) resentment at being constituted as an egoless receptacle for the suffering of others.'[37] Could this be a clue as to why mothers, particularly older mothers, are so often vilified in quality American television?

Modleski's work is a useful starting point in a study of possible viewing positions of the soap opera audience but, as the 'ideal mother', the viewer is offered limited pleasure and it does not explain the popularity of soaps. Ellen Seiter and Gabriele Kreutzner's work argues that Modleski's theories can be challenged by the 'possibility for *conscious* resistance to the soap opera text' (emphasis in original) and should allow for viewers positioned outside of the 'perfectly "successful" gender socialization entirely in keeping with a middle-class (and white) feminine ideal'.[38] When class, race and gender are taken into account, ethnographic research reveals that the viewership of soaps is actually a very different story. Seiter and Kreutzner argue that '[s]trongly held preferences for individual characters and dislikes for others prevented the ideal mother position as Modleski describes it from ever being fully taken up'.[39] Moreover, when it comes to the villainess, the women interviewed expressed a 'fond admiration' for her over the passive femininity of the 'ideal' mother:

> All of the women commented on their preference of strong villainesses; the younger respondents expressed their pleasure in and admiration for the powerful female characters who were also discussed in terms of transgressing the boundaries of a traditional pattern of resistance for women within patriarchy.[40]

If the villainess is considered a role model to women in the audience why do the mothers in quality American television series continue to get such short shrift? A possible answer is that the idea of women celebrating the villainess and the threatened destruction of 'the ideological nucleus of the text – the sacredness of the family',[41] is just too powerful – especially for a culture that depends upon the willingness of women to bear children and raise the next generation. By analysing the representation of motherhood on our television screens from a feminist perspective, however, we are offered a privileged insight into the role the media plays in maintaining 'the dominance of those ruling over [us]'.[42] In addition, understanding how the media and society are inextricably intertwined is vital if we are to understand why women continue to be oppressed.

Social philosopher and cultural theorist Nancy Fraser argues that in this era of neoliberalism, it is ever more urgent for feminism to re-group and move forward, as: 'No serious social movement, least of all feminism, can ignore the evisceration of democracy and the assault on social reproduction now being waged by finance capital.'[43] Fraser analyses two distinct stages of feminism. The first (encompassing both the first and second waves) fought for women's equality and made marginal progress towards political and economic parity for women; and the second, which, once women realized that they could do nothing other than ' "engender" the socialist imaginary', increasingly turned to a study of the representation of women in popular culture as a way of 'recognizing difference'.[44] For Fraser, the result has been a feminism defined by a lack of political will with an attention to identity politics that goes no further than describing women's place within a patriarchal neoliberal world. By focusing on the way women are represented, Fraser argues, the feminist battle has become one with distorted images rather than with the male-dominated industries that produced them. It seems to me that now is as good a time as any to take Fraser's call to arms seriously by understanding that 'a feminist theory worth its salt must revive the "economic" concerns of Act One – without, however, neglecting the "cultural" insights of Act Two'.[45] My study of motherhood on television is determined not to 'throw the baby out with the bath water' but to unite text with context in an effort to understand what we can learn from our mothers on television and how we can wield that knowledge politically.

With this in mind, Part I of this book lays out a history of how motherhood is positioned within a neoliberal patriarchal society and how this positioning finds its way onto network television screens. Chapter 1 outlines the origins of many of the motherhood 'norms' that we have grown to accept and how they have been consolidated through the years. This discussion of the mother and her positioning in society looks at the many ways that motherhood, or even the prospect of it, has historically been used economically, politically and culturally to discriminate against women. Chapters 2 and 3 offer a history of the mother on network television. Moving from the late 1940s up to the early twenty-first century, these two chapters argue that mothers have enjoyed a central role in the development of television history. While these chapters are about the representation of the television mothers and their relation to political and cultural change over the years, what is clear is that the soap opera and sitcom are two genres that focus on the family and prominently feature mothers. What is particularly interesting is how the sitcom is saturated in 1950s nostalgia which is, as Stephanie Coontz tells us, misleading as many mothers worked outside the home to supplement the family income. Nevertheless, this representation of American family life has become a powerful part of America's television history and provides a context to the discussion of the quality television sitcom that comes next.

Chapter 4 focuses on the representation of motherhood in *Sex and the City* (1998–2004). Screened at a pivotal moment in the emergence of HBO onto the global market, *Sex and the City* caught the attention of critics and viewers alike. Central to the series were four single Manhattanites, Carrie Bradshaw (Sarah Jessica Parker), Miranda Hobbes (Cynthia Nixon), Charlotte Yorke (Kristin Davis) and Samantha Jones (Kim Cattrall) as they lived lives of singledom and sampled the pleasures of New York man- (and occasionally woman-) hood. While none of the women have relationships with their own mothers,[46] by season four motherhood becomes central to the narrative. Miranda's surprise pregnancy and subsequent attempts to juggle her career, her friends and her sex-life as a single parent teaches us much about how this millennial woman negotiates motherhood in a culture that so firmly works to keep mothers in the home. In this chapter I argue that, regardless of whether the *Sex and the City* women can be claimed for feminism or not, in their focus on sex, shoes and shopping, most of the critical community missed the revolutionary potential of Miranda's mothering. Is this a deliberate elision of women's experience in an era embroiled in the media's mommy wars or is it symptomatic of a culture obsessed with the idealized mothers of network television?

Part II turns to the original dramas that launched HBO and the spectre of the terrible mother that haunts them. Chapter 5's focus is on *The Sopranos* (1999–2007), a series which stands, according to Mark C. Rogers, Michael Epstein and Jimmie L. Reeves, 'at the epicenter of a shift in the economic organization of the television industry'.[47] As such, *The Sopranos* has come to define HBO's move into the global television landscape and has become the series that most fully articulates HBO's brand equity on the global stage. Tony Soprano's (played by James Gandolfini) relationship with his mother was central, a fact not lost on commentators who described the mother/son relationship as: 'as the dark heart of *The*

Sopranos. ... Livia Soprano is the most terrifying character on a show populated with ruthless, cold-blooded killers – a manipulative monster in the guise of a doddering old lady'.[48] That Livia Soprano (Nancy Marchand) was based on David Chase's own mother was endlessly remarked upon at the time and, while the death of Nancy Marchand cut short her role, Livia's spirit lived on through Tony's therapy sessions with Dr Jennifer Melfi (Lorraine Bracco), a relationship that structured the entire *Sopranos* narrative.

The next two chapters consist of articles that have appeared elsewhere.[49] The inclusion of these previously published articles, albeit somewhat re-written, is deliberate. The subject of Chapter 6 – Alan Ball's first series written for television, *Six Feet Under* (2001– 5) – centres on another middle-aged mother, Ruth Fisher (Frances Conroy), who finds herself at the centre of a family of adult children after the sudden death of their father Nathaniel (Richard Jenkins) on Christmas Eve. This series offers us the opportunity to observe a grieving woman beset by the challenge of mothering her adult children. What happens to mothers at the heart of a family that, on the surface at least, no longer needs her? Ruth is another version of the post-menopausal maternal figure so vividly described in Philip Wylie's *A Generation of Vipers*[50] but, this time, the portrayal of the older mother is much more sympathetic. While David Chase's creation, Livia, is portrayed as maternity gone sour, Alan Ball's Ruth is a far more complex and sensitive portrayal of the complexities of middle-aged motherhood.

There are few women in the town of Deadwood, and even fewer mothers, and yet *Deadwood* (HBO, 2004–6) offers us a portrait of motherhood unlike any other. In Chapter 7 we learn that, if women are traditionally the civilizing force in the Western genre, then Deadwood, a mining town outside the rule of law, is innately and totally uncivilized – the West has never looked so Wild. David Milch's claim of historical verisimilitude, however, becomes increasingly problematic in the light of Al Swearengen's (played by Ian McShane) backstory. What is so compelling about this series, especially in this look at motherhood, is how it includes an event that overtly sexualizes Swearengen's relationship with his mother. This chapter argues that, in one short scene, much is revealed about the patriarchal unconscious and how it silences while simultaneously sexualizes the maternal.

Part III of the book turns away from HBO originals and focuses on adaptations. If the 1990s was a decade in which we saw the 'final moment in the age of television' when 'the centre of gravity of American popular television shifted away from the broadcast networks and towards the basic cable sector',[51] then it is clear that we are now at another transformational shift in viewing practices. Cable channels are losing audiences to Internet streaming sites as 'more than three-quarters (78%) of all US households has a subscription-video-on-demand service'.[52] Branding in this era is not only 'a powerful and commercially important strategy' but it enables television networks 'to compete efficiently in an increasingly crowded marketplace by creating strong, distinctive and loyal relationships with viewers'.[53] A strategy that has become increasingly vital as AT&T (which acquired Time Warner three years ago) agreed a deal in May 2021 to combine its streaming service, WarnerMedia, with Discovery to 'create a content powerhouse spanning Warner Bros film and TV … the HBO network … and Discovery's stable of reality-TV shows'.[54] With Amazon buying MGM in an US$8.45 billion deal the same month,[55] the stage is set for another era of multimedia conglomerate takeovers in the streaming wars in a concerted effort to combat the domination of Netflix. With this fierce competition and the rise of cord-cutting[56] in the US, the battle for acquisition has never been fiercer.

With the stakes becoming ever higher, Christine Conley's 2014 prediction that 'we're seeing more remakes and format adaptations because there simply aren't enough writers available to develop original programming'[57] has become even more apposite. With streaming services 'dropping' whole series onto their platforms, allowing viewers to binge-watch outside of the schedules, original content is a scarce and valuable commodity. This final part of the book will argue, through a study of some recent television adaptations, that the portrayal of motherhood, regardless of the original source story and how many women are involved in production, becomes subsumed by the patriarchal attitudes of the mass media and its (mainly) male executives. Chapter 8 is a substantially re-worked discussion of the adaptation of the Danish series *Forbrydelsen* (DR/ZDF Enterprises, 2007–12) to *The Killing* (AMC/Fox/Netflix, 2011–14). What is so interesting about this adaptation is that, having been cancelled and re-commissioned three times, its final series became a solo project for Netflix. Even with the loss of viewers, Netflix clearly thought that *The Killing* would attract subscribers, after all, a small audience is better than none. It is this final season that culminates in a startling hostility towards working mothers only hinted at previously, and this despite the creative input of its female showrunner, Veena Sud. How can we understand the overt disparagement of the mother in this final series and what can we make of the fact that not one critic mentioned this?

Chapter 9 turns to the adaptation of books to television with a specific focus on George R. R. Martin's *A Song of Ice and Fire*. HBO's *Game of Thrones* (2011–19) certainly exasperated and infuriated women in equal measure for its depiction of a misogynist world where rape is commonplace. And yet, for many, this fantasy world where women are valued only for their bodies and reproductive capacity is as enthralling as it is appalling. Martha Nussbaum's incisive assessment of the series tells us: ' "Game of Thrones" is elementally concerned with the way that meaningful consent dissolves when female bodies are treated as currency. War means raping the enemy's women; princesses go for a higher price, because their wombs are the coin of the realm, cementing strategic alliances.'[58] In this chapter I will argue that *Game of Thrones*' attitude towards its female characters is symptomatic of the commodification of wombs in patriarchal culture. As if to emphasize women's lack of agency, it is not just that their only significance is in the children they bear and their relationships to them, but that even the modicum of power given them in the source novels is nowhere to be seen in HBO's adaptation. My question here is, even with Martin as executive producer, what does this reveal about the television industry and who controls representation?

Unfortunately, there is a natural progression from the trade in wombs in *Game of Thrones* to Hulu's adaptation of *The Handmaid's Tale* (2017–). Originally published in 1985 when Republican and ex-B-list actor Ronald Reagan was president, Margaret Atwood's book tells of a world where civil war, climate change and pollution has decimated fertility. Gilead is a nation ruled by religious fundamentalists who deny women any of their basic rights and the few remaining fertile women are traded between Commanders in order to be impregnated by them. Once they have given birth they are removed from the household, given to another Commander and forced to endure the same humiliations. Known only by their Gileadean patronymic names – Offred (Of Fred), Ofwarren (Of Warren) – the women are policed by each other in a patriarchal dystopia where they are prohibited from reading, writing or earning their own money. It is clear that *The Handmaid's Tale* easily lends itself to a book on the way motherhood is represented on television but while it warns of a country where women are regarded as merely vessels of reproduction, the question remains, particularly in the light of the overturning of *Roe* v. *Wade*, is it Gilead or America itself that is under scrutiny?

Due to the growing international popularity of Nordic-noir series coupled with the success of showrunners like Amy Sherman-Palladino (*Gilmore Girls*, WB, 2000–7 and *The Marvelous Mrs Maisel*, Amazon, 2017–), Shonda Rhimes (*Grey's Anatomy*, ABC, 2005–, *Scandal*, ABC, 2012–18), Lena Dunham (*Girls*, HBO, 2012–17), Marti Noxon (*Dietland*, AMC, 2018 and *Sharp Objects*, HBO, 2018),[59] some television critics have claimed that there has never been such a golden age for women on television. In 2018, *The Huffington Post*'s Zeba Blay even went so far as to say that we are currently in a 'golden age of feminist TV', suggesting that we have entered an era when women have never enjoyed such exposure on our television screens.[60] However, when we move onto one of those later adaptations in Chapter 11 – *Big Little Lies* (HBO, 2017–19) – we will see that, even with a female-authored source novel and female producers, there is little difference in how mothers, particularly older mothers, are represented on television. Even though the villainess has been present throughout the final parts of this book, there are two in *Big Little Lies* – one black, one white – as if to prove that the fearful threat of the interfering mother knows no racial boundaries. In this chapter, the hopes that a move by independent filmmakers into the television arena will result in more 'feminist TV' are dashed with the crushing realization that television is still an industry that reproduces dominant (patriarchal) ideology. As 'subjects who are constituted through experience',[61] cultural attitudes, for those familiar with its constraints, become invisible over time – accepted 'norms'. What goes around comes around and, in *Big Little Lies*, it is possible to see just how invested our culture is in the demonization of the mother.

Notes

1. Gavin Bridge, 'Netflix Released More Originals in 2019 than the Entire TV Industry did in 2005', *Variety*, 17 December 2019, https://tinyurl.com/2p9dpchk (accessed 27 May 2022).
2. Ben Travers, '20 HBO Original Programs to be Excited about in 2020 – "The Outsider," "Perry Mason," and More', *Indiewire*, 2 January 2020, https://tinyurl.com/47mj93sx (accessed 25 June 2021).
3. Kevin Webb and Mara Leighton, '17 Critically Acclaimed Amazon Prime Video Original Shows to Add to Your Streaming Queue', *Business Insider*, 21 May 2020, https://tinyurl.com/mryd24w4 (accessed 27 May 2022).
4. Mark Sweney, 'Netflix and Amazon "will overtake UK cinema box office spending by 2020"', *Guardian*, 14 June 2017, https://tinyurl.com/2x9xrkbc (accessed 27 May 2022).
5. Subscription Video on Demand.
6. *Statista.com*, 'Consumer Spending on Digital Home Entertainment in the United States from 2012 to 2020 by Type', https://tinyurl.com/5b3x9tcj (accessed 27 May 2022).
7. Jessica Bursztynsky and Sarah Alessandrini, 'Netflix Closes Down 35% Wiping More than $50 Billion Off Market Cap', *cnbc.com*, 20 April 2022, https://tinyurl.com/2eth4k3v (accessed 28 May 2022).
8. Daniel Holloway, 'Number of Scripted TV Shows Declines in 2020, FX Says', *Variety*, 29 January 2021, https://tinyurl.com/25bmkr59 (accessed 27 May 2022).
9. Shane Romanchick, 'Here's Why You Can't Keep Up With TV Anymore; 550 Original Series Aired in 2021', *collider.com*, 15 January 2022, https://tinyurl.com/3umaenbt (accessed 28 May 2022).
10. Martha Lauzen, 'Boxed In: Women On Screen and Behind the Scenes in Television in 2019-20', 2020, p. 1, https://tinyurl.com/5n7c2eac (accessed 20 April 2022).
11. There is still debate about the correct term for these series. 'High End', 'Quality' and 'Complex' are just three. I am going to refer to the series in this book as simply 'quality television' or 'quality American television'.
12. Jean-Jaques Rousseau, *Emile* (Las Vegas: IAP 2009).
13. Laura Mulvey, *Visual and Other Pleasures* (London and New York: Palgrave Macmillan, 1989), p. 14.
14. Stuart Hall, 'Culture, the Media, and the "Ideological Effect"', in Stuart Hall and David Morley (eds), *Essential Essays, Volume 1* (Durham, NC: Duke University Press, 2019), p. 318.
15. *Ibid*.

16 James Lull, *Media, Communication, Culture: A Global Approach* (Ithaca, NY: Columbia University Press, 1995), p. 62.
17 Charlotte Brunsdon, Julie D'Acci and Lynn Spigel, 'Introduction', in Charlotte Brunsdon, Julie D'Acci and Lynn Spigel (eds), *Feminist Television Criticism: A Reader* (Oxford: Clarendon Press, 1997), p. 5.
18 Janet McCabe and Kim Akass, 'Feminist Television Criticism: Notes and Queries', *Critical Studies in Television*, 1:1 (2006): 108.
19 McCabe and Akass, 'Feminist Television Criticism', 109.
20 *Ibid.*
21 Ian Ang, *Watching Dallas: Soap Opera and the Melodramatic Imagination* (London: Routledge, 1985).
22 Jane Feuer, *Seeing Through the Eighties: Television and Reaganism* (London: BFI Publishing; Durham, NC: Duke University Press, 1995), p. 2.
23 Christine Geraghty, *Women and Soap Opera: A Study of Prime Time Soaps* (Cambridge: Polity Press, 2019).
24 Christine Geraghty quoted by Elke Weissmann, 'Provocation II: Not Another Article on the *Wire*: How Hierarchies of Gender Undermine TV Scholarship and Lead to Abuse', *Critical Studies in Television*, 15:4 (2020): 403.
25 *Ibid.*
26 Brett Martin, *Difficult Men: Behind the Scenes of a Creative Revolution* (New York: Penguin Group; London: Faber & Faber, 2013), p. 11.
27 Martin, *Difficult Men*, p. 13.
28 Mulvey, *Visual and Other Pleasures*, pp. 14–28.
29 Tania Modleski, 'The Search for Tomorrow in Today's Soap Operas', *Film Quarterly*, 33:1 (1979): 14.
30 *Ibid.*
31 Modleski, 'The Search', 15.
32 Modleski, 'The Search', 14–15.
33 Modleski, 'The Search', 14.
34 *Ibid.*
35 Modleski, 'The Search', 15.
36 Modleski, 'The Search', 14.
37 Modleski, 'The Search', 16.
38 Ellen Seiter and Gabriele Kreutzner, 'Resisting the Place of the "Ideal Mother"', in E. Seiter, H. Borchers, G. Kreutzner and E. Warth (eds), *Remote Control: Television, Audiences, and Cultural Power* (Abingdon: Taylor & Francis Group, 2013), p. 237.
39 Seiter and Kreutzner, 'Resisting', p. 238.
40 Seiter and Kreutzner, 'Resisting', p. 239.
41 Seiter and Kreutzner, 'Resisting', p. 240.

42 Hall, 'Culture, the Media', p. 318.
43 Nancy Fraser, *Fortunes of Feminism: From State-Managed Capitalism to Neoliberal Crisis* (London and New York: Verso, 2015), p. 5.
44 Fraser, *Fortunes*, p. 4.
45 Fraser, *Fortunes*, p. 5.
46 Except, of course, Miranda Hobbes (Cynthia Nixon) whose mother unexpectedly dies in season four, but only after vetoing her daughter's choice of lipstick ('My Motherboard, Myself', 4:8).
47 Mark C. Rogers, Michael Epstein and Jimmie L. Reeves, '*The Sopranos* as HBO Brand Equity: The Art of Commerce in the Age of Digital Reproduction', in David Lavery (ed.), *This Thing of Ours: Investigating The Sopranos* (New York: Columbia University Press; London: Wallflower Press, 2002), p. 43.
48 Scott Von Doviak, 'The Sopranos', *Culture Vulture*, n.d., https://tinyurl.com/2p8v2bmk (accessed 27 May 2022).
49 Kim Akass, 'Mother Knows Best: Ruth and Representations of Mothering in *Six Feet Under*', in Kim Akass and Janet McCabe (eds), *Reading Six Feet Under: TV to Die For* (London: I.B. Tauris, 2005), pp. 110–20; Kim Akass, 'You Motherfucker: Al Swearengen's Oedipal Dilemma', in David Lavery (ed.), *Reading Deadwood: A Western to Swear By* (London: I.B. Tauris, 2006), pp. 23–32.
50 Philip Wylie, *Generation of Vipers* (Illinois: Dalkey Archive Press, 1996).
51 Jimmie L. Reeves, Mark C. Rogers, and Michael M. Epstein, 'Quality Control: *The Daily Show*, the Peabody and Brand Discipline', in Janet McCabe and Kim Akass (eds), *Quality TV: Contemporary American Television and Beyond* (London: I.B. Tauris, 2007), p. 83.
52 Stephanie Prange, 'Study: Nearly 80% of US Households Subscribe to Netflix, Amazon Prime and/or Hulu', *mediaplaynews.com*, 28 August 2020, https://tinyurl.com/2p9ykh56 (accessed 26 May 2022).
53 Catherine Johnson, 'Tele-branding in TVIII: The Network as Brand and the Programme as Brand', *New Review of Film and Television Studies*, 5:1 (2007): 7.
54 Mark Sweney, 'AT&T Agrees Deal to Combine WarnerMedia with Discovery', *Guardian*, 17 May 2021, https://tinyurl.com/yckecjar (accessed 20 April 2022).
55 Joan E. Solsman, 'Amazon Buys MGM, Setting up Prime Video for James Bond, Rocky to Move in', *c/net*, 28 May 2021, https://tinyurl.com/2bhcy2y4 (accessed 27 May 2022).
56 The practice of cancelling subscriptions to streaming channels – this is very common in the US.

57 Christine Conley, Working Title Films, personal communication, 25 November 2014.
58 Martha Nussbaum, ' "The Aristocrats": The Graphic Arts of "Game of Thrones" ', *New Yorker*, 30 April 2021, https://tinyurl.com/3zpt5af6 (accessed 27 May 2022).
59 Anon, 'Women Showrunners Who Are Breaking the Glass Ceiling', *WMC News & Features*, 24 September 2020, https://tinyurl.com/yve7s9rt (accessed 27 May 2022).
60 Zeba Blay, 'How Feminist TV Became the New Normal', *HuffPost US*, 18 June 2015, https://tinyurl.com/yujf4zan (accessed 27 May 2022).
61 Joan W. Scott, 'Experience', in Judith Butler and Joan W. Scott (eds), *Feminists Theorize the Political* (New York: Routledge, 1992), p. 26.

Part I

Mothers on network television

1

Motherhood, culture and society

As feminist maternal scholar, Amber E. Kinser, notes: 'Feminist writers and activists in the United States have moved at various points in history between celebrating motherhood, critiquing it, using it as leverage to gain other rights, and reconceptualizing it so that mothering can be a more empowering experience for women.'[1] Clearly, if the human race is to survive, we must continue to reproduce, but, not only does motherhood lack agency in contemporary society, there is a tension between patriarchy, feminism, society's needs and women's basic rights. How can we be good mothers within a patriarchal world that works so hard to keep us out of the workplace? What constitutes good mothering anyway? Why are mothers continually scrutinized when fathers are not? How does the representation of mothers on television impact the way motherhood is regarded in the wider culture? In order to find answers to some of these questions, this first chapter will look at the way motherhood has historically been positioned within a western patriarchal society before turning to look at how this positioning has impacted mothers in the twenty-first-century workplace as a way of laying the foundations for my discussion of the representation of motherhood on television.

The way we regard motherhood in contemporary society is rooted in the seventeenth and eighteenth centuries and in how philosophers positioned women. For many, the gendered nature of motherhood feeds into essentialist notions of 'maternal instinct', something that all women 'naturally' possess, and which consigns them to the world of emotions – the body and the family – leaving men to the rational world of industry and commerce. 'Cartesian dualism' has its roots in philosopher René Descartes' seventeenth-century works and, according to Kinser, 'has significance for feminist thought because the world of the "mind" has generally been assigned to men (of the dominant class and race) and the world of the "body" has typically been assigned to women (and also to men of lower social status)'.[2] As Kinser notes, a justification for the removal of women from public life was the fear that intellectual development would cause women's uteruses to shrivel, and '[w]hile we don't see such outlandish arguments operating today, we certainly see residual arguments that women's natural roles as mothers are their primary function and that their energies are properly channelled into the home, even if they work outside the home or attend school'.[3]

It is no coincidence that this thinking was reinforced with the split between public and private that was ushered in with industrialization. Eighteenth-century philosopher Jean-Jacques Rousseau's attitudes reinforced those of Descartes when, in 1762, he controversially published his musings on education and the relationship between the individual and society. Publicly burned on its first publication, *Emile* formulated distinctions between the gendered division of labour as well as laying out his treatise on how children should be educated within a modern western society. Writing in the throes of the industrial revolution, Rousseau makes clear that, in his opinion, and in a modern society, it is a woman's job to rear children in their early stages of childhood, as it is in this first stage of maturation that children need to be 'civilized'. As the world of emotion guides childhood until the age of twelve, for Rousseau it naturally falls to the mother to inculcate her offspring into adulthood, as '[i]f the author of nature had meant to assign [this role] to men he would have given them milk to feed the child'.[4]

From the early days of the industrial revolution, and as the separation of home and work life became more defined, mothers were increasingly confined to the home as, biologically determined, they had little room for manoeuvre and were destined to a life of domesticity and dependence upon a male breadwinner. Even if Rousseau was writing in the eighteenth century, his theories anticipated the modern bourgeois family and have become central to notions of gendering in contemporary society, particularly his idea that the subordination of women is essential for both the public and political realms to function. This state of affairs led early feminists like Mary Wollstonecraft to openly criticize Rousseau for containing women within the domestic sphere[5] and, although she sits uneasily within the canon of feminist writings, believing that women should be educated only according to their class and if they have responsibility for bringing up future generations, Wollstonecraft's writing nevertheless quite usefully set the tone for much subsequent writing about motherhood when, in 1792, she pointed to a central contradiction: 'To be a good mother – a woman must have sense, and that independence of mind which few women possess who are taught to depend entirely on their husbands.'[6] When it comes to motherhood Wollstonecraft argues that women are caught in a double-bind, they either neglect their children or spoil them, and even worse, in so doing disregard their duties towards their husband: 'the common relationship that binds the whole family on earth together'.[7] Maternal instinct for Wollstonecraft is not a natural state, it can only grow out of 'habitual exercise' and is not, as many would have us believe, innate to all women.

Part of the problem for feminism has always been that, in the face of entrenched patriarchal thinking, feminist theorists often find themselves mired in these dualisms. In order to find value in women's domestic work, for example, second-wave feminists based 'their arguments in essentialism – in their belief in natural differences between women and men'.[8] Writing in 1976, feminist and poet Adrienne Rich offered a way out of this impasse by positing the thought that the only useful way to theorize maternity within a patriarchal world is to describe motherhood and mothering as two distinct entities: '*the potential relationship* of any woman to her powers of reproduction and to children; and the *institution*, which aims at ensuring that that potential – and all women – shall remain under male control' (emphasis in original).[9] Not only does Rich's thinking release women from being intrinsically tied to their biology but it allows us to see how it is the patriarchal institution of motherhood that has historically 'ghettoized and degraded female potentialities'[10] and not the actual act of mothering itself. For feminist maternal scholar Andrea O'Reilly: 'Rich's distinction between mothering and motherhood was what enabled feminists to recognize that motherhood is not naturally, necessarily, or inevitably oppressive.'[11]

To understand how this all impacts on mothers and their representation on television, it is necessary to first understand how workplace practices continue to feed into early essentialist thinking by favouring men and, to some extent, childless women. As one of the leaders in the western world, America still has the worst maternity rights (bottom in all the Organisation for Economic Co-operation and Development countries with no right to any paid leave[12]) and sees childcare as a problem for the individual (or woman), open to the free market, a choice for those that can afford it. That this is a 'Hobson's choice' is of little interest for most as the neoliberal job market becomes ever more antagonistic towards women with children who are told that they should choose between a family or career if they are to compete equally. UK Independence Party leader, Nigel Farage, may have been berated in 2014 for his opinion that women with children are 'worth less' in the workplace than their childless counterparts because of biological 'choice'[13] but he revealed a widely held, deeply misogynist secret: that even though men and women both procreate, only women are expected to choose between family and a paid occupation.

Since industrialization, motherhood has been confined to the private sphere, separated from the male-dominated workplace and expected to be paid for by a 'family wage', a concept so ingrained that mothers continue to earn substantially less than their childless counterparts. While our child-free sisters are very slowly crawling towards fairer pay policies, mothers continue to fight the battle of unequal economic discrimination, based on their perceived inability to juggle career and childcare: 'Mothers suffer a penalty relative to non-mothers and men in the form of lower perceived competence and commitment, higher professional expectations, lower likelihood of hiring and promotion, and lower recommended salaries. This evidence implies that being a mother leads to discrimination in the workplace.'[14] As a result of this motherhood penalty women's incomes drop 30 per cent after giving birth.[15] With reduced economic power, it is little wonder that most mothers feel that feminism has passed them by as, post-childbirth, they simply replace the 'glass ceiling' with a 'maternal wall' and are often restricted to 'mommy track' jobs that see them valued less than their childless counterparts.

In addition, women continue to experience pregnancy discrimination at work with women pushed out of their jobs due to pregnancy or maternity every year,[16] with most forced to sign Non-Disclosure Agreements preventing their cases ever coming to court.[17] Research conducted by Childbirth Connection, an initiative focused on improving maternity care, estimates that over 250,000 women are denied requests to accommodate their workplace pregnancies each year.[18] The Equal Employment Opportunity Commission suggests that approximately 5,300 pregnancy discrimination claims are filed a year, a figure that has been rising each year for the past twenty, and a sum that is hardly representative with many more women too scared or impoverished to sue their American employers.[19] Despite claims that companies like Walmart, Merck and AT&T (among myriad others) actively support and empower pregnant women, in the past few years '[t]ens of thousands of women have taken legal action alleging pregnancy discrimination'.[20] It should be no surprise that the recent COVID-19 pandemic impacted even more on working mothers than fathers, with mothers forced to do most of the childcare and home-schooling regardless of whether they had a full-time job or not. In fact, this problem has become so acute that the *New York Times* reported that, in the United States, '[a]lmost 1 million mothers have left the workforce – with Black mothers, Hispanic mothers and single mothers among the hardest hit'. Despite this, according to the article's author, 'the cultural and policy response enacted at this point has been nearly nonexistent'.[21] A shameful state of affairs that prompted the Biden administration to use Equal Pay Day (24 March 2021) to issue a proclamation admitting that: 'Due in large part to the impact of the pandemic, there are 4.2 million fewer women working now than there were in February 2020.'[22]

Women's biology may have historically been used as a way of forcing them to stay home, but it is their lack of earning power and prohibitively expensive childcare that continues to work against them. Keeping women in work is not just a question of choice in the twenty-first century but an economic necessity as, in the low to middle income bracket, female employment has become increasingly vital to bolster an ever-decreasing family income and maintain living standards. Despite this, American mothers are paid 75 cents for every dollar earned by men, 'a gap that translates to a loss of $1,275 a month or $15,300 annually'.[23] As if that is not bad enough, the wage gap for non-white working mothers is even worse with black women, for example, being paid 63 cents for every dollar a white father earns.[24] In addition, the warning is that, under current conditions, the pay gap will not be closed until 2059, with working women who are just starting their career standing 'to lose a staggering $406,280 to the wage gap', and of course this is more for non-white working mothers as 'Latinas face typical lifetime losses that total over $1.1 million and for Black and Native American women, it is nearly $1 million'.[25] Add this to the extortionate cost of childcare, losing your job due to pregnancy and how men often enjoy pay hikes of 6 per cent after starting a family, while working mothers lose up to 4 per cent pay with each child,[26] and any mother could be forgiven for giving up the struggle to work post-childbirth and retire gracefully into the home. Yet the truth is, in keeping with the long history of working mothers, and despite what newspaper reports would have us believe, maternal employment remains high. Even if they have to work longer and harder to earn the same kind of money as their male counterparts, women increasingly have to work post-childbirth if they are to avoid the poverty trap.

Mindful of the parlous nature of childcare and maternity leave, and with economic and social fault-lines exposed during the COVID-19 pandemic, on 28 April 2021 President Biden's administration proposed a transformational shift. 'The American Families Plan' lays out the revolutionary ideas of Biden's administration, stating that 'unlike in past decades, policies to make life easier for American families must focus on bringing everyone along'. These 'once-in-a-generation investments' in American's future include plans to 'add at least four years of free education' to the existing provision by providing 'universal, quality-preschool to all three- and four-year olds'. In addition, the proclamation pledges that the federal government will provide 'direct support to children and families', ensuring that 'low- and middle-income families spend no more than seven percent of their income on child care'. So far, so amazing. Coupled with the promise that, to keep America competitive and in line with other nations, the federal government will create 'a national comprehensive paid family and medical leave program' and it seems like a dream come true for American mothers. Particularly when there is a guarantee of 'twelve weeks of paid parental, family, and personal illness/safe leave by year 10 of the program'.[27] We would be well-advised not to hold our breath, however, as much could happen between now and the final stages of this proposed plan in 2031 but, nevertheless, the Biden administration has acknowledged that maternity pay, high-quality affordable childcare and funded early years education are vital to the economic well-being of a nation.

We could also be forgiven for thinking that maternity pay and high-quality childcare are vital to seeing ourselves truthfully represented on television screens. For Ellie Peers, the Writer's Guild of Great Britain's General Secretary, the gender inequality in key roles within the industry impacts not only on employment of women, but if 'key creative roles on film productions are held predominantly by men ... this is influencing female representation on screen'.[28] Something that holds true for television and other creative industries. Without the incentive to tell women's stories, the media we receive is inevitably formed by the attitudes and prejudices of white male creatives and, while it is not impossible for male writers and directors to produce stories about and for women (and vice versa),[29] it is commonplace for those characters and stories to promote an unapologetically male agenda. In addition, while there are no figures related to how many mothers work within the creative industries, anecdotal evidence points to the fact that long days and seven-day working weeks are incompatible with childcare and, unless women have willing partners to take on a major caring role, mothers are effectively barred from working in the television industry. Little wonder then that stories about our mothers are inevitably told from male and single women's perspectives.

The recent rise in streaming sites and subsequent demand for content to fill them has had a positive impact on female representation, with streaming services featuring 'substantially more female protagonists than programs on cable or broadcast networks'.[30] Before we start celebrating however, 2020–1 saw a decrease of 2 per cent (down to 33 per cent from 35 per cent) of women in key roles such as creators, directors, writers, executive producers, producers, editors and directors of photography on both broadcast and cable programmes.[31] It should also be noted that the recent historic high of women working as directors of photography on broadcast television remains at only 7 per cent (6.8 per cent)[32] with 94 per cent of broadcast programmes employing no female directors of photography.[33] Additionally, the percentage of women working in key behind-the-scenes positions is still remarkably low with an increase in 2020–1 of 1 per cent to 31 per cent on broadcast television and a decrease on streaming programmes down from 35 per cent to 33 per cent.[34] When considering that 'programs with at least 1 woman creator employed substantially greater percentages of women in other key behind-the-scenes roles and featured more female characters than programs with exclusively male creators',[35] it should be no surprise that gendered inequality in representational terms is still an issue for US cable and network television.

The impact of this inequality behind the scenes is even more depressing when we see that, on broadcast television: 'Female characters experienced a precipitous decline in numbers from their 30s (39%) to their 40s (17%)'[36] and, despite the fact that 2016–17 saw broadcast programmes becoming 'more racially and ethnically diverse',[37] the latest report does not reveal the ethnicity of women behind the scenes. A quick look at the representation of women in front of the camera, however, tells us that:

> In 2020–21, 57% (56.9%) of all female characters in speaking roles were White (down 3 percentage points from 60% in 2019–20), 23% (23.2%) were Black (down 3 percentage points from 26% in 2019–20), 8% (7.5%) were Latina (up 3 percentage points from 5% in 2019–20), 9% (9.3%) were Asian (up 1 percentage point from 8% in 2019–20), 2% (1.9%) were multiracial/multiethnic, less than 1% (0.8%) were MENA5, and less than 1% (0.5%) were of some other race or ethnicity.[38]

The Geena Davis Institute tells us 'If She Can See It, She Can Be It',[39] which should be a watchword for women working behind the scenes of mass entertainment. This is a subject that feminist television scholars have, over the years, returned to repeatedly. For example, cultural studies scholar Kathryn Woodward argues that as a society our understanding of motherhood is often 'through cultural representations which present us with ideas – for example, about what constitutes good or bad mothering, or even about for whom motherhood is or is not appropriate'.[40] If it is true that the way mothering on television is portrayed offers us insight into the way mothers are politically and economically oppressed offscreen, then surely it is time for us to look beyond representation and wield that knowledge politically?

Notes

1. Amber E. Kinser, *Motherhood and Feminism* (California: Seal Press, 2010), p. 1.
2. Kinser, *Motherhood*, p. 10.
3. Kinser, *Motherhood*, p. 11.
4. Jean-Jaques Rousseau, *Emile* (Las Vegas: IAP, 2009), p. 5.
5. Mary Wollstonecraft, *A Vindication of the Rights of Women* (California: CreateSpace Independent Publishing Platform, 2014).
6. Wollstonecraft, *A Vindication*, p. 141.
7. *Ibid*.
8. Kinser, *Motherhood*, p. 18.
9. *Ibid*.
10. Adrienne Rich, *Of Woman Born: Motherhood as Experience and Institution* (New York, London: W.W. Norton & Company, 1986), p. xv.
11. Andrea O'Reilly, *Feminist Mothering* (New York: State University of New York Press, 2008), p. 3.
12. Miranda Bryant, 'Maternity Leave: US Policy is Worst on List of the World's Richest Countries', *Guardian*, 27 January 2020, https://tinyurl.com/mu52yyhu (accessed 8 June 2022).
13. Nigel Farage made this (now infamous) faux pas when he asserted at a City event in January 2014 that women who have children are 'worth less' to their employers than single, childless women as they make 'different choices, simply due to biological reasons' and choose to have families rather than a career. Peter Dominiczak, 'Nigel Farage: Mothers are Worth Less to Finance Firms than Men', *Telegraph*, 20 January 2014, https://tinyurl.com/2p9xwhuu (accessed 8 June 2022).
14. Shelley J. Correll, Stephen Benard and In Paik, 'Getting a Job: Is There a Motherhood Penalty?', *American Journal of Sociology*, 112:5 (2007): 1297–339.
15. Jessica Dickler, 'First Time Moms See a 30% Drop in Pay. For Dads, There's a Bump Up', *CNBC*, 30 April 2019, https://tinyurl.com/2kt79ra8 (accessed 8 June 2022).

16 Simon Read, 'Pregnant Women to Get More Job Protection', *BBC News*, 24 January 2019, https://tinyurl.com/yckn3sfd (accessed 8 June 2022).
17 *Pregnant Then Screwed*, http://pregnantthenscrewed.com/ (accessed 8 June 2022).
18 Nora Ellmann and Jocelyn Frye, 'Efforts to Combat Pregnancy Discrimination', *Center for American Progress*, 2 November 2018, https://tinyurl.com/3emwmjwv (accessed 8 June 2022).
19 Carly McCann and Donald Tomaskovic-Devey, 'Pregnancy Discrimination at Work: An Analysis of Pregnancy Discrimination Charges Filed with the US Equal Employment Opportunity Commission', 26 May 2021, pp. 8–9, https://tinyurl.com/22ccn2xf (accessed 8 June 2022).
20 Natalie Kitroeff and Jessica Silver-Greenberg, 'Pregnancy Discrimination Is Rampant Inside America's Biggest Companies', *New York Times*, 8 February 2019, https://tinyurl.com/3a52bnfh (accessed 8 June 2022).
21 Jessica Grose, 'America's Mothers are in Crisis: Is Anyone Listening to Them?', *New York Times*, 4 February 2021, https://tinyurl.com/ymr8edx5 (accessed 8 June 2022).
22 The White House, 'Proclamation on National Equal Pay Day', 24 March 2021, https://tinyurl.com/49umf6rw (accessed 8 June 2022).
23 Jasmine Tucker, 'The Wage Gap Has Robbed Women of Their Ability to Weather CoVid-19', *National Women's Law Center*, March 2021, https://tinyurl.com/mrx2yzrm (accessed 8 June 2022).
24 *Ibid.*
25 *Ibid.*
26 Kitroeff and Silver-Greenberg, 'Pregnancy Discrimination'.
27 Jen Psaski, 'Fact Sheet: The American Families Plan', The White House, 27 April 2021, https://tinyurl.com/2p8b94bh (accessed 8 June 2022).
28 Ellie Peers, 'Introduction', in Alexis Kreager with Stephen Follows, *Gender Inequality and Screenwriters: A Study of the Impact of Gender on Equality of Opportunity for Screenwriters and Key Creatives in the UK Film and Television Industries*, May 2018, p. 3, https://tinyurl.com/ydhrty7b (accessed 9 June 2022).
29 HBO's *Mare of Easttown* (2021) is a good example of a well-rounded portrayal of motherhood on American television. Created by Brad Ingelsby, the series stars Kate Winslet and Jean Smart as a truly sympathetic representation of three generations of mothers and daughters.
30 Martha Lauzen, 'Boxed In: Women On Screen and Behind the Scenes in Television in 2019–20', 2020, p. 1, https://tinyurl.com/5n7c2eac (accessed 20 April 2022).

31 Martha Lauzen, 'Boxed In: Women On Screen and Behind the Scenes on Broadcast and Streaming Television in 2020–21', 2021, https://tinyurl.com/4f2brdjz (accessed 27 April 2023).
32 Lauzen, 'Boxed In, 2020–21', p. 16.
33 *Ibid.*
34 Lauzen, 'Boxed In, 2020–21', p. 4.
35 Lauzen, 'Boxed In, 2020–21', p. 6.
36 Lauzen, 'Boxed In, 2020–21', p. 12.
37 Lauzen, 'Boxed In, 2019–20', p. 3.
38 Lauzen, 'Boxed In, 2020–21', p. 9.
39 *Geena Davis Institute for Gender in Media*, https://seejane.org/ (accessed 8 June 2022).
40 Kathryn Woodward, *Identity and Difference* (London, Thousand Oaks and New Delhi: SAGE, 1997), p. 240.

2

Motherhood on network television, 1940s to 1980s

October 2010 and Barbara Billingsby, the actress that played June Cleaver in *Leave it to Beaver* (CBS, 1957–63) died peacefully in her sleep at the age of ninety-four. According to the *Wall Street Journal*: 'Billingsley not only created a mold for TV moms that other actresses would follow, she also conjured up an image of infinitely patient and pearl-necklace-wearing parenthood that real-life moms would try, often with frustration, to emulate.'[1] Of course, *Leave it to Beaver* was not the only sitcom to feature that ever-smiling mother and a brief historical overview of the way mothers have been represented on US network television arguably reveals much about how the viewing experience 'gets determined by, but also determines, a gendered sense of self'.[2] For example, feminist writers like Ashley Sayeau have argued that television has, over the years, acted as 'not merely a window on the world for women, but a door to it',[3] revealing much about how women's politics and their lives intersect on US television series. Nelson persuasively argues for a political and feminist television approach, beginning with Lucille Ball on *I Love Lucy* (CBS, 1951–7), through the sitcoms of Norman Lear (*All in the Family* [CBS, 1971–9], *The Mary Tyler Moore Show* [CBS, 1970–7] and *Maude* [CBS, 1972–8], in particular) through to *Sex and the City* (HBO, 1998–2004) and, like many feminist television scholars before her, looks to television's progressive potential to describe women's cultural and societal positioning. With this in mind, a look at the history of mothers on network television reveals much about the power of the relationship between the mother's role in the home and her fictional representation.[4] While the mothers under scrutiny here often appear in sitcoms, it is the representation of mothers and their cultural and political context that is of interest here, not the situation comedy itself.

From *Mary Kay and Johnny*'s (DuMont, 1947/CBS, 1948–50) central couple that not only shared a bed (unheard of on American television) but also included Mary Kay Stearns' real-life pregnancy within the fictional world, to shows like *The Goldbergs* (CBS, 1949–51) and *Mama* (CBS, 1949–57), early sitcoms were focused on the family with a central maternal character. Looking back to this post-Second World War period, however, journalist and author Susan Faludi contends that even though women were represented as an 'angel in the home', the reality of most women's lives was often in stark contrast.[5] Despite what books like Betty Friedan's *The Feminine Mystique*[6] and our television sitcoms would have us believe, '[w]hile 3.25 million women were pushed or persuaded out of industrial jobs in the first year after the end of the Second World War ... 2.75 million women were entering the work force at the same time'.[7] Compared to the war years, however, women entered more menial jobs than ever before as public opinion on them working outside the home changed.

> The culture derided them; employers discriminated against them; government promoted new employment policies that discriminated against women; and eventually women themselves internalized the message that, if they must work, they should stick to typing ... The fifties backlash, in short, didn't transform women into full-time happy housewives, it just demoted them to poorly paid secretaries.[8]

By 1947 more women had managed to re-enter the workplace, with employment levels returning to the inter-war years, and with a greater number of women employed 'by 1952 ... than at the height of the war'.[9] According to media historians Susan Douglas and Meredith Michaels, by '1955, there were more women with jobs than at any point in the nation's previous history, and an increasing number of these were women with young children'.[10] For Faludi, the, now infamous, media backlash against feminism was fed by 'women's unrelenting influx into the job market, not a retreat to the home',[11] a claim confirmed by Judith Warner, who tells us that 'at the height of the period [which] we tend to think of as the at-home-mom Feminine Mystique years, one third of the workforce was female. About two-thirds of those working women were married, and more than half of those married women had children of pre-school or school age'.¹²

I Love Lucy was one of the first US imports to appear on British television (ITV in 1955). The show starred Lucille Ball as housewife Lucy Ricardo who, while enjoying a happy marriage to (real-life) husband Ricci Ricardo (Dezi Arnaz Jr), tried weekly (and some might say weakly) to escape a life of domesticity. Ball is famous for a whole string of television breakthroughs. Along with her husband, she formed and headed up the production company Desilu which produced the series and recorded the show in front of a live studio audience, on a fixed sound stage with a multiple camera shoot, so that coast-to-coast America could enjoy the same high standard of telecasting while also allowing for global syndication.¹³ The innovative decision to underwrite the expense of filming in exchange for retaining copyright of the series led to Ball and Arnaz becoming the most powerful couple in showbiz at that time, changed the industrial practices of network television and ensured their dominance in the television industry.¹⁴ Even wielding this amount of power, it took mammoth negotiating skills for Ball to avoid enforced maternity leave and to include her real-life pregnancy with second child Desiderio into the storyline of *I Love Lucy*. At that time, and despite the series being a runaway success, CBS personnel insisted that it was undesirable to feature a pregnant woman on television, fearing a loss of sponsorship.¹⁵ Even after gaining approval from religious groups, the powers-that-be decided that her condition could not be referred to as 'pregnancy', choosing instead to call it 'expecting' and using the French word 'Enceinte' as the episode title ('Lucy is Enceinte', 2:10). Ball timed her caesarean to coincide with the day her character gave birth in the sitcom. The ensuing publicity put the family on the first ever cover of the *TV Guide* in 1953, shot *I Love Lucy* to the top of the ratings, and ensured Lucille Ball a place in television history. Not bad for a ditzy redhead that never quite escaped her fictional life of domestic containment.

Despite the ground broken by Lucy Ricardo, countless television mothers were forever consigned, however cheerfully, to a lifetime of servitude. Married women in those early television days rarely worked and were portrayed as living a life of devoted maternal and domestic bliss. It was during this period, according to family historian Stephanie Coontz, that the image of the 'traditional family' was created from two opposing and, in many ways, mutually exclusive family ideals: the first (from the mid-nineteenth century), which favoured the strong mother–child bond; and the second (from the 1920s) focusing 'on an eroticized couple relationship, demanding that mothers curb emotional overinvestment in their children'.[16] Betty Friedan confesses to being one of the journalists that helped create this image of womanhood, which was principally 'designed to sell washing machines, cake mixes, deodorants, detergents, rejuvenating face-creams, hair tints'.[17] We should not be surprised by her observation that '[t]he hybrid idea that a woman can be fully absorbed with her youngsters while simultaneously maintaining passionate sexual excitement with her husband was a 1950s invention that drove thousands of women to therapists, tranquilizers, or alcohol when they actually tried to live up to it'.[18] Once a job was added to the mix it soon became clear that the romanticized ideal, so often used as something for mothers to aspire to, was bound to fail, especially in the light of gendered expectations that asked:

> Why ... should men with the capacities of statesmen, anthropologists, physicists, poets, have to wash dishes and diaper babies on weekday evenings or Saturday mornings when they might use those extra hours to fulfil larger commitments to their society?[19]

Of course, no such questions were asked about wasting women's skills and, despite only a decade earlier being deemed capable of holding down men's jobs while the country was at war, women were once again, by the end of the 1950s, considered capable only of domestic labour with the world of work deemed outside of their realm, or so the media would have us believe. As the career woman was slowly subsumed by her identity as wife and mother, the notion of 'togetherness' was coined by the publishers of *McCalls* in the mid-1950s and became the watchword for a happy family life. As Friedan notes, this was 'a movement of spiritual significance [used] by advertisers, ministers, newspaper editors'[20] and trod a fine line between marital bliss and co-dependence.

Back in television-land, it was not until 1962 that Lucille Ball managed to again push televisual boundaries, this time by finally breaking out of the home, getting that job and playing a widowed single mom raising two children in *The Lucy Show* (CBS, 1962–8). Despite the fact that, by the 1960s, '40 percent of women were in the work force ... almost half were mothers of school-age children ... [and] the figures were even higher for African American women',[21] Ball remains anachronistic in the 1960s television landscape as other television mothers were stuck in an impasse. Despite the progress being made by feminists in the real world, the only way our television mothers seemed to be able to break out of dull domesticity was by magic: Samantha Stephens (Elizabeth Montgomery in *Bewitched* [ABC, 1964–72]), Morticia Addams (Carolyn Jones in *The Addams Family* [ABC, 1964–6]) and Lily Munster (Yvonne de Carlo in *The Munsters* [CBS, 1964–6]) proved that, even if we were stuck in the home we could enliven things considerably if only we harnessed our magic powers and followed their weird and wacky ways. Even then it was remarkable that Samantha, who with a twitch of her nose could get most domestic jobs done, yearned only to be an ordinary housewife and mother.

Here it is worth briefly mentioning one of the least successful sitcoms of this era, NBC's *My Mother the Car*, which aired for thirty episodes, one single season, from September 1965 to April 1966. Billed as a fantasy sitcom, it is revealing of just how the unconscious of many a television writer and executive works. The premise is this – Jerry Van Dyke plays David Crabtree who, while browsing at a used car lot, sees an old jalopy – a 1928 Porter – labelled as a 'Fixer Upper'. Taking a liking to it and thinking that it might be suitable as a second family car, Crabtree gets inside. Of course, as a rein*car*nation of his mother, the car talks to him through the radio. Entitled 'Come Honk Your Horn' (1:1) the episode sees Crabtree guilt-tripped into driving the car home as his mother demands: 'Did I raise my very own son to leave his very own mother on a used car lot?' Later, his wife's incredulity peaks when he tells her that the car 'did talk to me and beg and plead to take her home'. It has to be asked why the creative team behind the show, Allan Burns and Chris Hayward, did not get the same kind of response when pitching the idea. Jerry Van Dyke's brother had much more success in *The Dick Van Dyke Show* (CBS, 1961–6). Considered one of the most successful sitcoms of all time, Dick Van Dyke starred with Mary Tyler Moore who, despite being a very traditional stay-at-home mom to son Ritchie (Larry Matthews), broke with convention and caused a mild media storm by wearing capri pants instead of the usual dresses and skirts of other sitcom mothers. Despite being risqué in her dress, however, Laura never shared a bed with husband Rob (Dick Van Dyke), a strict network rule that neatly sidestepped the issue of motherhood and sexuality even if it did lead many to ponder methods of conception.

Whereas the 1950s have been immortalized as a period when families attempted to create a post-war idyll, the 1960s were characterized by violent uprisings and images of war which, for the first time in television history, were beamed straight into living rooms. American network television turned to more socially relevant programming as it became impossible for executives and creators to ignore the tumultuous events of the decade. The Vietnam War, the assassinations of John F. Kennedy (22 November 1963), Dr Martin Luther King Jr. (4 April 1968) and, only two months later, Robert F. Kennedy (5 June 1968) led to riots in over one hundred American cities[22] and, coupled with the turning of opinion against the Vietnam War, the nation was engulfed in an outpouring of grief. Primetime television found itself trying to perform an increasingly difficult balancing act as network executives attempted to package dramatic politicized youth culture without subverting and alienating traditional middle-class, capitalist, post-war norms. The rise of broken families in the late 1960s, due in part to the introduction of the 'no-fault' divorce in 1969[23] and the subsequent decline in notions of the traditional family, led to portrayals of what would become known as the 'blended family'. *The Brady Bunch* (CBS, 1969–74) is a good example of network television trying to come to terms with what could happen in an increasingly fractured and fracturing society. American networks were still reluctant to allow divorcées onscreen and the series never revealed what had happened to the father of Carol Brady's (née Martin, played by Florence Henderson) three daughters. Nevertheless, the conjoining of Carol's and widower Mike Brady's (played by Robert Reed) families represented a break away from the past, chipped away at familial stereotypes and, for many, was considered the last of the old-style family sitcoms.

In the late 1960s NBC screened *Julia* (1968–71) starring Diahann Carroll as Julia Baker – the first television sitcom to feature a black single mother. Topically, Julia's husband had been killed in the Vietnam War and, much to six-year-old son Corey's (played by Marc Copage) chagrin, his mother is forced to find work to support them. Leaving Corey alone in the apartment, Julia suffers the opprobrium of a neighbour, prompting her son to ask why she can't get a husband instead of a job ('Mama's Man', 1:1). The series may be remembered as ground-breaking but it was far from unproblematic at the time with Diahann Carroll herself remarking on the invisibility of women of colour in the world of television:

> With black people right now, we are all terribly bigger than life and more wonderful than life and smarter and better – because we're still proving ... For a hundred years we have been prevented from seeing accurate images of ourselves and we're all overconcerned and overreacting. The needs of the white writer go to the superhuman being. At the moment we're presenting the white Negro. And he has very little Negroness.[24]

In terms of television history *Julia* ensured that, by the end of the 1960s, our televisual mothers were beginning to edge their way out of the June Cleaver mould forever.

Perhaps one of the most famous single parents of this era, to David Cassidy fans at least, was the working mother of five, Shirley Partridge (Shirley Jones) in *The Partridge Family* (ABC, 1970–4) who proved that it was possible to successfully combine single motherhood with a musical career. The first season episode 'My Son, The Feminist' (1:12) must be instrumental in the feminist awakening of a generation of teenage girls when the group are booked to sing at a POW (Power of Women) event. Not everyone is happy with the idea of a junior 'women's liberation' event taking place at the local high school but Keith Partridge (David Cassidy) is coerced into appearing by his girlfriend, Tina (Jane Actman). The episode revolves around debates on women's equality, censorship and freedom of speech. Coming so close to the events of 1968, the uprising of the Civil Rights Movement and second-wave feminism, the episode is striking in its overtly political tone.

Paul Wells suggests that the sitcom is often ideologically progressive, a place where challenging ideas and images can be 'smuggled in' under the guise of humour,[25] and Tina's description of the family as a site of oppression for women is radical for the time, particularly in a network sitcom aimed at teenagers. Tina tells the assembled family: '[W]omen are discouraged from having careers. We're supposed to get married, become housewives and sit around waiting for the babies to come.' Getting into her stride, she adds: 'The family unit is decadent. It's only pleasurable and beneficial to the husband.' Even after being told by Shirley Partridge that she may want to wait until she has a family before making speeches about it, Tina's retort, '[t]he family unit dehumanizes a woman. It makes her nothing more than a drudge and a childbearer', could have come straight from the second-wave feminist manifesto. To be sure, *The Partridge Family* could never be anything other than fantastic with teen heartthrob David Cassidy as lead singer in the family band but, with speeches like Tina's and Shirley Partridge at the centre of the family, *The Partridge Family* was an unexpected standard-bearer for mothers working outside the home.

The 1970s were noteworthy for being the decade that the networks attempted to respond to social shifts while appealing to a 'quality' demographic – young, urban, educated and high-earning audiences. This period is dominated by sitcoms produced by two independent production companies: MTM, who made their name through *The Mary Tyler Moore Show* (CBS, 1970–7) and Tandem/TAT who, helmed by Norman Lear, became famous for their working-class and socially relevant sitcoms. While the MTM writer's room is credited as the springboard for the quality television series that came after it, it was *The Mary Tyler Moore Show* that is remembered by viewers.[26] Mary Richards (Mary Tyler Moore) was originally intended to be a divorcée herself but, coming fresh out of *The Dick Van Dyke Show*, television executives worried that viewers would think she had divorced the incredibly popular Dick Van Dyke. To avoid this issue, the first episode shows Mary breaking up with her boyfriend Bill (Angus Duncan) after her move to Minneapolis, thus neatly sidestepping any issues of divorce and Van Dyke ('Love is All Around', 1:1). *The Mary Tyler Moore Show* ran for seven years and, for many, is the epitome of a second-wave feminist television show and one of the first workplace sitcoms. Despite having boyfriends, the mainstays of the series were Mary's relationships with neighbour Rhoda Morgenstein (Valerie Harper), landlady Phyllis Lindstrom (Cloris Leachman) and her work colleagues Lou Grant (Ed Asner), Murray Slaughter (Gavin MacLeod) and Ted Baxter (Ted Knight).

Just one year later and the Norman Lear years sprang to life with *All in the Family* (CBS, 1971–9), a sitcom originating in the UK as *Till Death Us Do Part* (BBC, 1965–80) and re-written to accommodate the social and political mores of American society. *All in the Family* was ground-breaking and gritty, showed the generation gap in all its glory and featured hapless Edith Bunker (Jean Stapleton) who, despite being at the sharp end of her husband Archie's (played by Carroll O'Connor) insults, does her best to keep the peace between him, daughter Gloria (Sally Struthers) and son-in-law Michael 'Meathead' Stivic (Rob Reiner). Animating the real-life generation gap between baby boomers and their 1950s parents, *All in the Family* provided an antidote to the utopian vision of the traditional ever-smiling middle-class mother gladly serving her family and featured such memorable moments as Gloria being fired for being pregnant ('Mike Faces Life', 7:7). Being screened in 1975 it was three years before the Pregnancy Discrimination Act was passed in the United States (1978), and it highlighted an issue that continues to face many women today.

It was through a guest appearance on *All in the Family* that Maude Findlay, cousin to Edie (played by Bea Arthur), was introduced to the American public and was soon starring in her own series, *Maude* (CBS, 1972–8). Arch-enemy of Archie, Maude is a liberal, feminist, upper-middle-class, four times married, middle-aged mother who visits the Bunkers, against Archie's will, to support Edie who is struggling to look after the family during a 'flu outbreak ('Cousin Maude's Visit', 2:12). In no time at all battle lines are drawn as Maude, the polar opposite of the Republican blue-collar misogynist Archie, makes clear her antipathy to everything Archie holds dear. Maude's next appearance is in the back-door pilot 'Maude' (2:24) at daughter Carol's (played by Marcia Rodd) wedding. This episode sees the complexities of Maude's life laid bare. Not only has she buried two husbands and is married to a fourth, Walter (Bill Macey), but live-in daughter Carol, already a divorcée with an eight-year-old son, Philip (Brian Morrison), is prospective bride to a man who reveals himself to be such a misogynist that she refuses to marry him on the eve of their wedding. Only ten minutes into the episode and Maude's family configuration has single-handedly destroyed any illusion of the domestic bliss portrayed in early sitcoms.

Maude was, for many reasons, even more controversial than *All in the Family*. Not only was the titular character a liberal feminist, but she was outspoken and, partway through the first season, found herself pregnant at the age of forty-seven – something never seen before on network television ('Maude's Dilemma', Parts 1 & 2, 1:9 and 1:10). First screened in November 1972, the double episode sees Maude debating the many issues around pregnancy termination. As her daughter and husband point out, abortion is now legal in New York, although it would be two more months before *Roe v. Wade* was passed in the United States (in 1973). For Carol it is clear-cut, there is no need for Maude to have a baby at her age – she tells her mother that a termination is 'as simple as going to the dentist'. After all, it isn't just that Maude and Walter are worried about being the 62-year-old parents of an Eagle Scout, as Maude acerbically remarks but, as neighbour Arthur Harmon, a doctor, warns, 'pregnancy at her age carries risks'. Part 2 not only revolves around Maude's decision to have an abortion but Walter's avoidance of a vasectomy. Clearly pregnancy is not merely a female problem in this household and, despite Walter worrying about the procedure, he tells Maude: 'I never wanted to become a father before, why should I want to become one later on? ... I'm happy to become a father because you want to have a baby, not because I want to become a father.' A confession that allows Maude to decide that, despite being happily married, having a surprise baby at forty-seven is not desirable for her or her family.

Maude is certainly not typical of the kind of mothers represented on network television but, as the 1970s progressed, there was a steady increase in the representation of mothers working outside the home. *Family Ties* (NBC, 1982–9) is notable in this period for attempting to bridge the divide between the left-leaning Lear-era sitcoms with all their gritty realism and the new decade of right-leaning Reaganite policies. Despite being sold to the NBC with the pitch 'hip parents, square kids',[27] by episode four the series had begun to focus on Michael J. Fox's character, the Reaganite Alex P. Keaton, and left his mother Elyse (played by Meredith Baxter-Birney) in the background. The show that had originally planned to revolve around the ex-hippie liberal parents and the problems of childrearing without boundaries soon left the parents on the sidelines with the focus skewed onto their more conservative offspring.

By the time the mid-1980s hit, the 'have-it-all' mother was firmly entrenched in both visual and printed media. The meteoric rise of lifestyle guru, Martha Stewart, who published no less than eleven books during the decade, confirmed what every mother was being told, that if you worked hard enough and long enough you could successfully continue your career and combine motherhood with the ability to earn as much as your husband – all that was needed was the instruction manual, superhuman strength and good childcare. *The Cosby Show* (NBC, 1984–92) was not only television's fourth longest running series to date, but it 'changed the face of American television and set a new standard for representing African American families in non-stereotyped roles'.[28] Phylicia Rashad starred as Clair Huxtable, a successful lawyer and happily married mother of five who must surely go down in television history for raising the bar to unnatural heights for superwomen everywhere. Not only did she negotiate a high-flying law career, but successfully raised five children at the same time. True, their oldest child was already twenty when she first made an appearance halfway through season one, but with three teenagers and a five-year-old, Clair Huxtable was surely the epitome of the 1980s have-it-all heroine. Despite accusations that the Cosbys were, like Julia before them, hardly representative of the majority of African American families, Phylicia Rashad is spirited in the series' defence, arguing that it is just as realistic to portray middle-class black neighbourhoods with a doctor and a lawyer living in the same house as it is to feature black working-class households. For Rashid, if people do not believe that they exist, 'Well, they didn't grow up in my community.'[29]

As the have-it-all 1980s ended, network television would become more political than ever. The next chapter looks to the 1990s and beyond to see how motherhood and representation changed.

Notes

1 WSJ Staff, 'Barbara Billingsley, June Cleaver on "Leave It To Beaver", Dies at 94', *Wall Street Journal*, 16 October 2010, https://tinyurl.com/2p97v3ke (accessed 8 June 2022).
2 *Ibid.*
3 Ashley Sayeau, 'As Seen on TV: Women's Rights and Quality Television', in Janet McCabe and Kim Akass (eds), *Quality TV: Contemporary American Television and Beyond* (London: I.B. Tauris, 2007), p. 53.

4 A more in-depth study of feminism and the sitcom can be found in Bonnie J. Dow's *Prime-Time Feminism: Television, Media Culture, and the Women's Movement Since 1970* (Philadelphia: University of Pennsylvania Press, 1996).
5 Susan Faludi, *Backlash: The Undeclared War Against Women* (London: Chatto & Windus/Vintage, 1992), p. 74.
6 Betty Friedan, *The Feminine Mystique* (New York: W.W. Norton, 1963).
7 Faludi, *Backlash*, p. 74.
8 Faludi, *Backlash*, p. 75.
9 *Ibid.*
10 Susan J. Douglas and Meredith W. Michaels, *The Mommy Myth: The Idealization of Motherhood and How It Has Undermined Women* (New York: Free Press, 2005), p. 34.
11 Faludi, *Backlash*, p. 75.
12 Judith Warner, *Perfect Madness: Motherhood in the Age of Anxiety* (New York: Riverhead Books, 2005), p. 137.
13 Leigh Allen, 'Filming the *I Love Lucy* Show', *American Cinematographer*, 1 April 2020, https://tinyurl.com/mt9b2fvb (accessed 8 June 2022).
14 *Ibid.*
15 Despite *I Love Lucy* often being cited as the first sitcom to ever feature pregnancy that accolade must go to *Mary Kay and Johnny*, the first sitcom to be shown on network television in the United States. However, the show was not recorded and the writing-in of Mary Kay's real pregnancy and subsequent introduction of her son into the storyline remains only in production notes, scripts and in interviews with the couple.
16 Stephanie Coontz, *The Way We Never Were: American Families and the Nostalgia Trap* (New York: HarperCollins/Basic Books, 1992), p. 9.
17 Friedan, *Feminine Mystique*, pp. 63–4.
18 Coontz, *The Way We Never Were*, p. 9.
19 Friedan, *Feminine Mystique*, p. 42.
20 Friedan, *Feminine Mystique*, p. 41.
21 Douglas and Michaels, *The Mommy Myth*, pp. 34–5.
22 Daniel Bukszpan, 'America's Most Destructive Riots of All Time', *cnbc.com*, 13 September 2013, https://tinyurl.com/2p83xwz4 (accessed 8 June 2022).
23 W. Bradford Wilcox, 'The Evolution of Divorce', *National Affairs*, 51 (2009), https://tinyurl.com/yae886rw (accessed 9 June 2022).
24 Quoted in Aniko Bodroghkozy, ' "Is This What You Mean by Color TV?": Race, Gender, and Contested Meanings in Julia', in Joanne Morreale (ed.), *Critiquing the Sitcom: A Reader* (Syracuse: Syracuse University Press, 2002), p. 138.

25 Paul Wells, quoted in Joanne Morreale, 'Introduction', in Joanne Morreale (ed.), *Critiquing the Sitcom: A Reader* (Syracuse: Syracuse University Press, 2002), p. xii.
26 Jane Feuer, Paul Kerr and Tise Vahimagi (eds), *MTM Quality Television* (London: BFI, 1985).
27 David Haglund, 'Reagans's Favorite Sitcom', *Slate*, 2 March 2007, https://tinyurl.com/2p9yynye (accessed 8 June 2022).
28 Timothy Havens, '"The biggest show in the world": Race and the Global Popularity of *The Cosby Show*', *Media Culture & Society*, 22 (2000): 371. DOI: 10.1177/016344300022004001.
29 Lisa Capretto, '"The Cosby Show" and Race: Phylicia Rashad Weighs In On Sitcom's Portrayal of a Black Family', *Huffpost*, 9 July 2013, https://tinyurl.com/3pzbhupr (accessed 8 June 2022).

3

Motherhood on network television, 1980s onwards

Motherhood in the 1980s may have been characterized by happily married have-it-all superwomen like Clair Huxtable but, for feminist scholar Bonnie J. Dow, sitcoms like *Kate and Allie* (CBS, 1984–9), *The Golden Girls* (NBC, 1985–92) and *Designing Women* (CBS, 1986–93) dragged network television into the 1990s by showing what motherhood and women's ensemble sitcoms could look like.[1] For Dow, *Designing Women* is driven by the kind of conversation that is often 'devalued as gossip, chatter, or bitching' and the very fact that four women talk about 'women's issues' means that the show is 'a regeneration of feminist consciousness that often vigorously resists postfeminist attitudes'.[2] The result is that women's talk is treated as 'worthwhile'[3] and, while the women in the series may not all be feminists and every episode may not focus on feminist issues, '*Designing Women*'s rhetorical strategy of framing its feminist discourse within a conservative, even postfeminist setting, and with a collection of amusing and hardly militant characters, may increase, rather than decrease its power'.[4]

This is certainly true of the episode 'Working Mother' (5:3), which aired on 1 October 1990 and articulated the issues raised a decade earlier by the *New York Times* article 'Many Young Women Now Say They'd Pick Family Over Career'.[5] The report kicked off a few similar stories, but the debate died down until midway through the 1980s when another surfaced that confirmed the sentiments of the *New York Times*' story. Faith Popcorn, a former advertising executive, argued that women were abandoning careers post-childbirth and instead choosing 'nesting' or 'cocooning'. Based on very little evidence Popcorn's prediction that women were abandoning the office in droves for a life of blissful domesticity quite quickly became reported as the latest trend.[6] The notion of 'trend reporting', according to Susan Faludi, 'attains authority not through actual reporting but through the power of repetition. Said enough times, anything can be made to seem true'.[7] For example, Popcorn's MBA figure was taken from a 1986 *Fortune* cover story called 'Why Women Managers are Bailing Out', a story based on the 'cocktail chatter' of a couple of female graduates who were overheard talking about their intention to stay home and look after their babies. The story went to print claiming that: 'After ten years, significantly more women than men dropped off the management track.'[8] *Fortune*'s senior reporter Alex Taylor III neglected to report, however, that a decade after graduation 'virtually the same proportion of women and men were still working for [the same] employers' and that even if 30 per cent of 1,039 women from the class of 1976 had dropped off the management track, so had 21 per cent of the men.[9] Taylor's 'significantly more women' boiled down to 9 per cent and, given that women still bear most of the responsibility for childcare, the big news should surely be that the employment gap was so small.

Going back to *Designing Women*, it is possible to see how this media debate is animated through the four friends' attitudes towards working mothers as it is revealed that a particularly challenging client, Randa Oliver (Lexi Randall), is a demanding nightmare because she has been left at home while her parents travel Europe. Julia Sugarbaker (Dixie Carter) is quick to blame Randa's 'evil devil-child' attitude on her mother's regular absences but Mary-Jo (Annie Potts) leaps to her defence, asking 'Why do we always blame the mother?' as she confesses that her son, Quinton (Brian Lando) has been caught housebreaking to play a friend's Nintendo while she was at work. Bearing in mind that, by the mid-1980s, '59 percent of married mothers worked ... 46.8 percent of mothers with a child under one worked. Black married mothers were even more likely to be in the labour force than their white counterparts',[10] and it is easy to see how the four friends' conversation is a good example of feminist consciousness raising, particularly when Charlene (Jean Smart) decides to give up work after missing her daughter's first steps.

Mary-Jo's snarky comments about Charlene's daytime television viewing habits and Charlene's rejoinder about Mary-Jo's son cause an argument that raises the issue: Is it a choice to 'opt-out' of the working world (Charlene) or is working motherhood a necessity (Mary-Jo)? Of course, this being sitcom-land, the issue must be resolved before episode end but not before the conversation between Charlene and Mary-Jo articulates both sides of the debate: 'stay-at-homers – lazy or dumb. Working mums – selfish yuppies'. For Mary-Jo, who refused alimony from her ex-husband to prove to her sons that you could 'pick yourself up', working as a divorced mother was never a debate, yet, for Charlene, who has a rich husband, it is clearly a 'choice'. Both Mary-Jo and Charlene agree that, whichever side you are on and whether working is through necessity or choice, it is vital that mothers do not turn on each other, particularly when bringing up children 'stopped being just child care and started being [about] the ethics of parenting choices'.[11]

The ethics of parenting choices were again thrust centre stage with the decision for *Murphy Brown* (CBS, 1988–2018) to feature single career woman, Murphy Brown, falling pregnant after a night of unprotected sex ('Uh Oh', Parts 1–3). Even if second-wave feminism (and the invention of the contraceptive pill) gave single women sexual freedom, the networks still pandered to a conservative agenda and had Brown have sex with an old flame rather than a one-night-stand with a stranger. In the run-up to the 1992 presidential election, Dan Quayle propelled the sitcom into the centre of a media storm by blaming the fictional character for being partly to blame for the 'poverty of values' that led to that year's Los Angeles riots. Dan Quayle's now infamous speech argued that the fictional character epitomized 'today's intelligent, highly paid, professional woman – mocking the importance of fathers, by bearing a child alone, and calling it just another "lifestyle choice"'.[12] A storm in a media teacup maybe, but the *Murphy Brown* incident is a good example of how seriously we should take images of the television family, particularly those of the mother. Quayle later claimed that he meant his speech to merely 'stir a debate' over family values and Candice Bergen herself said some years later that his 'was a perfectly intelligent speech about fathers not being dispensable'[13] but the truth is that, in his rush to condemn single mothers, Quayle clean forgot about the fictional father's role in the pregnancy.

This fact was not lost on commentators such as *Time* magazine, which argued that the storyline was not about the selfish and careless attitudes of women but an accurate reflection of the growth in fatherless families, which was 'encouraged less by television than by welfare policies that punish poor mothers who marry'.[14] Other critics suggested that the speech was a strategy 'to suggest that L.A.'s rioters, who were mostly black and Hispanic, have in common with feminists and other Democrats a shoddier moral standard than nice people'.[15] Stephanie Coontz, professor of family history, goes even further to say that Quayle's criticism of Murphy Brown was responsible for '[kicking] off more than a decade of outcries against the "collapse of the family"',[16] and was seen by many as a turning point in the American culture wars. Proving just how powerful television can be, however, *Murphy Brown* aired a rejoinder to Dan Quayle, when she told fictional viewers that 'in a country where millions of children grow up in non-traditional families' the senator's views on her choice seemed 'painfully unfair' ('You Say Potatoe, I Say Potato', 5:2). Having the last word on mothering and the family on television had rarely seemed as politically powerful than in this particular instance.

Into the 1990s and single moms continued to be prominent with shows like *Grace Under Fire* (ABC, 1993–8) and *Home Improvement* (ABC, 1991–9) showing how network television sitcoms were changing as we ushered in the new millennium. Raising children alone through divorce, widowhood or choice, and using myriad forms of childcare, mothers on American television were, by the 1990s, relatively well-rounded, sometimes career-oriented and represented maternity in all its guises. We even had a working-class mum grace our screens when *Roseanne* (ABC, 1988–97, 2018) became one of the decade's most unlikely hits. Not only was the sitcom set in a blue-collar family but the central character, Roseanne, mother to three, flew in the face of expectations from the off with her no-nonsense, tough love attitude, and was one of the few sitcom mothers to have been afforded any extensive critical appraisal.[17] *Roseanne* certainly broke barriers for the way motherhood could be represented and arguably opened doors for later sitcoms featuring out of the ordinary mothers, particularly HBO's *Sex and the City*, which I will return to later, and *Friends*, which, as a pivotal series in the history of network television, will be discussed at some length.

There is a moment in the 2002 episode of *Friends* ('The One with the Baby Shower', 8:20) when it dawns on Rachel Green (Jennifer Aniston), heavily pregnant with Ross Geller's (played by David Schwimmer) child, just what is in store for her: 'I've spent so longing planning the pregnancy and birth that I have forgotten what comes after. I'm going to have a baby. I don't know what to do.' The episode ends with Ross quizzing her in the style of *Bamboozled* – a game show that Joey Tribbiani (Matt LeBlanc) has auditioned for. Flustered by the speed of the questioning Rachel gets an answer wrong and Ross, completely in the thrall of the game, blurts out 'Wrong answer. You are going to be a terrible mother.' Rachel's horrified expression reveals how, carried away by the pregnancy and the 'how to give birth' sessions, preoccupied with where to live, and what she is going to do about her relationship with Ross, like many prospective mothers, she has overlooked life after birth, has no idea how she is going to manage their baby, what kind of mother she is going to be, and where to turn for help.

Friends ran on NBC from September 1994 to May 2004 and should need no introduction as one of the most popular sitcoms of all time, nominated for sixty-four Primetime Emmy Awards (among myriad others), winning seven, including one for 'Outstanding Comedy Series' in 2002, and consistently ranked in the top ten of the final primetime ratings. Such was the show's popularity that the series finale, aired on 6 May 2004, was seen by 52.5 million American viewers, making it the fourth most watched series finale in television history and the highest of that decade. The show has consistently been at the top of the ratings: it was at the top of the *Hollywood Reporter*'s one hundred favourite television shows of 2016,[18] it is the most binge-watched series on Netflix[19] and was voted the favourite television show for the sixteen to twenty-five age group in the UK.[20] Such is the perennial popularity of the series that, in May 2021, HBO Max staged a reunion. 'The One Where They Get Back Together' drew over five million viewers for SkyOne in the UK and an estimated '29% of US streaming households'[21] watching on HBO Max. Suffice to say, the reunion was hotly anticipated and eagerly discussed in the media.

Friends certainly chimed with the zeitgeist of mid-1990s America with its focus on young singletons who spent most of their time 'hanging out' together in a pseudo family configuration not unusual of later US sitcoms. Of course their love lives were complicated, as were their family ties, but their portrayal of unwavering mutual support and involvement in each other's lives extended offscreen as the stars became close friends (most notably Jennifer Aniston and Courtney Cox-Arquette), opted to collectively negotiate their contracts with Warner Brothers (against the studio's preference for individual contract negotiations) and insisted that each character had exactly the same amount of screen time, earning the series the reputation of being US television's first truly ensemble sitcom.[22]

From the very first episode, *Friends*, despite being ostensibly about single, twenty-something Manhattanites, promised a wide variety of mothers as far away from June Cleaver as could be imagined with the pilot episode featuring Ross in the midst of divorcing his wife, Carol Willick (Anita Barone) due to her affair with Susan Bunch (Jessica Hecht) ('The Pilot' or 'The One Where Monica Gets a Roommate', 1:1). The added twist was Carol's pregnancy with Ross' child in the second episode ('The One with the Sonogram at the End', 1:2) a situation that not only introduced lesbian mothering into a network sitcom, but also did so in a time slot that children could watch.[23] This was not the only twist on motherhood that would feature over the decade-long run of the series, however, as Chandler Bing's (played by Matthew Perry) transvestite father is, in a clear example of transphobia, squarely blamed for the breakup of his marriage to Chandler's erotic novelist mother. Phoebe Buffay's (played by Lisa Kudrow) complex background (her adoptive mother committed suicide when Phoebe was 14) did not interfere with her decision to become surrogate mother for her brother and sister-in-law's triplets, despite the fact that her birth mother, Phoebe Abbott (Teri Garr), was well aware of how difficult it was to give up her own twins and tried to dissuade her daughter from the decision. And while much of season eight revolved around Rachel's pregnancy, the focus of season nine is not how she managed as a single parent with a tangled love life, but Monica and Chandler's efforts to get pregnant, a storyline including references to a multitude of mothering alternatives and ending in the surrogate birth of their twins in the series finale ('The Last One' or 'The One Where They Say Goodbye', 10:17 and 10:18).

Strangely, for all its global popularity and critical acclaim, *Friends* has received very little scholarly attention,[24] due partly to the fact that, as a comedy, it belongs to a notoriously undervalued genre, suffering from a cultural and theoretical elitism that sees it as low art as opposed to the high standing of tragedy. And while comedy is a staple fare of television it, along with television itself, is often categorized as mere entertainment for the masses with little or no ideological or cultural value. *Friends* was not renowned for being a particularly political or ideologically topical show and its move to Netflix in 2018 provoked accusations of racism, misogyny, homophobia and transphobia. The series did, however, present a conflict between traditional and modern family values, particularly with topics such as 'surrogate motherhood, adoption, infertility, out-of-wedlock births, lesbian parenting, interracial dating, premarital sex, even impotence'.[25] Indeed *Friends* may well not be remembered for its searing political commentary but in a show about 'a drifting group of friends [who] forged their own family, one of unflappable devotion and support with the theme-song mantra of "I'll be there for you"',[26] its focus on new familial configurations and non-traditional maternity are clearly in conflict with traditional values and yet, due to the lack of attention paid to the cultural significance of both the show and its portrayal of motherhood, this goes virtually unnoticed.[27] With an eye to Paul Wells' 'progressive' sitcom that smuggles in challenging ideas under the guise of humour,[28] what are we to make of the way the series dealt with its potentially progressive portrayals of motherhood? And surely it is disingenuous to suggest that mothering is peculiarly absent from the series, particularly when pregnancy and motherhood were central to at least three seasons?

Despite the birth of Rachel and Ross' baby, it did not go without comment that Emma was rarely seen and there was very little focus on the actual affective labour of mothering. Emma, like Ross' other child, Ben, remained part of the narrative but only as they impacted upon the main characters' storylines, and while this may in part be due to the fact that *Friends* was filmed live, thus limiting the amount of time a child could actually be on set, Rachel's onscreen mothering soon became subsumed under the 'will they, won't they?' narrative that culminated in the couple's eventual romantic pairing. Is it possible that the progressive potential of motherhood in *Friends* was ultimately squandered in its need to attract a young, mainstream and affluent audience? And, more to the point, is this unusual? *Friends* appeared in a decade that, according to David Bushman, was 'pretty prosperous and safe. We were not at war, the economy was doing pretty well – and … it was a time where a show like "Friends" was sort of perfect'.[29] It was also a time when feminism had been labelled 'post-' and Generation X women were accused of focusing on existential angst and identity politics rather than fighting for equality. In fact, for some postfeminist women, there was a distinct sense that there was nothing left to fight for, women were on a par with men both within the workplace and without. *Friends* then came at a time when the characters within the show who were 'wrestling with the exhilaration and angst of their 20s'[30] were as representative of their viewers as *The Mary Tyler Moore Show* had been of second-wave feminists in the early 1970s and, as such, the erasure of issues relating to motherhood is fairly representative of a general lack of cultural and feminist interest in mothering.

Friends did, at least, put motherhood on the map, whereas sitcoms such as *2 Broke Girls* (CBS, 2011–14), *The Big Bang Theory* (CBS, 2007–19) and *How I Met Your Mother* (CBS, 2005–14), while clearly trading on the success of the surrogate sitcom family of friends, take the representation of mothers to levels that are, in many cases, retrogressive. *The Big Bang Theory*, for example, puts the responsibility for the shortcomings and neuroses of each of the lead characters firmly onto their mothers' shoulders: Leonard Hoefstadter's (played by Johnny Galecki) mother, Beverley, for example, is played (by Christine Baranski) as a judgemental, cold, analytical and unforgiving neuroscientist who, despite being an award-winning psychiatrist, is blissfully unaware of other people's feelings, including those of her son and his friends. This archetypal 'bad' mother is played against Sheldon Cooper's (played by Jim Parsons) 'good' mom, an endlessly supportive, warm and caring Texan belle (played by Laurie Metcalf), who infantilizes her son but is often called upon to expertly negotiate his neuroses. Both of these, however, pale by comparison to Howard Wolowitz's monstrous mother who, like Maris Crane (*Frasier*, NBC, 1993–2004) and Vera Peterson (*Cheers*, NBC, 1982–93) before her, is never to be seen although she is most definitely heard. Mrs Wolowitz (Carol Ann Susi), is described as a vastly overweight, mustachioed woman who dominates her son by yelling at him from off-screen – as stereotypical a 'castrating' mother as ever there was. This notion of the overbearing mother continues through Howard's marriage to Bernadette Rostenkowski-Wolowitz (Melissa Ivy Rauch), whose voice, the actress has claimed, is based upon her own mother's dulcet tones.[31] And while *How I Met Your Mother* is ostensibly focused on the woman in the title, she actually remains anonymous until the final season, when it is revealed that she has already died, in a remarkable sleight of hand that ensures her centrality while simultaneously rendering her invisible and totally lacking in subjectivity.

From 1998 onwards mothers became more central to primetime series than ever before, migrating out of their traditional stomping ground of the sitcom and soap opera and into mainstream teenage dramas. Series like *Charmed* (The WB, 1998–2006), which, while obviously indebted to magical sitcoms *Bewitched* and *Sabrina, the Teenage Witch* (ABC, 1996–2000; The WB, 2000–3), and riding the success of *Buffy the Vampire Slayer* (The WB, 1997–2003), centred around the lives of three sisters whose magical gifts were passed down through the female line. The brainchild of Constance M. Burge, *Charmed* was one of a slew of series that were clearly aimed at mothers and their teenage daughters and, despite the absence of both the Halliwell sisters' mother and grandmother, was imbued with motherly love. Only two years later *The Gilmore Girls* (The WB, 2000–7) not only dealt with issues arising out of single motherhood (mother Lorelai Gilmore [Lauran Graham] was a pregnant teen runaway) but also focused on her problematic relationship with her own mother (Emily [Kelly Bishop]) as well as the dynamics arising out of the small age gap between her and daughter Rory (Alexis Bledel).

By the beginning of the twenty-first century motherhood had moved out of teenage television and murdering in the name of motherhood was no longer *verboten* on the networks. Who could ever have imagined the global popularity of shows like *Desperate Housewives* (ABC, 2004–12)? Premiering in October 2004, the series won multiple awards at the Emmys, Golden Globes and Screen Actors Guild and maintained an audience of over twenty million viewers. In 2006 it was reported that the series was the most popular show in its demographic worldwide with an audience of approximately 115–119 million viewers[32] and it was the third most watched television show in twenty countries.[33] No mean feat for a narrative inspired by the story of young mother Andrea Yates who drowned her five young children in the bathtub while suffering severe postpartum depression and psychosis. That motherhood is not always a bed of roses was never so true or so deftly animated as in the first five minutes of the pilot episode when mother and housewife Mary Alice Young (Brenda Strong) commits suicide for (as yet) unknown reasons ('Pilot', 1:1). Narrated from beyond the grave, *Desperate Housewives* quickly established itself as the zeitgeist hit for new millennium as, much like Betty Friedan's *The Feminine Mystique* some forty years earlier, it exposed the angst beneath the outwardly polished lives of the women of Wisteria Lane, most of whom either were, or would soon become, mothers.

The post-1996 US television era, in which US television was deregulated, allowed unprecedented freedom to 'let anyone enter any communications business – to let any communications business compete in any market against any other'[34] and resulted in an overhaul of the US television network system. Key to this change was the inclusion of the Internet into the broadcasting spectrum and the relaxation of rules allowing for media cross-ownership. HBO was quick to take advantage of its status as an independent cable company screening uncut Hollywood films, adult documentaries and Pay Per View sports specials and, being low in the ratings but owned by the third largest television network globally, Time Warner, could afford to take risks. Commissioning and airing prison series *Oz* in 1997 (HBO, 1997–2003) showed how far HBO was prepared to gamble on original content with the series pushing boundaries in terms of its subject matter, as well as containing violence, sexuality and profanity never before seen on US television. Available only to those able to pay the subscription and free from sponsorship worries, HBO neatly sidestepped censorship issues that continue to dog its fellow network and cable competitors, meaning that it could invest in adult-themed dramas for a discerning audience.

Hot on the heels of the testosterone-fuelled world of *Oz* came a succession of breakout hits for the little known (at least outside the United States) but increasingly successful cable channel with shows like *Sex and the City* (1998–2004), *The Sopranos* (1999–2007),

Six Feet Under (2001–5) and *Deadwood* (2004–6) ensuring HBO's place on the twenty-first-century digital media landscape. If the series were not as successful as their network companions in terms of audience numbers, they certainly attracted critical attention and the desired demographic for HBO, discerning adults that could afford to pay the US$10 monthly subscription cost (currently on average US$12–20 per month). This educated, liberal and distinctly middle-class audience, HBO anticipated, could deal not only with uncensored content but complex narratives, ensemble casts and subjects not usually aired on the more conservative US television networks. The resultant critical and commercial success of the HBO original series came at a time when, threatened with being overwhelmed by the explosion of cable channels, branding was crucial.

It would be HBO's next two original series that would put the cable channel well and truly on the map, ensure its place in US television history and raise the stakes of the television game forever.

Notes

1 Bonnie J. Dow, *Prime-Time Feminism: Television, Media Culture, and the Women's Movement Since 1970* (Philadelphia: University of Pennsylvania Press, 1996), pp. 101–34.
2 Andrea Press, *Women Watching Television: Class, Gender, and Generation in the American Television Experience* (Philadelphia: University of Philadelphia Press, 1991), p. 47.
3 Dow, *Prime-Time Feminism*, p. 105.
4 *Ibid*.
5 Dena Kleiman, 'Many Young Women Now Say They'd Pick Family Over Career', *New York Times*, 28 December 1980, https://tinyurl.com/3zuz2yt3 (accessed 9 June 2022).
6 Susan Faludi, *Backlash: The Undeclared War Against Women* (London: Chatto & Windus/Vintage, 1992), p. 109.
7 Faludi, *Backlash*, p. 104.
8 Quoted in Faludi, *Backlash*, p. 111.
9 Faludi, *Backlash*, pp. 110–11.
10 Susan J. Douglas and Meredith W. Michaels, *The Mommy Myth: The Idealization of Motherhood and How It Has Undermined Women* (New York: Free Press, 2005), p. 56.
11 Tracy Thompson, 'A War Inside Your Head', *Washington Post*, 15 February 1998, https://tinyurl.com/46uykr34 (accessed 8 June 2022).

12 Dan Quayle, Address to the Commonwealth Club of California, 19 May 1992, https://tinyurl.com/2p8ctfy (accessed 4 June 2022).
13 Mark Armstrong, 'First Look: The News in Brief, July 11, 2002', *eonline*, 11 July 2002, https://tinyurl.com/mr9x52ek (accessed 2 June 2022).
14 Anon, 'Dan Quayle vs Murphy Brown: The Vice-President Takes on a TV Character Over Family Values', *Time*, 1 June 1992, https://tinyurl.com/5n6uk7na (accessed 7 June 2022).
15 Quoted in *ibid*.
16 Stephanie Coontz, 'What "Killed" the Institution of Marriage? L-O-V-E', *History News Network*, 5 January 2005, https://tinyurl.com/59mwwree (accessed 1 June 2022).
17 Kathleen Rowe, *The Unruly Woman: Gender and the Genres of Laughter* (Austin: University of Texas Press, 1995).
18 THR Staff, 'Hollywood's 100 Favorite TV Shows', *Hollywood Reporter*, 16 September 2015, https://tinyurl.com/mry8fc3c (accessed 8 June 2022).
19 Todd Spangler, '"Friends", "Grey's Anatomy" Were Most Binge-Watched TV Shows of 2018, Study Finds', *Variety*, 20 December 2018, https://tinyurl.com/49f4kf2 (accessed 30 May 2022).
20 Ian Youngs, 'Friends is the UK's Most Popular Subscription Streaming Show', *BBC.com*, 9 August 2018, https://tinyurl.com/4rj7ec2u (accessed 8 June 2022).
21 Roxie Pell, 'Friends Reunion Nearly Matches Wonder Woman 1984 Views on HBO Max', *ScreenRant*, 29 May 2021, https://tinyurl.com/36xej9nf (accessed 10 June 2022).
22 Christina McCarroll, 'A "Family" Sitcom for Gen X – "Friends" Cast a New TV Mold', *Christian Science Monitor*, 6 May 2004, https://tinyurl.com/y8f92p3n (accessed 8 June 2022).
23 It is the inclusion of storylines such as these, plus sexually charged themes, that led L. Brent Bozell, President of the Parents Television Council, to accuse *Friends* of continuously exposing children to 'lewd and offensive programming ... with adult themes including explicit sexual references or adult sexual situations'. Tania Branigan, 'Friends and Buffy Slayed in Parents' Hate-list', *Guardian*, 24 August 2002, https://tinyurl.com/dtham23j (accessed 10 June 2022).
24 An issue raised by both Eleanor Hersey Nickel in '"I'm the Worst Mother Ever": Motherhood, Comedy and the Challenges of Bearing and Raising Children in "Friends"', *Studies in Popular Culture*, 35:1 (2012): 25–45, www.jstor.org/stable/23416364 (accessed 8 June 2022) and Hannah Hammad, 'The One with the Feminist Critique: Revisiting Millennial Postfeminism with Friends', *Television & New Media*, 19:8 (2018): 692–707.

25 McCarroll, 'A "Family" Sitcom'.
26 *Ibid.*
27 Since writing this chapter, *Friends: A Reading of the Sitcom* by Simone Knox and Kai Hanno Schwind (New York: Palgrave Macmillan, 2019) has been published.
28 Wells, quoted in Morreale, *Critiquing the Sitcom*, p. xii.
29 Quoted in McCarroll, 'A "Family" Sitcom'.
30 *Ibid.*
31 Lane Vasquez, 'The Truth About Bernadette's Voice on "The Big Bang Theory"', *theThings*, 17 May 2021, https://tinyurl.com/ycyndzhk (accessed 8 June 2022).
32 TVSA Team, 'Desperate Housewives On SABC3 Confirmed', *TVSA*, 3 April 2007, https://tinyurl.com/2xxp7h7c (accessed 8 June 2022).
33 Anon, 'CSI Show "Most Popular in World"', *BBC News*, 31 July 2006, https://tinyurl.com/38azzefn (accessed 8 June 2022).
34 Federal Communications Commission (FCC), 'The Telecommunications Act of 1996', para. 1, fcc.gov (accessed 8 June 2022).

Part II

Original dramas

4

Sex and the City (HBO, 1998–2004)

According to Andrea Press, 'television "discovered" the female prime-time market in the 1970s', as evidenced by a spate of '"hybrid" prime-time shows, which combine melodramatic elements with traditionally male genres like the cop show or the action show'.[1] Fast-forward to 1998, and it was a hybrid of television sitcom format and the filmic romantic comedy, that saw HBO's breakout hit series *Sex and the City*, shine a light on a specific milieu of millennial women and how they negotiated life as single women. Screened in an era defined by postfeminism and in an economy that was enjoying the largest growth that we would see this century, the series had much to reveal about women and friendship and became synonymous with consumerist culture and have-it-all feminism. As many feminist scholars have argued, *Sex and the City* was about so much more than fashion, shoes and sex. A fact evidenced by the size of the audience and how quickly the series became compulsory viewing with the finale reaching an audience of 10.6 million in the United States and over 4.1 million in Britain.[2] Not bad for a show on what was then a relatively minor cable channel exported onto the third most popular terrestrial channel in Britain.[3]

Much of the discourse around *Sex and the City* focused on the potential feminism of the show – with a great deal of discussion centring on whether the women (principally Carrie Bradshaw) could be read as either feminist, postfeminist or third-wave feminist icons – or whether they were feminists at all with their obsession with shoes, clothes and men. The fact that the series was about four single women meant that the characters were always going to have to bear the burden of representation in this way and

HBO's commercial decision to consciously attract affluent female subscribers make any feminist credentials seem like an afterthought. Despite author Naomi Wolf claiming that the series was 'the first global female epic – the answer to the question posed in Virginia Woolf's essay "A Room of One's Own". What will women actually do when they are free?',[4] most of the media hype surrounding the first seasons of *Sex and the City* focused on the sex of the title with very little thought given to the possible ramifications of the act itself. In addition, the lack of restrictions by HBO meant that *Sex and the City* could follow in the footsteps of prison drama *Oz*, showing and saying what had previously been prohibited on American television but, while *Oz* had focused on male relationships in the pressure cooker of a high security prison, *Sex and the City* would do the polar opposite and feature four glamorous and decidedly white, middle-class Manhattan women.

Famously adapted from Candace Bushnell's 1996 book, *Sex and the City*,[5] the series' opening gambit – whether women can have sex 'like men', without emotion or attachment – is soon brought up short with Carrie's pregnancy scare ten episodes into the first season. A storyline framed by the four friends' reactions to their invitation to Laney Berlin's (played by Dana Wheeler-Nicholson), baby shower ('The Baby Shower', 1:10). Described by Carrie as 'hell on earth', the women discuss the prospect over popcorn and a movie. Miranda tells her friends that they couldn't 'drag her to that thing with a grappling hook in her mouth' adding: 'It's a cult ... They all think the same, dress the same and sacrifice themselves to the same cause. Babies. I've lost two sisters to the motherhood.' While the friends' reactions are mixed, Miranda remains hostile. Samantha's eventual justification for attending – 'just imagine how fat she's going to be' – sends the four friends on a road trip to Connecticut to observe former wild-child, Laney, in full maternal glory. If Samantha's gift of a bottle of scotch is wildly inappropriate for a pregnant woman, then Miranda's present of a packet of pastel condoms reveals much about her attitude towards reproduction. Once inside Miranda warns Carrie: 'We can't separate. Once they isolate you from the herd it's all over.' And while three of the friends, Miranda, Carrie and Samantha, are appalled at the performance of 'idealized' motherhood at the party – with mothers breastfeeding toddlers and Laney's nude, Demi Moore style painting in the bathroom – Charlotte, who is the only one of the friends to long for marriage and motherhood, is in her full beribboned glory. Miranda and Carrie eventually escape to sit on the steps of Laney's house where Miranda bemoans that the witch in *Hansel and Gretel* was very misunderstood: 'I mean the woman builds her dream house and those brats come along and start eating it.'

From this early episode, the series steadily works towards exposing the myths of motherhood that have, according to Susan Douglas and Meredith Michaels, been peddled in the media since the 1980s. In their book, *The Mommy Myth*, they argue that the media works to pit woman against woman and, more importantly, mother against mother. For Douglas and Michaels, the myth of new momism 'seeks to contain and, where possible, eradicate, all the social changes brought on by feminism', adding: 'It is backlash in its most refined, pernicious form because it insinuates itself into women's psyches just where we have been rendered most vulnerable: in our love for our kids.'[6] Douglas and Michaels offer two media stereotypes: the ideal/Madonna/nurturing mother and the bad working mother that are used to judge mothers against and, simultaneously, set women impossible standards by which to judge themselves.[7] Douglas and Michaels propose that it is time to 'exhume what feminists really hoped to change about motherhood' and 'to go back to a time when many women felt free to tell the truth about motherhood – e.g. that at times they felt ambivalent about it because it was so hard and yet so undervalued'.[8]

Miranda's ambivalence towards motherhood is identified early on in season four. While Charlotte and Trey's (played by Kyle MacLachlan) attempt to have a child is the focus of their married life, Miranda's surprise pregnancy only three episodes after the death of her own mother[9] is a narrative fillip that deflates any romantic notion of motherhood and conception: a single woman with a lazy ovary knocked up after a 'mercy fuck' with ex-boyfriend Steve Brady (David Eigenberg), a man with 'only one ball' ('Coulda, Woulda, Shoulda', 4:11). As Miranda tells Carrie, 'it's like the special Olympics of conception'. At brunch she tells her friends the news. Charlotte, who has devoted herself to being an exemplary wife to Trey, a full-time homemaker and is desperate to conceive their baby, leaves the restaurant abruptly when Miranda tells them she is thinking of terminating the pregnancy. A conversation about abortion ensues. If you consider that it was only in the 1950s that Lucille Ball revolutionized pregnancy on our television screens, the early 1970s that Maude terminated her abortion and the early 1990s that Vice President Dan Quayle had berated the sitcom character Murphy Brown for having a child out of wedlock, you can see how radical this discussion was. Despite telling Carrie that she can barely find time in her busy life to schedule an abortion let alone have a baby, Miranda finds herself in the clinic and, at the very last moment, cancels the procedure. It may, after all, be her last chance and even the cynical Miranda cannot pass up the opportunity to experience motherhood, which according to Peggy Orenstein has 'supplanted marriage as the source of romantic daydreams for childless, unmarried women in their twenties and early to mid-thirties'.[10]

It is not only that Miranda chooses to keep her baby (much to her friends' delight), but her swelling body, with its fatigue, uncontrollable flatulence and out-of-control sex drive, are a constant source of comedy. As she so eloquently puts it, 'I don't know why they call it "morning sickness" when it's all fucking day long' ('Just Say Yes', 4:12). Told that she is expecting a boy, Miranda finds herself 'faking her sonogram' ('Change of a Dress', 4:15) telling Carrie that 'everyone else is glowing about her pregnancy' and wondering whether she ever will. When Magda (Lynn Cohen) finds the sonogram photograph of the baby and tells Miranda that a boy is good luck, Miranda is compelled to perform her, now perfected, ritual of fake joy. She pulls a muscle in her neck as a result. If this is not a good enough example of how women are expected to possess an innate 'maternal instinct', it is reinforced by Carrie's reluctance to marry Aidan and her question 'are we just programmed?' to want marriage and babies – a question partly answered by Miranda's rant two episodes later: 'The fat ass, the farting, it's ridiculous! I am un-fuckable and I have never been so horny in my entire life. That's why you're supposed to be married when you're pregnant – so somebody is obligated to have sex with you' ('Ring a Ding Ding', 4:16). Miranda's nine-month abjection is eventually complete when, interrupting Carrie's last fairy-tale date with Mr Big (Chris Noth) – a horse-drawn carriage ride through New York's Central Park – her waters break over Carrie's coveted, beautiful and expensive new Christian Louboutin shoes (Figure 4.1). Never before has

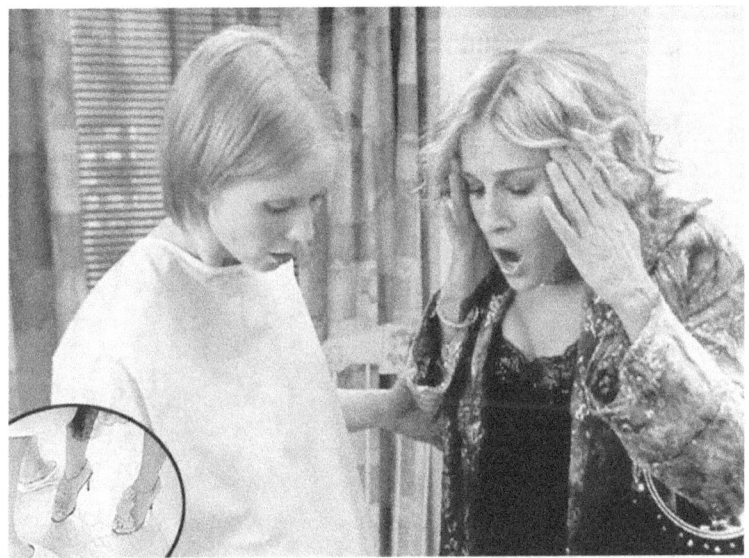

Figure 4.1 'I Heart NY', *Sex and the City*, season 4, episode 18

the reality wave of motherhood been exposed so starkly as when Miranda's amniotic fluid gushes over Cinderella's fairy-tale glass slippers ('I Heart New York', 4:18).

In addition to exposing the indignities of pregnancy, *Sex and the City* re-works existing representations of new motherhood away from the more usual glowing idealized Madonna-and-child imagery. Throughout season five, Miranda struggles with the trauma of being a new mother surrounded by single women without children who are patently unqualified to guide her through this particular maze. In 'Anchors Away' (5:1), Samantha bundles Miranda and baby Brady into a cab with indecent haste so that the child-free friends can go shopping. Carrie's spontaneous visit to Miranda later that day finds her friend unable to coax Brady to breastfeed or concentrate on their conversation. The sight of Miranda's swollen, veiny, milk-filled breasts (Figure 4.2) fills Carrie with horror and, taking her leave abruptly, ignores Miranda's assurances that she can now focus as Brady has latched on successfully. Carrie kisses her friend on the head and tells her, 'Miranda, you're a mother, but it's OK, I won't tell anyone'. This phrase, although offered with

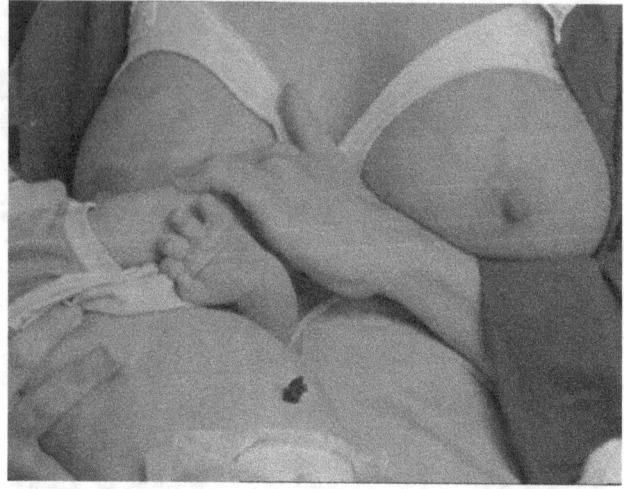

Figure 4.2 'Anchors Away', *Sex and the City*, season 5, episode 1

love, exposes a gulf between the two friends, identifying Miranda's transformation from 'one of the girls' to 'mother'. Considering how ambivalent all four women have been about marriage and motherhood, it is no reassurance to Miranda when Carrie tells her that nothing will affect their friendship and that she is still one of them.

Not only is this scene revealing of the gulf between pre- and post-motherhood women, but it also exposes the steep learning curve that women have to undergo to become confident, breastfeeding mothers. Breastfeeding is often in the headlines as women continue to be criticized for turning their backs on the practice even while they are harassed for nursing their babies in public spaces,[11] but the difficulties women face with the act itself are rarely seen in fiction or addressed in the mainstream media. Far from being 'natural' to all women, something that all mothers should want to do, Miranda's difficulties with feeding Brady show us that this is yet another skill to be learned and is not instinctive to all new mothers. The appearance of Miranda's breasts leaves no doubt that, for the foreseeable future at least, they will be feeding and not titillating, which may hint at the truth behind the complaints against breastfeeding in public. It is not that women expose their breasts while nursing that is the problem, but how onlookers (usually male) react to the sight of fully functional, non-sexual and un-objectified breasts.

There are two bastions of motherhood that Miranda attempts to storm in season five: sex and work. Telling an old flame that she has had a baby but she's 'still allowed to have sex', Miranda takes him back to her apartment. As Carrie's voiceover tells us, 'Miranda was trying to prove that she could still do it all. Bring home the bacon, bring home a baby and bring home an orgasm'. Giving a whole new meaning to the phrase 'mummy's coming', Miranda eventually concedes defeat, accepts that her life has to change and that motherhood and dating are mutually incompatible, for the time being at least ('Plus One Is the Loneliest Number', 5:5). In 'Critical Condition' (5:6) Miranda's exhaustion with Brady's constant crying reaches its peak as she tells her friends that she has not slept for days, all her clothes smell of barf and she hasn't had time to have a haircut: 'If he was 35, this is when we would break up! This 13-pound meatloaf is pushing me over the edge. I feel disgusting.' Pleading with Brady to stop crying that night, a neighbour complains. The next day sees a distraught and bedraggled Miranda snapping at Carrie on the phone, worrying that she's a bad friend as well as a bad mother. Her fear of being distanced from her single friends is only exacerbated by the neighbourhood community of mothers who prove Douglas and Michaels' assertation that we are often 'judged by the toughest critics out there: other mothers'[12] and show how isolating and terrifying new motherhood can be. It is only the intervention of one of those neighbours, Kendall (Lisa Gay Hamilton), that gives voice to the problem that has, so far, remained unspoken. Offering Miranda an oscillating chair to stop Brady crying, she learns that Miranda has only childless friends and tells her: 'Well then, you're screwed. If they don't have kids, they don't have a clue.' While this comment arguably undermines the show's commitment to respecting single, child-free women's lives it also cuts in the opposite direction, reminding us that childcare is a matter of effective props and knowing friends rather than natural instinct, and proves Douglas and Michaels' assertion that 'motherhood *is* a collective experience' (emphasis in original).[13]

The challenges of new motherhood and dating are nothing compared to the impossibility of Miranda's attempt to combine her successful law career with single parenthood. It can be no coincidence that the episode 'Hop, Skip and a Week' (6:6) was originally screened in 2003, the same year that the *New York Times* published Linda Belkin's article 'The Opt-Out Revolution'.[14] This article, which ignited a fierce debate known as the US media's 'mommy wars' also made its way to UK newsprint,[15] and spoke of the pressures on working mothers in the twenty-first century. Featuring a select group of well-educated women with first degrees from Princeton, and some MBAs from Columbia and Harvard, the article focused on the way they had 'opted-out' of high-flying careers in order to stay home and look after their children. Journalist Linda Belkin argues that this is not how it should have been, and that second-wave feminism should have led to equality in the workplace but, on the evidence of the women interviewed for this article, once they had children, no matter how good their careers, women seemed to stall. Yet, rather than address the real issues at stake here, such as the lack of support for working mothers, the women talked about their 'choice' and decision to 'opt-out' of the workplace in order to stay at home. For Joan Williams[16] and Miriam Peskowitz, it is this rhetoric of choice that has done so much to undermine women's careers post-childbirth and has betrayed the idea of equality in the workplace. As Peskowitz points out, we 'talk about the glass ceiling and the mommy track so regularly that these phrases seem passé, yesterday's news',[17] and yet they still hold much currency in twenty-first-century American life. She adds:

> Scratch the surface and there's the glass ceiling. Peer into the company accounts and there's the persistent gender wage gap. Look at who's taking family leave, or why our public life seems so devoid of fortysomething women, and why it's still mostly men running for office or men running the TV news, and it's pretty clear that we aren't as postfeminist as we'd like to be.[18]

As she puts it, 'the gains for women in the past decades have not meant a similar gain for mothers ... childraising remains mothers' work, and in many families it's the mother's salary that is balanced against daycare costs'.[19] In an environment where long working hours and intense competition are the norm, mothers often find themselves 'at odds with the workplace, and ... bearing the brunt of this mismatch'.[20] In fact, as Peskowitz argues, 'today's workplace makes it increasingly difficult for two people who are really committed to their jobs to also raise a family'.[21]

It is in this cultural context that Miranda's narrative is as poignant as it is revealing. Her return to her job as partner in a law firm finds her 'politically incorrectly happy to be there'. Thinking that she is being called into a meeting about progress on her latest case, Miranda is faced by two colleagues – Maurice (Lee Shepherd) and Fern (Rosemarie DeWitt) – who accuse her of tardiness and struggling with her caseload. It is Miranda's female colleague, Fern, that (rather smugly) lists the times that Miranda has been late, with full details of when, where and how. Miranda's rejoinder – 'way to watch my back Fern' – points to the gap between mothers and non-mothers and also exposes the myth of sisterhood in the neoliberal workplace. As she leaves the room Miranda tells her colleagues that, in terms of her workload she is, in fact, 'kicking ass' but it is 'at home that she is doing a bad job'. If, as Peskowitz argues, it is difficult for two parents to commit to their jobs and raise a family, Miranda's narrative emphasizes the impossibility of being both an ideal worker and a single parent. After Brady begins to prefer Magda's company over his mother's, Miranda eventually succumbs to the pressure and decides that she has to cut her working week to around 50 or 55 hours maximum if she is to survive motherhood.

Sex and the City may well have exposed the truth behind the fiction but the celebrity discourse surrounding the series constantly undermined that process. Nowhere is this more evident than in the magazine stories that regularly appeared about the stars' real-life pregnancies and motherhood. Pregnant throughout season five (although not in the series) Sarah Jessica Parker gave birth to her first child, James, in autumn 2002. Six months later she was reported to be 'back in shape'. Promotional shots for the final season revealed no trace of her recent pregnancy.[22] Compare this to Miranda's tortuous narrative in seasons five and six and her struggle with postpartum weight which, according to the media, Parker did not share: 'She'll slip into motherhood as easy as she does her Manolo Blahniks.'[23] Read alongside Miranda's story of lugging around a puking baby, and defending her 'fat ass' in Atlantic City ('Luck be an Old Lady', 5:3) the 'blissfully wed' Parker story confirmed the 'have it all' discourse so vehemently dismantled within the show. It also adds rather interesting reading to what Douglas and Michaels call the 'celebrity mom profile', which, in their analysis, snowballed in the 1980s and became a fixture in the 1990s. According to them, the celebrity-mom profile 'was probably the most influential media form to sell the new momism, and where its key features were refined, reinforced, and romanticized'.[24] They add that the celebrity-mom profile has been an 'absolutely crucial tool in the media construction of maternal guilt and insecurity, as well as the romanticizing of motherhood, in the 1980s and beyond'.[25] Not only does it present mothers who have allegedly found a balance between working and caring for children, but there is an added pressure. If the celebrity mom is willing to give up her glittering showbiz career in order to nurture and mother her children, the suggestion is, why aren't we? Douglas and Michaels argue that the celebrity-mom portraits resurrect many of the stereotypes that women had hoped were buried thirty years ago, including the notion that '[w]omen are, by genetic composition, nurturing and maternal, love all children, and prefer motherhood to anything, especially work, so should be the main ones responsible for raising the kids'.[26] This discourse, add Douglas and Michaels, exemplifies what motherhood has become in our intensified consumer culture: a competition. One that pits mother against mother and leaves the notion of sisterhood in the dust.

The radical potential of *Sex and the City*'s Miranda is that she forces us to look at the messiness of mothering and gives agency to the actual affective labour of caring for a child, whether single parent, stay-at-home mom or working woman. This representation offers an alternative version to the 'idealized motherhood' stereotypes that exist in the media. Dragged into motherhood with a 'grappling hook in her mouth', Miranda faked her sonogram, let a friend's baby fall off the sofa at her baby shower ('A Vogue Idea', 4:17) and had difficulty coping with and bonding with Brady. She was never someone for whom mothering would come easily and it is fair to say that Miranda's maternal journey shows us how motherhood causes exhaustion and guilt, is isolating and demands impossible standards of perfection. In fact, Miranda Hobbes' narrative is a perfect example of Adrienne Rich's theorization of female-centered and female-defined 'mothering' and how it rebels against the steely grip of the patriarchal institution of 'motherhood'.[27]

This is not where her story ends, though, as Miranda has to, despite her misgivings, move out of Manhattan to Brooklyn for the sake of her family ('Out of the Frying Pan', 6:16) and must take on the next stage of her life's journey, which includes caring for Steve's mother, Mary (Anne Meara). Despite their difficult relationship, it is Miranda who offers Mary a home after her mother-in-law's stroke. Sitting at her kitchen table with Charlotte, the women acknowledge each other's problems and how 'amazing' they both are – Charlotte and Harry have just lost a baby girl by surrogate and Miranda has gained an unruly adult child in the guise of Mary ('An American Girl in Paris (Part Deux)', 6:20). Rescuing her mother-in-law after she wanders off in a confused mental fugue, Miranda is forced to care for Mary as a mother would a child. Framed in the bathroom, their red hair linking them and Brady's bath toys emphasizing Mary's child-like state, the mise-en-scène suggests that Miranda has finally accepted a role that she fought against for so long. Later that night Magda tells her 'What you did, that was love. You love'. Kissing her on the head gently, Magda gives Miranda the approval that was missing from her relationship with her own mother. Over six seasons, and through her cynical world view, Miranda's journey in *Sex and the City* offered us an unusually rich and previously unseen insight into mothering and all its messiness.

Sex and the City: the films

This seems as a good a time as any to return to the films that came after *Sex and the City* to ask what went wrong? Especially as the narrative arc set up in the first season episode, 'The Baby Shower', was brought to its ultimate expression in the second film. In many ways, Big and Carrie's decision not have children in *Sex and the City 2* (Michael Patrick King, 2010) was foreshadowed in 'Catch-38' (6:15) when, confronted with Alexander Petrovsky's (played by Mikhail Baryshnikov) vasectomy and her realization that indecision may mean that Carrie has left motherhood too late, she asks: 'Did we want babies and perfect honeymoons, or did we think we *should* have babies and perfect honeymoons?' While Charlotte and Harry Goldenblatt (Evan Handler) now have two longed-for children, the 'terrible twos' and reality of stay-at-home mothering has hit Charlotte hard. Miranda has learned to juggle childcare and a demanding job, but we are shown how precarious this balancing act is through the arrival of her misogynist and vengeful boss who eventually forces her out of her job. Even Samantha struggles with the onset of menopause, not because she mourns the end of her childbearing years but because she worries about losing her sex drive.

Even before *Sex and the City 2* premiered, the critical community was scathing. *Newsweek* had already asked (about the first film) 'if it's not a case of "Sexism in the City". Men hated the movie before it even opened [and] ... gave it such a nasty tongue lashing you would have thought they were talking about an ex-girlfriend'.[28] By the time the second film was released, the knives were again already out and, before it even premiered, had been given savage reviews. The women were too old, the storyline too thin and the ostentatious consumerism was too out of place in a post-recession world. For Lindy West of *The Stranger*: '*SATC2* takes everything that I hold dear as a woman and as a human – working hard, contributing to society, not being an entitled cunt like it's my job – and rapes it to death with a stiletto that costs more than my car.'[29] The worst criticism, however, was aimed at the women. For Sukhdev Sandhu the women's crime was 'getting older', aiming his most vitriolic attack on Sarah Jessica Parker for 'looking, if you happen to go for human pipe-cleaners, absolutely fabulous ... like a cross between Wurzel Gummidge and Bride of Chucky'.[30] Andrew O'Hagan in the *London Evening Standard* went one further by describing the women as 'greedy, faithless, spoiled, patronising ... morons', calling Samantha a 'blond slut' whose inner life 'stops at her labia' and possessing 'the desperate mentality of the School Bike'.[31]

True, there is a misplaced trip to Abu Dhabi complete with burqa-clad women and the storyline around the all-expenses luxury trip (actually filmed in Morocco rather than the United Arab Emirates) was ill-advised. What was even more stark, however, was the exposure of the reality behind the 'happy-ever-after' fairy tale, which was always going to sit awkwardly on the big screen. *Sex and the City* (Michael Patrick King, 2008) had already threatened this narrative with Big and Carrie's overblown wedding replaced with a simple one and, with all the critical opprobrium, the radical nature of the women's stories in this second outing was largely overlooked. For *The Hollywood Reporter*, at least, the women had never seemed so 'proudly feminist' as they were in *Sex and the City 2* and, even if for the same critic, the film could be understood as 'blatantly anti-muslim',[32] the sheer chutzpah of this final outing, which was openly critical of a patriarchal ideology that oppresses women, was subsumed under near-hysterical criticism. *Sex and the City 2* did, however, speak directly to legions of loyal fans. Always famed for its honest and forthright depiction of women, the film, while flawed, delivered on its original promise. Of particular note for this chapter is how it lays bare the expectations associated with motherhood and the real affective labour of mothering. Miranda, sick of being dumped on by her boss, decides to leave work and become a stay-at-home mom. Something that we would never have expected from the most feminist of the friends, leading many to wonder whether she had truly been picked off from the herd and become part of the 'cult of motherhood' identified by her back in 1998.

In their opulent Abu Dhabi hotel suite Miranda invites Charlotte for a pre-dinner drink (Figure 4.3). Dressed in gold and sipping their signature Cosmopolitans, Miranda raises her glass and tells her friend 'being a mother kicks your ass'. Charlotte's well-rehearsed rejoinder – 'the benefits make it worth it' – hides the despair that has driven her on the trip in the first place. Miranda takes the situation in hand and in a moment of feminist consciousness raising tells her friend: 'OK. We're sixty-seven hundred miles

Figure 4.3 *Sex and the City 2*

away from everyone. You can say it to me, I'm a mother too ... all the things you're thinking but won't allow yourself to say out loud.' When Charlotte looks at Miranda quizzically, Miranda takes a swig of her drink and says: 'OK. I'll go first. As much as I love Brady, and I do love him more than words, being a mother is not enough. I miss my job.' That being a stay-at-home mother is not a role that fulfils all women has never been said so plainly. Gathering her courage, Charlotte confesses that as much as she loves her girls, she enjoys being away from them as her daughter's crying is driving her crazy. Emboldened by Miranda's sympathy and fuelled by cosmopolitans, Charlotte tells her friend: 'Sometimes, I go in the other room, close the door and just let her scream. Isn't that awful?' She continues: 'Can I tell you something else? I feel guilty. I feel so guilty because all I ever prayed for was to have a family and now, I have these two beautiful girls and they're driving me crazy. And I feel like I'm failing. I just feel like I'm failing all the time.' Many critics have commented on the fact that the *Sex and the City* women are far removed from 'normal' women's lives, particularly in this luxurious setting, but Charlotte names this very problem by saying that, despite having a nanny, mothering 'is so hard ... How do the women without help do it?' Miranda's simple answer, 'I have no fucking idea', reveals a simple truth, and one that undercuts that myth of motherhood that the *Sex and the City* series did so much to explode. If two privileged women like Miranda and Charlotte find mothering hard and unfulfilling (even with nannies) what do we make of the 'new momism' outlined in Douglas and Michaels' 2004 book?

While it is true that *Sex and the City* does not speak to all women, the maternal narrative arc played out across twelve years is truly revolutionary and has never been equalled. It exposed the fact that not all women want to be mothers, mothering is not an instinct, breastfeeding is tough, not all mothers want to stay at home and, even if they do, it is not always perfect. While mothering is often a job that is gladly embraced, it is just as often full of guilt and, furthermore, it is mothers that are castigated by society for not doing a good enough job. These stories, told through the eyes of our *Sex and the City* women, expose the inconsistencies between a fictional narrative, the myth of ideal motherhood and the celebrity mom discourse. In the end, Miranda clearly shows us not only the

Figure 4.4 Advertisement for *And Just Like That ...*

ambivalence towards motherhood that many women feel, but also the difficulties of trying to fit the role into a neoliberal workplace organized around a full-time ideal worker 'who works full time and overtime and takes little or no time off for childbearing or child rearing'.[33]

Afterthoughts on *And Just Like That ...* (HBO Max, 2021–)

HBO Max premiered *And Just Like That ...* on 9 December 2021 (Figure 4.4). Set eleven years after the last film, HBO later announced that it was 'the most viewed series premiere of a new HBO or HBO Max series on the streaming service'.[34] It was certainly hotly-anticipated and contained some surprises from the get-go. The creators of the series' decision to kill off Big (Chris Noth) in the first episode ('Hello It's Me', 1:1) was a surprise to everyone, not least Carrie, who finds her husband suffering a heart attack after his record-breaking session with a Peloton. In retrospect, this was a fortuitous sleight of script in the light of accusations of historical sexual assault levelled at Chris Noth which forced a rapid re-editing, removing him from Carrie's flashback scenes, ensuring that the series was not affected by negative publicity. This was not the only problem with the revived series. Willie Garson, who played Stanford Blatch, suffered pancreatic cancer during shooting and had to be written out after four episodes due to his death in September 2021 and Kim Cattrall famously refused to have anything to do with the sequel.

And Just Like That … picks up with Miranda and Charlotte both struggling with older children. Miranda and Steve's marriage is in a sexual hiatus while their son is so sexually active that Miranda worries that they have done the right thing allowing Brady (Niall Cunningham) to sleep with his girlfriend at home ('Hello It's Me', 1:1). Meanwhile Charlotte is conflicted about her daughters' competing needs – Lily (Cathy Ang), a model child, plays concert piano and wears dresses chosen by Charlotte in direct contrast to Rose (Alexa Swinton), who wants to be a boy named Rock ('When in Rome', 1:3). It is not that Miranda and Charlotte are totally unprepared for sexual activity and gender fluidity, after all we have seen what they have experienced in the past, but here we can see how uncomfortable children's developing sexuality often is for mothers – pre-pubescence and adolescence are universally disliked – whether suffering the process or remembering it as an adult. In addition, as if to remind us that motherhood is not easily attainable for everyone, Miranda's new friend college professor Dr Nya Wallace (Karen Pitman) is struggling with infertility issues, a subject that she and Miranda regularly discuss. Charlotte's new friend, documentarian Lisa Todd Wexley (Nicole Ari Parker), is part of the 'power moms' group who run school events. A 'super woman' with three children, and effortless glamour, Lisa and Charlotte prove that stay-at-home moms and working moms can get along without rancour.

While motherhood is still central to the series, some twenty years since Miranda and Charlotte's initial pregnancy and infertility storylines, *And Just Like That …* revisits motherhood but with less revolutionary potential. Times have changed and the fact remains that none of the women even hint at relationships with their own mothers. At least we can celebrate that at the end of the first season no soap opera villainess has reared her ugly head, except potentially

Lisa's mother-in-law Eunice (Pat Bowie). It's a pity that we can't say this about the first drama series to put HBO so firmly on the map. A subject I will explore in the next chapter.

Notes

1. Andrea Press, 'Gender and Family in Television's Golden Age and Beyond', *Annals of the American Academy of Political and Social Science* (September 2009), 143.
2. Joe Flint, '"Sex and the City" Finale Scores Series' Highest Ratings Ever', *Wall Street Journal*, 25 February 2004, https://tinyurl.com/4j8bxjuu (accessed 9 June 2022).
3. The first run of the show appeared in the UK on Channel 4 between 1999 and 2005.
4. Quoted in Heather Hodson, 'The Sex and the City Girls are Back in Town', *Daily Telegraph*, 17 May 2008, https://tinyurl.com/2p87nmv9 (accessed 9 June 2022).
5. Candace Bushnell, *Sex and the City* (New York: Warner Trade Books, 1996).
6. Susan J. Douglas and Meredith W. Michaels, *The Mommy Myth: The Idealization of Motherhood and How It Has Undermined Women* (New York: Free Press, 2005), p. 23.
7. Douglas and Michaels, *The Mommy Myth*, pp. 11–12.
8. Douglas and Michaels, *The Mommy Myth*, p. 27.
9. 'My Motherboard Myself', 4:8. It is noteworthy that this is the only episode in which any of the women's mothers are mentioned. And this despite the fact that the men remain close to theirs.
10. Quoted in Douglas and Michaels, *The Mommy Myth*, p. 25.
11. Julie Mazziota, 'Breastfeeding in Public is FINALLY Legal in All 50 States', *People*, 25 July 2018, https://tinyurl.com/2p9bv8rf (accessed 9 June 2022).
12. Douglas and Michaels, *The Mommy Myth*, p. 19.
13. Douglas and Michaels, *The Mommy Myth*, p. 25.
14. Lisa Belkin, 'The Opt-Out Revolution', *New York Times Magazine*, 26 October 2003, https://tinyurl.com/yc42z9s3 (accessed 8 June 2022).
15. Lucy Cavendish, 'Motherhood: Stay-at-Home or Back-to-Work? The Battle Continues', *Observer*, 28 March 2010, https://tinyurl.com/4m45bjau (accessed 8 June 2022) and Gaby Hinsliff, 'I Had It All, But I Didn't Have a Life', *Observer*, 1 November 2009, https://tinyurl.com/2ap9edp6 (accessed 9 June 2022).

16 Joan Williams, *Unbending Gender: Why Work and Family Conflict and What to Do About It* (Oxford: Oxford University Press, 1999).
17 Miriam Peskowitz, *The Truth Behind the Mommy Wars: Who Decides What Makes a Good Mother?* (New York: Seal Press, 2005), p. 67.
18 Peskowitz, *The Truth*, p. 66.
19 Peskowitz, *The Truth*, pp. 66–7.
20 Peskowitz, *The Truth*, p. 70.
21 Peskowitz, *The Truth*, p. 71.
22 Anon, *Hello!*, 758, 1 April 2003, p. 82.
23 Holly Millea, 'Oh Baby!', *Elle*, September 2002, p. 338.
24 Douglas and Michaels, *The Mommy Myth*, p. 113.
25 *Ibid*.
26 Douglas and Michaels, *The Mommy Myth*, p. 138.
27 Adrienne Rich, *Of Woman Born: Motherhood as Experience and Institution* (New York, London: W.W. Norton & Company, 1986), p. xv.
28 Ramin Setoodeh, 'Criticism of "Sex and the City" is Mostly Sexist', *Newsweek*, 2 June 2008, https://tinyurl.com/3bndc2xs (accessed 9 June 2022).
29 Lindy West, 'Burkas and Bikinis: I Watched 146 Minutes of *Sex and the City 2* and All I Got Was This Religious Fundamentalism', *Stranger*, 27 May 2010, https://tinyurl.com/mvbbzvw9 (accessed 9 June 2022).
30 Sukhdev Sandhu, 'Sex and the City 2, a Review', *Telegraph*, 28 May 2010, https://tinyurl.com/musfrwzn (accessed 8 June 2022).
31 Andrew O'Hagan, 'Sex and the City 2 is Ugly on the Inside', *London Evening Standard*, 28 May 2010, https://tinyurl.com/5x5kcnxu (accessed 8 June 2022).
32 Stephen Farber, 'Sex and the City 2: Film Review', *The Hollywood Reporter*, 14 October 2010, https://tinyurl.com/ytabzsbd (accessed 9 June 2022).
33 Williams, *Unbending Gender*, p. 2.
34 Alexandra Del Rosario and Mellie Andreeva, ' "And Just Like That …" Delivers HBO Max's Strongest Series Debut; "The Sex Lives of College Girls" Peaks in Viewers with Finale', *Deadline*, 10 December 2021, https://tinyurl.com/5dvjzhnt (accessed 2 June 2022).

5

The Sopranos (HBO, 1999–2007)

If *Sex and the City* showed us that motherhood is not necessarily a natural and desired state for all women, the next series from HBO, as well as consolidating the cable channel's success in the original drama market, offered us an alternative insight into attitudes towards motherhood – particularly the impact of mothers on their male offspring. Shortly after the premiere of *Sex and the City*, HBO launched *The Sopranos*, a landmark series which quickly became the most successful original drama for the cable channel and synonymous with the channel's branding strategy.[1] Central was Tony Soprano's (played by James Gandolfini) visits to therapist Dr Jennnifer Melfi (Lorraine Bracco), due to the stress-induced anxiety attacks which threaten his ability to retain power in a world in which he came 'in at the end' ('Pilot', 1:1). Also central to the early seasons is the complex relationship Tony has with his mother, Livia Soprano (Nancy Marchand), a bitter and resentful woman who is squarely blamed for the precarious state of his mental health. This chapter will focus on the first two seasons of *The Sopranos* as an insight into the way motherhood is viewed within very patriarchal worlds while setting the tone for many of the quality television series that come after.

Before moving on to discuss the representation of motherhood in this series I am going to offer an outline of the mother's positioning within psychoanalysis and how it has impacted on the way mothers have historically been situated within culture. This approach is particularly apposite due to the centrality of psychoanalysis in the narrative of *The Sopranos*. Particularly useful is sociologist Miriam M. Johnson's work on misogyny and motherhood, specifically her discussion of how motherhood has been used by psychoanalysts to 'explain why men are motivated to denigrate and dominate women'.[2] Johnson argues that '[t]he devaluation of women (by both men and women) is not an inevitable reaction formation to women's prominence in early child care. It is a choice, helped along by the male dominance institutionalized in political and economic structures and supported in male peer groups'.[3] Understanding the positioning of motherhood within the millennial series emerging from HBO is particularly powerful when read alongside this statement as they see mothers and motherhood through a specifically patriarchal lens. Further, as the critical community comments on these women, they reveal a cultural antipathy towards motherhood that is as misogynistic as the representation itself. As Johnson argues, 'attempts to effect real change (as opposed to a change in the forms male misogyny takes) may fail *unless we recognize unconscious motivational tendencies and their underlying dynamics*' (my emphasis).[4] This chapter is my attempt to bring these unconscious motivational tendencies and underlying dynamics to the fore.

There can be little doubt that the work of Sigmund Freud has influenced the way western society thinks about its mothers. Central to Freud's formulation of the maturation of children is his 1909 case study of an equinophobic boy, 'Little Hans', and his subsequent theory that all children desire their parent of the opposite sex and have to repress those feelings; a process resulting in the Oedipus Complex, which takes place between the ages of three and six.[5] According to Freud, faced with the sight of their mother's genitals (or lack of a penis), boys worry that they too will suffer from castration and, rejecting their mother (their first love object), turn to the father as possessor of the penis and symbol of power and privilege.[6] It was during the 1940s that Freudian theory impacted on US culture through psychoanalysts like Helene Deutsch who theorized that good motherhood depended upon women rejecting their 'masculine wishes' and accepting their passive 'feminine' role. For psychoanalysts like Deutsch, ideal or 'complete motherliness' was considered vital if children were not to be burdened by pathologies in their later lives.[7] This idealized (and culturally sanctioned) version of motherhood was soon put to the test during the Second World War when examinations performed by army psychologists, most notably the Selective Service Administration, reported that '[n]early one-fifth of all the men called up to serve in the war were either rejected or unable to complete their service for "neuropsychiatric" reasons'.[8] Of course, the reason for this was firmly placed at the feet of mothers who were blamed for over-protecting their sons, at least according to Edward A. Strecker, an adviser to the secretary of war and consultant to the surgeon general of the army and navy. Based on his war-time experiences, Strecker argued that the nation's men had suffered negatively from women, 'whose maternal behavior is motivated by the seeking of emotional recompense for the buffers which life has dealt her own ego'. A major fault of 'mom', he added, was that she had failed 'in the elementary mother function of weaning her offspring emotionally as well as physically'.[9]

This criticism of mothers was supported by magazine articles like the 1945 *Ladies' Home Journal* article which asked: 'Are American Moms a Menace?' Author, Amram Sheinfeld, linked national security to the way mothers raised their children, arguing that 'mom is often a dangerous influence on her sons and a threat to our national existence'.[10] For Sheinfeld, one of the ways to counteract the problem of neurotic mothers raising neurotic sons was for them to breastfeed 'only as long as is absolutely necessary'. But, the author noted, this was too late for many as Adolf Hitler, for example, was cited as the 'only son and spoiled darling of his not-too-bright mother'. A sentiment shared by authors Ferdinand Lundberg and Marynia F. Farnham, who warned that, when studying despots like Hitler and Mussolini it should be remembered that 'their true subject is hardly the man (or woman) they have chosen to scrutinize ... but the mother or her substitute. Men, standing before the bar of historical judgment, might often well begin their defense with the words: "I had a mother ..." '.[11]

This outrageous misogyny was most notoriously reinforced in Philip Wylie's 1942 book, *Generation of Vipers*,[12] in which he aimed a vicious invective at America's mothers for raising a nation of sons 'unmanned' by excess maternal affection. Although Wylie's book attacked many groups in American society – scientists, the government, doctors, the military and priests – his most vitriolic rant was reserved for post-menopausal American mothers who, according to Wylie, emasculated their sons. Wylie praised Freud for drawing attention to the 'fierce and wonderful catalogue of examples of mother-love-in-action which traces its origin to an incestuous perversion of a normal instinct',[13] and talks of the Oedipus Complex becoming 'a social fiat and a dominant neurosis in our land'.[14] Obviously striking a nerve, the book stirred up a hornet's nest of outrage and, by its twentieth printing in 1954, had sold over 180,000 copies. For Wylie, a whole generation of men were the victims of women who he describes as having 'raped the men, not sexually, unfortunately, but morally'.[15]

It is into this world that the fictional Tony Soprano's mother, Livia, is born. In *The Sopranos*, the domestic jostles for importance within the patriarchal worlds of the mafia and the Roman Catholic Church, constantly threatening to overwhelm as Tony's relationships with his more elderly relatives, Uncle Junior (Corrado 'Junior' Soprano [Dominic Chianese]) and mother Livia Soprano, as well as those of his immediate family – wife Carmela (Edie Falco) and children, Meadow (Jamie Lynn-Siegler) and A.J. (Robert Iler) – prove to be as challenging as the mobster world he inhabits. Tony's mother, Livia, has been universally condemned by critics, described as 'monstrously manipulative, chronically cantankerous, and utterly unchic',[16] a character whose presence was so overbearing that, according to Todd VanDerWerff, 'she was even more powerful in death, as though she were a ghost that had cold hands seized around Tony's heart, ready to squeeze at any instant and bring on another panic attack'.[17]

Our introduction to Tony links him inextricably to his relationships with his mother as, waiting for his first therapy session, he is framed between the naked legs of a female statue. For Joseph S. Walker, who has written one of the most sustained analyses of the relationship between Tony, his psychiatrist and Livia Soprano,[18] this visual composition is 'a symbolic foreshadowing of the program's central drama of Tony's conflict with his mother. Livia – a shorthand reference to the complex relations of birth, subservience, sex, fear desire, and guilt which connect them, and which have essentially incapacitated Tony'.[19] It is through his therapy sessions that we come to know Tony Soprano, mobster boss and family man, and, despite the fact he has been warned by Dr Melfi that he cannot reveal illegal acts to her, the viewer is granted privileged knowledge of Tony's violent gangster life. For Walker it is the juxtaposition of these two worlds that reveals

Tony's battle between two constructed identities, asking: '[I]s Tony to be a coherent subject, or a hysterical object?'[20] A question animated in the sequence opening 'Meadowlands' (1:4), the first time we experience Tony's dream world first-hand.[21] Following his lingering and lustful gaze at his therapist's legs and then onto a series of improbable scenarios – Hesh Rabkin (Jerry Adler) passing by the window in time for his 3pm appointment, A.J. (Robert Iler) looking through a gap in the door/exchanged with Tony who sees Silvio Dante (Steven Van Dante) in flagrante delicto with an unidentified woman. The sexually fuelled grunts and groans of Silvio continue as the camera pans to Paulie 'Walnuts' Gaultieri (Tony Sirico) and Salvatore 'Big Pussy' Bonpensiero (Vincent Pastore) in Melfi's waiting area. The shot then cuts to Tony addressing the back of Melfi's head with 'What the hell's going on?' and then onto Jackie Aprile Sr (Michael Rispoli), hooked up to chemo and 'smelling rain in the air'. This montage of disjointed shots ends with Tony asking the back of his therapist's head: 'Dr Melfi what the hell you doing to me?' Of course, Dr Melfi is revealed as Tony's own mother which, considered alongside his earlier lascivious gaze, reveals a decidedly and overtly Oedipal longing.

Analysed through Melfi's psychoanalytic framework, Tony's mother is firmly established as 'the one' at the bottom of his anxiety issues despite the various stresses associated with the nature of his work and the generational chasms between the older and younger members of his crew. In the past Janet McCabe and I argued that, through Tony's therapy sessions, 'the assimilation of Jennifer's psychoanalytical vernacular by Tony ... allows a feminine voice to penetrate into a generic text that has traditionally excluded it'.[22] Complicating this assertion is the patriarchal voice that insinuates itself through these therapy sessions, with Melfi's authoritative positioning giving expression to a therapy that is rooted in an overtly male Freudian psychoanalytic discourse and a series created by male showrunner, David Chase. Although the words are spoken by Melfi, it should be remembered that this is a male perspective that ensures Livia's positioning as a truly monstrous mother and, through a traditionally Freudian lens, the source of Tony's anxiety. While there is no doubt that maternal power is an issue for Tony, it is remarkable that there is so little acknowledgement that his father, the violent mafia don, may also be the source of his psychological traumas.

It is not long before we are given valuable insight into Tony's childhood. Called into A.J.'s school for a parent/teacher conference for A.J. and two of his friends when they have been discovered drunk after stealing sacramental wine from church, Carmela and Tony are confronted by the possibility that their son may have ADHD (attention deficit hyperactivity disorder) ('Down Neck', 1:7). While Carmela remains calm, Tony is sent into a spiral of self-doubt and recrimination over the effect that his line of work may be having on A.J. and the possibility that his 'disease' may be genetic. At dinner that night, and as if to exacerbate Tony's fears, Livia and Uncle Junior support A.J., telling the family that his mother 'practically lived at the Vice-Principal's office' and that Tony only remembers 'what he wants to remember'. To Tony's increasing discomfort, and A.J.'s incredulous expression, both Livia and Uncle Junior regale the family with stories of Tony's childhood misdemeanours: stealing a car 'before he was ten years old' and selling stolen lobsters for 'a buck apiece down on Bloomfield Avenue'. A series of flashbacks throughout this episode, punctuated by therapy sessions, reveal how his father's line of work was disclosed to the young Tony. Remembering how his elder sister Janice (Madeline Blue) was taken for mystery car rides every Sunday, Tony tells Melfi that his heart 'was broken' at his father's favouritism, only to be assuaged when Johnny Boy is arrested at the fairground along with his mafia cronies. Rather than a preference for his sister, the mafia men were using their daughters as a front for illegal activities. Despite his therapist's suggestion that this would have been 'devastating' to a young child, Tony tells her that he was proud of his father, considered him a 'freedom fighter' and recounts how he bragged about Johnny Boy's violence to his friends. His mother, on the other hand, was always 'a night at the opera' who threatened to stick a fork in his eye when he wouldn't stop complaining and would sooner 'smother' the children than let their father take them to Reno ('Down Neck', 1:7).

When Livia eventually discovers that Tony is seeing a psychiatrist, she tells A.J. (with some insight) that 'he goes to talk about his mother – that's what he's doing. He talks about me – he complains, she didn't do this, she did that. I gave my life to my children on a silver platter and this is how he repays me'. It is in these sessions that Dr Melfi focuses on Livia's emotional hold over Tony, telling him: '[S]he's very powerful.' And yet, Tony is reluctant to admit that 'this little old lady' has such an impact on his emotional life, telling Melfi: '[S]he's a good woman. She put food on that table every night. I'm the ungrateful fuck because I come here, complain about her, and I let my wife exclude her from my home.' And this despite Carmela's assurances that Livia is welcome to live with the family ('46 Long', 1:2). When Carmela takes her to lunch unexpectedly, Livia immediately suspects the worst, and well she might as Tony stashes his guns and illegal contraband in her room while she is out ('The Legend of Tennessee Moltisani', 1:8). Her son clearly sees an opportunity to use the retirement home as a prime hiding place for incriminating evidence and, like the fairground meetings of his father before him, a good place to meet his gangland cronies. Livia is certainly nobody's fool though and, after living with Johnny Boy so long, she knows the rules of the mafia world.

Yet, despite this, the narrative never gives Livia a break with *Sopranos* folklore firmly blaming her for ordering a hit on her son. Filicide does not seem overblown in a world where the matriarch has been depicted as a monstrous force from the start. As the story goes, Livia is unhappy about the way her son moved her into the retirement home and, coupled with the possibility that he could be revealing family secrets to his psychiatrist, engineers his demise at the hands of Uncle Junior. So far, so dysfunctional. Yet, subsequent re-viewings of the episodes in question reveal a slightly different narrative; Livia may well be expert in revealing truths to suit her own agenda, but it is the way that knowledge is traded and subsequently utilized that is crucial here. Livia chooses her moment to impart her news about Tony, complaining that 'he goes to talk about his mother' only after her brother-in-law has told her that they have a 'bad apple' in the crew. Of course, Tony is immediately suspected by Uncle Junior, who is paranoid about the meetings held at the retirement home fearing his demise during an 'end game' and, ignoring Livia's plea that she doesn't 'want there to be any repercussions', orders the hit.

It is only after the failure of the mission that Livia's narrative truly begins to unravel. Tony tells everyone that he was the victim of a carjacking but he knows that this attempt on his life was at the hands of Uncle Junior. Of course, depression ensues and Melfi ups his dosage of Lithium, thus rendering Tony unable to move beyond the bedroom and seeing him in the thrall of daydreams of

Isabella – a beautiful and seductive Italian dental student living next door ('Isabella', 1:12). Over the course of this episode Tony's hallucinations take hold as the depressed mafia don stumbles around with a vacant look on his face and the inability to 'get a grip' on his depression. His mother is quick to tell everyone that she cannot understand his behaviour and, complaining about Tony to her brother-in-law, is confused when Uncle Junior tells her: 'It's done.' Melfi hints to Tony that his mother may have been behind the attempt on his life telling him that she is 'always talking about infanticide' and it is only later, when the FBI play Tony edited highlights of conversations between his mother and uncle, that the therapist's accusations appear to be confirmed. While it is true that Livia has likened Tony's appearance to her lobotomized cousin, telling Junior 'better he died than went on living like that – that's what his mother used to say' ('I Dream of Jeannie Cusamano', 1:13), the conversation that is replayed to Tony is edited alongside other snippets of dialogue between sister and brother-in-law, conjoined to make Tony believe that his mother wished him dead.

In terms of narrative motivation, it is clear that the FBI are cognizant of the fact that, in order to get Tony to talk, they must use all means necessary to motivate him. But what of Melfi? Is she so enamoured of Freudian theory that she can only believe that his mother is at the heart of Tony's emotional issues and behind an attempt on his life? Set in a society that blames the maternal for all things psychologically damaged and underscored by a training in Freudian psychoanalysis, this could be true. But Melfi's continual and pernicious deprecation of Livia to her client are also due to the nature of Tony's therapy sessions and his inability to reveal his criminal activities to his psychiatrist. For David Chase the sessions with Melfi and her client are 'flawed from the start: "What people forget is that Melfi was compromised from the get-go"'[23] and necessarily restricted to what he can tell his therapist. In this case it is easy to see that, while the audience knows that Tony's criminal activities are central to his stress, for his psychiatrist, who can only work with what he tells her, his anxiety attacks can only be attributable to his difficult relationship with his mother. For David Pattie, 'the various violent deaths in Tony's life are glossed over in the therapy sessions ... because the two narratives they are involved in are fundamentally incommensurate'[24] with the therapeutic process dependent upon full and 'final disclosure' whereas Tony works 'towards the maintenance of the criminal status quo'.[25]

In addition, and as Douglas L. Howard argues, language in *The Sopranos* is subject to an 'inherent ambiguity' with the interpreter 'often forced to rely upon nonverbal cues or to consider context and intent in order to make sense of a linguistic statement'.[26] Livia is certainly an expert in wielding nonverbal clues and, like all the mafia wives inhabiting this world, has learnt how '[m]afia dialogue is predicated on suppression, misdirection and euphemism'.[27] The eventual culmination of their therapeutic process in these early days is precipitated by Melfi who, reading from a book, tells Tony that his mother suffers from borderline personality disorder: 'She suffers from intense anxiety; real people are peripheral – these people have no love or compassion and create bitterness and conflict between others in their circle' ('I Dream of Jeannie Cusamano', 1:13). Tony's violent reaction leads to the termination of their relationship as his therapist oversteps the mark, openly discussing his mother's pathology. In the world of mafia-speak the therapeutic relationship, built upon bringing what is repressed into the open, cannot survive and Melfi is not only alienated from Tony, but finds herself removed to a motel as her association with the mafia don threatens her life and her livelihood.

Of course, their relationship does not end there. After another anxiety attack in season two, Tony finds it impossible to replace his psychiatrist and eventually persuades her to take him back. But, and as Janet McCabe and I have argued in the past, Melfi's relationship with Tony, along with her place in *The Sopranos* narrative, never really recovers as she becomes 'ever more entangled in her enthrallment of his performance of male power and her knowledge of its untenable reality'.[28] For Jason Jacobs, 'Tony may not understand himself but he understands the world better than Melfi ... In this way the show challenges us to consider a mob leader as a better human being than his therapist'.[29] In addition, after Melfi blurts out her diagnosis of Livia's issues, her lack of skill in negotiating these linguistic hurdles becomes increasingly apparent (surprisingly for a therapist whose work depends on interpretation of silences and ambiguities). After Livia's stroke at the end of season one, and due to Nancy Marchand's illness, Livia's power wanes and 'the Oedipal story arc more or less ended'.[30] But the impact of the mother/son bond does not end with her death as Melfi continues to shore up Tony's dysfunctional relationship with his mother throughout the series. It is not until much later that Tony muses to Melfi that he realizes that mothers 'are the bus. They're the vehicle that gets you here. They drop you off, then they go their own way, continue on their own journey. The problem is we keep tryin' to get back on the bus when we should just be lettin' it go' ('Kennedy and Heidi', 6:18). Maybe the therapeutic relationship has had more of an impact on Tony than we think.

If Tony is ready to let go of Livia's hold on him then what of the critical community that insist on Livia's guilt and a culture that continues to blame the mother for society's ills? If the world of *The Sopranos* is so heavily weighted against understanding the insidious misogyny against the mother, then surely the world outside should be more sympathetic to the mobster mom, left widowed by her husband's risky lifestyle and powerless in this most patriarchal of worlds. Not so. For cultural commentators writing about *The Sopranos*, Livia will go down in history as the monstrous mother that ordered a hit on her son. Regina Barreca, for example, while identifying with 'almost every female character ... at some point during the first three seasons' maintains that Livia 'arranges to have her son whacked for putting her in a retirement community'.[31] She goes on to describe Livia as anticipated in Simone de Beavoir's *The Second Sex*: ' "[She] lies in wait like the carnivorous plant," passive and lethal. "She is absorption, suction, humus, pitch and glue, a passive influx, insinuating and viscous".' She continues: 'the patriarchal matriarch is scary; she batters those around her into action while seemingly only to beguile them with the powers of the weak and thereby effectively disguises her iron maiden malevolence'.[32] Barecca's insistence on Livia's guilt and damning description of her nature arguably smacks of the same kind of unconscious motivation that fuelled Philip Wylie's *Generation of Vipers* some sixty years previously.

On the other hand, as Joseph S. Walker argues, despite Livia's immense power in the series, her ability to wreak havoc on her son and his family, and her reputation as the mother that ordered that hit, 'it is surely worth noting that she never once utters such a command, or even such a suggestion; her agency is expressed through silence, analogy, innuendo'. Despite this, Walker suggests 'that her manipulation of Junior is clear – to the audience, to Tony, to the FBI, even to Junior himself – it is nonetheless silent and invisible'.[33] This is not the only controversy surrounding Livia. It is noteworthy that there is still dispute over her illness and whether she feigns dementia and a stroke. Her smile as she is wheeled off on a gurney could easily be read as facial paralysis but season two begins with the idea that even if her symptoms are real, her stroke could be psychologically induced. What is clear is that, such is our cultural antipathy towards the mother that we readily accept Livia's guilt and, like the soap opera villainess, she easily becomes someone on which to project our own negative maternal experiences.

In the end, amidst all the controversy around Livia Soprano, David Chase admits that he actually 'had a really good childhood' and that, while he did go into therapy to deal with his childhood issues, he was not haunted and daunted by his mother in the same way. He tells Mark Lawson: '[F]or everyone who writes about *The Sopranos* … Tony Soprano's mother is [his] mother, [and] that there is a strong degree of identification.'[34] Certainly, by his own admission, his mother was a 'handful' but she was also 'funny',[35] something that Livia Soprano is never allowed to be, particularly amongst the cultural commentators that have written about the show. It would be HBO's next series that would again shine a light on the centrality of the mother in the American family but this time her representation would be a much more sympathetic portrayal and allow *Six Feet Under*'s matriarch, Ruth Fisher (Frances Conroy), the kind of compassion and subjectivity denied Livia Soprano.

Notes

1 Jimmie L. Reeves, Mark C. Rogers and Michael M. Epstein, '*The Sopranos* as HBO Brand Equity: The Art of Commerce in the Age of Digital Reproduction', in David Lavery (ed.), *This Thing of Ours: Investigating The Sopranos* (New York: Columbia University Press; London: Wallflower Press, 2002), p. 48.
2 Miriam M. Johnson, 'Women's Mothering and Male Misogyny', in Andrea O'Reilly (ed.), *Maternal Theory: Essential Readings* (Canada: Demeter Press, 2007), p. 202.

3 Johnson, 'Women's Mothering', pp. 204–5.
4 Johnson, 'Women's Mothering', p. 201.
5 Based on the Greek myth of Oedipus who mistakenly kills his father and marries his mother.
6 This necessary turning away from the mother is, for Freud, more complex for girls as, with no penis to start with, their journey towards adulthood is more fraught, a 'negative Oedipus Complex' which results in 'penis envy' rather than the castration anxiety suffered by boys.
7 Judith Warner, *Perfect Madness: Motherhood in the Age of Anxiety* (New York: Riverhead Books, 2005), p. 73.
8 Ibid.
9 Quoted in Warner, *Perfect Madness*, p. 74.
10 Ibid.
11 Ibid.
12 Philip Wylie, *Generation of Vipers* (Illinois: Dalkey Archive Press, 1996).
13 Wylie, *Generation*, p. 198.
14 Wylie, *Generation*, p. 194 (footnote).
15 Wylie, *Generation*, p. 200.
16 Virginia Rohan, 'Marchand's Death Hits "Sopranos" Hard', *Orlando Sentinel*, 28 June 2000, https://tinyurl.com/2kky7f3b (accessed 8 June 2022).
17 Todd VanDerWerff, 'A Ghoul in Angels' Clothing: *Mad Men's* Betty Draper is *The Sopranos*' Livia Soprano. Or She Will Be', *avclub.com*, 5 October 2010, https://tinyurl.com/y5t6y73p (accessed 8 June 2022).
18 Joseph S. Walker, ' "Cunnilingus and Psychiatry Have Brought Us to This": Livia and the Logic of Falsehoods in the First Season of *The Sopranos*', in David Lavery (ed.), *This Thing of Ours: Investigating the Sopranos* (New York: Columbia University Press; London: Wallflower Press, 2002), pp. 109–23.
19 Walker 'Cunnilingus and Psychiatry', p. 110.
20 Walker 'Cunnilingus and Psychiatry', p. 114.
21 Although he has already revealed much about his unconscious anxieties through the discussion of his dream about his penis (being grabbed by a seagull) in the pilot.
22 Kim Akass and Janet McCabe, 'Beyond the Bada Bing! Negotiating Female Narrative Authority in *The Sopranos*', in David Lavery (ed.), *This Thing of Ours: Investigating the Sopranos* (New York: Columbia University Press; London: Wallflower Press, 2002), p. 153.
23 Brett Martin quoted in David Pattie, ' "Whatever Happened to Stop and Smell the Roses?": *The Sopranos* as Anti-therapeutic Narrative',

in David Lavery, Douglas L. Howard and Paul Levinson (eds), *The Essential Sopranos Reader* (Lexington: The University Press of Kentucky, 2011), p. 168.
24 Pattie, 'Whatever Happened?', p. 169.
25 *Ibid.*
26 Douglas L. Howard, '"Soprano-Speak": Language and Silence in HBO's *The Sopranos*', in David Lavery (ed.), *This Thing of Ours: Investigating the Sopranos* (New York: Columbia University Press; London: Wallflower Press, 2002), p. 195.
27 Pattie, 'Whatever Happened?', p. 172.
28 Kim Akass and Janet McCabe, '"Blabbermouth Cunts"; or Speaking in Tongues', in David Lavery, Douglas L. Howard and Paul Levinson (eds), *The Essential Sopranos Reader* (Lexington: The University Press of Kentucky, 2011), p. 97.
29 Jason Jacobs, 'Violence and Therapy in *The Sopranos*', in Michael Hammond and Lucy Mazdon (eds), *The Contemporary Television Series* (Edinburgh: Edinburgh University Press, 2005), p. 155.
30 Akass and McCabe, 'Blabbermouth Cunts', p. 98.
31 Regina Barreca, 'Why I Like the Women in *The Sopranos* Even Though I'm Supposed Not To', in Regina Barreca (ed.), *A Sitdown with The Sopranos: Watching Italian American Culture on T.V.'s Most Talked-About Series* (New York: Palgrave Macmillan, 2002), p. 30.
32 Barreca, 'Why I Like the Women', p. 34.
33 Walker, 'Cunnilingus and Psychiatry', p. 118.
34 Mark Lawson, 'Mark Lawson Talks to David Chase', in *Quality TV: Contemporary American Television and Beyond* (London: I.B. Tauris, 2007), p. 187.
35 Lawson, 'Mark Lawson Talks', p. 188.

6

Six Feet Under (HBO, 2001–5)

If Livia Soprano's depression at the loss of her husband is paid short shrift in *The Sopranos*, the loss of *Six Feet Under*'s patriarch is central to the narrative and the Fisher family. The series premiered on HBO in June 2001 and, coming hot on the heels of HBO's breakout hits *Sex and the City* and *The Sopranos*, meant that much was riding on their next original series. For many, being about death, the show was never going to make the grade and critics were open about the pressure they felt to like it: 'I'm supposed to like *Six Feet Under*. I know this because it's on HBO … But it's hard to imagine anyone watching Sunday night's plodding and pretentious pilot and coming back for more.'[1] The series' central character – Ruth Fisher (Frances Conroy) – was also compared unfavourably to her predecessor, Livia Soprano. Wendy Lesser of the *New York Times*, for example, claimed that Ruth Fisher was a mere 'doormat for the show's producers to step on' and 'an infinitely less compelling' character whose biggest problem was that 'she embarrasses her kids'.[2] Other critics were also less than complimentary about Ruth, including Phil Rosenthal who described her as 'the increasingly cartoonish matriarch whose misguided search for direction in her life will become a running gag'.[3] Linda Stasi's reaction was equally damning: 'Ruth is so wooden, she makes Mary Tyler Moore in *Ordinary People* look like an emoting machine', adding 'she is a ready-to-explode mess in ankle socks and housedresses'.[4] These early opinions, over the course of *Six Feet Under*'s four-year run, did change but, with the benefit of hindsight, is this even a fair early assessment of the central character or just another knee-jerk reaction betraying a cultural antipathy towards older mothers? Is it not true to say that there is more to Ruth than meets the eye and that she is far more complex than these initial responses would suggest? Surely to dismiss Ruth in this way was to totally miss the point as, within the world of *Six Feet Under*, her centrality reveals an aspect of mothering that is routinely missing from quality television series. For Robert Tobin at least, Ruth is a good example of 'a generation of women who had spent their lives entirely under the thumb of patriarchy'.[5]

Before turning to Ruth's place in *Six Feet Under* it is worth briefly considering the intervention of French linguist and psychoanalyst, Jacques Lacan, in the world of psychoanalytic thinking. Updating Freud's Oedipal Complex, Lacan argued that it is actually structured by the child moving from the space of the Imaginary, ruled by the mother, through the acquisition of language to the Symbolic, a space determined by the father ('The Law of the Father').[6] For Lacan, this movement from the Imaginary through to the Symbolic takes place between the ages of 6–18 months through the 'Mirror Phase' – a critical stage in the child's life when he/she recognizes their reflection in the mirror as a more complete version of themselves. Crucially, the mother is always aligned with the Imaginary, the place before language, as 'Other' for the child, and defined by her 'lack'. Just like the castration complex theorized by Freud, mothers are always equated with their lack of a penis (Freudian) or, for Lacan, the lack of a phallus or signifier. Feminists have, over the years, attempted to revise and update Lacan's thinking but, despite their attempts, there is still a tendency within patriarchy to reduce the mother to her role as the nurturing, breastfeeding, pre-Oedipal mother who only has meaning in relation to her young children. With this in mind, any attempt to understand what happens to the mother once the child becomes independent is negligible and motherhood is inevitably repressed and silenced, invisible to society and reduced to metaphor.[7]

Ruth's positioning within *Six Feet Under* complicates this repression and offers us an innovative subject position which allows the 'unrepresentable to emerge from the patriarchal restrictions of representation'.[8] If the sex-gender divide in modern society is due to 'natural and biological' functions which assume that 'women's primary social location is domestic'[9] then Ruth's initial framing in the kitchen confirms our expectations. It is not long before this positioning is complicated as, in a phone call with her husband,

Nathaniel (Richard Jenkins), Ruth fires off a list of chores for him to do and scolds him for smoking in the new hearse. Nathaniel's rebellion against the mother's powerful voice (as the soundtrack ironically plays Bing Crosby's 1943 classic 'I'll be home for Christmas') leads to his untimely death brought about by a sneaky cigarette and a bus. Ruth's reaction to the news of Nathaniel's accident shows us just how complex this maternal representation is going to be as, in a sudden and violent explosion, she throws the phone across the kitchen, followed by the dinner, dishes and knives, all the while howling like a wounded animal. Telling her son David, '[t]here's been an accident. The new hearse is totalled. Your father is dead ... Your father is dead and my pot roast is ruined' foreshadows the fact that, nestled in the heart of a cast of extraordinary characters, Ruth is certainly not going to be a run-of-the-mill mother.

Ruth's centrality to the family home and workplace, particularly a funeral home, troubles our understanding of the domestication of motherhood at the turn of the millennium. It is no coincidence that we are introduced to the matriarch of the Fisher family preparing a Christmas feast. For Alan Ball, the creator of *Six Feet Under*, the kitchen is usually 'the heart of the home, the source of nourishment and sustenance, the congregating place, the hearth'.[10] Despite the fact that the kitchen holds a central place in the lives of the Fisher family, and especially Ruth, Ball warns us that 'it's not a completely warm and rosy place, because the Fishers live in the constant presence of death'.[11] The kitchen in this series also becomes so much more than just a space to cook and eat meals as Ruth becomes estranged from domesticity, trapped in a domestic space that threatens to overwhelm her. In addition, Ruth's inner emotional journey is symbolized by a kitchen which threatens to engulf her as she gradually becomes lost in her attempt to find a place in the world after the death of her husband. In 'The Room' (1:6) she stands, statue-like, gripping a saucepan with her children bustling about her. In 'The Invisible Woman' (2:5) Ruth dreams of a bare house – stripped of furniture and devoid of life – the cavernous domestic space rendered cold and unforgiving. A solitary dinner of a pork chop, potatoes and a few Brussels sprouts in 'Back to the Garden' (2:7) tells of Ruth's overwhelming loneliness; the dark domestic space emblematic of her spiritual and emotional journey, made visible through low camera angles, wide lenses and sinister lighting that turn the cosy space into her uncanny prison.

On the other hand, the kitchen is where Ruth feels comfortable enough to divulge her innermost secrets to her adult children. After discovering that David is gay, Claire (Lauren Ambrose) finds her mother sitting at the kitchen table reading *Now That You Know: A Parents' Guide to Understanding Their Gay and Lesbian Children*[12] ('In the Game', 2:1). Ruth asks Claire how she feels about David's sexuality and, attempting to open a dialogue about the subject, asks her daughter if she has ever had feelings of same-sex attraction. Ruth's attempt to establish an intimate relationship with her adult daughter is painful as she clumsily divulges that she 'once had a little crush on Jane Fonda', leading to Claire's caustic rejoinder: 'Well she's single again so now's your chance.' Later that same evening, the awkward relationship with her children again rears its ugly head when Ruth tells David, Nate and Claire that she is inviting Nikolai (Ed O'Ross) to dinner on Sunday and confesses that she's having a sexual relationship with him. Telling her aghast children that '[w]e're all adults – we're all sexual beings – we should acknowledge that' sees Ruth asserting her role as an adult with the right to speak about such matters which results in her adult children sniggering and behaving like, well, children.

According to E. Ann Kaplan, 'by 1986, the mother/sexual woman split was healed'[13] but, as we can see here, there is no such healing for the post-menopausal/middle-aged mother/sexual woman, as '[h]er sexuality simply does not exist beyond her reproductive potential'.[14] Safely ensconced in the family home with their mother taking care of them, the Fisher children are understandably reluctant to bear witness to their mother's sexual revelations and, while they tolerate Ruth's various eccentricities, it is her sexuality that causes them the most consternation and shows how in 'patriarchal terms the feminine should be either woman or mother, never both'.[15] The first time Claire meets Hiram Gunderson (Ed Begley, Jr) ('Brotherhood', 1:7) she envisions her mother having energetic sex with him on the kitchen counter; later David imagines his mother reaching under the table and informing the assembled company that she 'can't get enough of [Hiram's] cock'. The kitchen is, of course, the room that George Sibley (James Cromwell) brings up the subject of his and Ruth's energetic and vocal lovemaking which has been keeping her children awake ('Falling Into Place', 4:1).

Ruth's use of language, her weird juxtaposition of tones – practical and sharp/caring and nurturing – emphasizes her role as a mother and yet strains her efforts to connect with her children. Her cajoling yet critical voice is reminiscent of the role of the mother's voice in early childhood, associated as it is with sphincteral training.[16] We are privy to these clashing emotional responses repeatedly over the course of the series as Ruth struggles to come to terms with becoming the sole parent of adult children while mourning the loss of her husband. Coming across his mother cleaning silver in the kitchen Nate confesses that he found nude Polaroids of her in his father's belongings. Looking at the photos of her younger self, Ruth tells her son the history of the photos, taken by her husband before he went to Vietnam. She tells him that when he was a baby, in order to get some privacy, they went to a seedy motel room and made love like maniacs, like it was the last time. Adding, 'It's frightening how much we change. Are you staying for dinner dear?' ('The Room', 1:6). When David finally comes out to his mother, an emotional discussion ensues during which Ruth admits that life was so much easier when her children were small as they 'used to tell her everything', she finally composes herself to ask if he is staying for dinner. Through tears she adds the non-sequitur: 'We're having veal' ('A Private Life', 1:12). This equation of food with comfort is not restricted to her children. Hiram takes her out for dinner to tell her, guilt-stricken, that he has met somebody else. Ruth takes the news calmly and tells him: 'Let's order dessert. That'll cheer you up' ('Knock Knock', 1:13). Refusing the toast that Ruth has prepared for breakfast finds Claire accused of having an eating disorder ('Pilot', 1:1) and it is ultimately that solitary dinner in a cavernous kitchen that signals the end of domestic bliss for Ruth ('Back to the Garden', 2:7).

If the Fisher children seem intent on keeping their mother confined to the domestic, like the soap opera mother before her, this works against the psychoanalytic fiction that it is the mother who keeps her children down with her in the Imaginary to fulfil her needs. Realizing that her children do not need her anymore is a shock for Ruth, but also shows how the mother's role becomes redundant and, along with her sexuality, has to be denied. 'Life's

Too Short' (1:9) sees Ruth and Hiram planning a camping trip. Ruth's ecstatic midnight wandering, later that night, after inadvertently taking David's rogue ecstasy tablet (hidden in a bottle of aspirin), reveals a rampant sexuality hidden beneath her prim repressed façade. Hallucinating her dead husband, she tells him that she misses what they had, to which he replies, 'Well, go find it again.' The next morning Hiram tells a flushed Ruth that she had never before been so passionate with him. Ruth's laugh here is reminiscent of the 'Laugh of the Medusa'[17] and while it is a source of discomfort for Hiram, it offers the viewer some insight into Ruth's hidden depths.

We have seen how Ruth's sexuality is a source of discomfort for her children, but what of the other side of the binary, the 'domesticated image of the Virgin Mary, the mother devoid of sexual desire'?[18] This side of Ruth is revealed in the pilot episode the day after hysterically confessing her affair to her sons at Nathaniel's funeral. With flowing hair, she asks Nate to stay for a few more days. Evoking memories of the idealized mother of Nate's childhood, Ruth gets her way. Later in this first season, waiting at the hospital for the outcome of Nate's surgery, Ruth, again with hair loose and tousled, is surrounded by her children and reminiscent of Michelangelo's 'Pieta', the iconic sculpture of maternal suffering ('The Last Time', 1:13). This may initially seem unproblematic and in keeping with the binary of Virgin Mary/Eve that is traditionally sanctioned by patriarchy, but Ruth's assertion that 'a woman's hair is the gateway to her sensuality' retrospectively problematizes this assumption and proves her grasp of the way she is positioned along with her ability to manipulate it ('The Eye Inside', 3:3).

Ruth may be keenly aware of her positioning, but it is clearly not going to be an easy route out of domesticity for her. Having tried to fill the void left by the death of Nathaniel, Ruth attends a self-actualization course – 'The Plan' – and is attracted to the idea that she can achieve self-fulfilment, regardless of how unhappy her past may have been ('Out, Out, Brief Candle', 2:2). Inspired by the speeches of graduating students, especially a forty-one-year-old woman who speaks 'fiercely from the "I"', Ruth leaps at her chance of subjectivity and confronts Nate and David about the whereabouts of the US$93,000 she invested in the business. Seeing the new casket wall bought by her sons, she demands to know how they paid for it and asks to see receipts and accounts. To the bemusement of her sons, she tells them 'I am speaking *fiercely* from the "I"', and fierce she is: body shaking, clenched fists and angry expression on her face. Unaccustomed to this kind of power she adds, 'Do you mind?' before leaving the room with a flourish.

The Plan proves to be cathartic for Ruth and, exhilarated by her angry outburst at the seminar – 'fuck my lousy parents ... my selfish bohemian sister and her fucking bliss ... my legless grandmother ... my dead husband and my lousy children and their nasty little secrets' – the following day sees her again speaking fiercely from the 'I' ('The Plan', 2:3). Forgiving old enemies, Ruth writes a letter to her dead mother absolving her of 'all the terrible things she did' to her and speaks to her bemused family in building metaphors. It is not until she discusses Keith's (played by Mathew St Patrick) niece Taylor (Aysia Polk) with David, that he is moved to tell her: 'Mom, I'm happy for you if this whole Plan thing of yours has enabled you to draft your own blueprint or patch up some of the cracks in your foundation but ... just between you and me you're starting to sound like a crazy person and I think it's time you kept that shit to yourself and minded your own fucking business' ('Driving Mr. Mossback', 2:4). By this time her children have learned to accept Ruth's foibles, as well as her right to be an adult with her own sexual life, but here she goes too far. Like Jennifer Melfi before her, the subjectivity accorded to the critical voice renders it far too powerful and, while The Plan may offer resolution from past hurts and possible happiness for Ruth, it does not offer an unproblematic solution to her dilemmas. As if to emphasize this, the next episode finds Ruth, alone, looking through photos of her young family ('The Invisible Woman', 2:5). It is a moment of heart-wrenching poignancy as Ruth realizes that her role as a 'stay at home' mother to her young children is firmly behind her. This is obviously the downside to an occupation so lauded by society and rarely finds expression in cultural representations, unless through the vitriol of the likes of Philip Wylie. Left alone, Ruth faces the reality of her situation and loses hope of ever finding happiness and a place within the world again.

Discovering that she is grandmother to Nate's daughter, Maya (Brenna and Bronwen Tosh), gives Ruth a chance to relive the maternal role that she had so reluctantly left behind. Happily falling back into the role of nurturing mother, cradling her granddaughter, hair loose and flowing, Ruth again evokes the Madonna, the ultimate icon of idealized maternity ('I'll Take You', 2:12). However comfortable she feels in this role, Maya is not her child and it is not long before the cracks begin to appear in Ruth's relationship with her new daughter-in-law, Nate's wife Lisa (Lili Taylor). Unaware of how mothering has changed in the past thirty years, Ruth gives her granddaughter peanut butter ('Perfect Circles', 3:1). Lisa agitatedly explains that her mother-in-law has made a big mistake due to allergen dangers while a bewildered and distressed Ruth explains that peanut butter was no problem when her children were young. Being a mother in the late 1960s and 1970s has not prepared her for being a grandmother now and Ruth's adeptness at nurturing is sharply juxtaposed with her ignorance of modern-day mothering practices. Dr Spock may have been the expert on parenting in Ruth's day but this one mistake shows how things have moved on. In order to continue her role as childminder to Maya, Ruth has to re-educate herself. A shocking fact that proves that not only is mothering not innate but that Ruth can no longer rely on the now outdated mothering skills that have carried her through her key role in life.

Bettina (Kathy Bates), a straight-talking, irreverently mischievous and unruly woman, appears in Ruth's life just as she is feeling most lost. Kathleen Rowe argues that the unruly woman's power comes from the fact that she threatens patriarchal belief systems: 'What most threatens that set of beliefs is not (or is not only) the vagina, but the female mouth and its dangerous emanations – laughter and speech.'[19] Ruth is appalled when Bettina steals a scarf on their shopping trip ('The Eye Inside', 3:3). Laughingly telling her friend that 'fortunately, women our age are invisible, so we can really get away with murder', Bettina opens Ruth's eyes to how women of their age, as long as they are silent, can fly under the radar of patriarchy. The shopping trip proves to be liberating for Ruth as the banter between the women reveals a hidden facet of her personality. Embracing the newly discovered invisibility, Ruth shoplifts a lipstick and, under Bettina's watchful eye, reveals the woman that, up until now, has been submerged underneath her all-encompassing role as mother. The culmination of Ruth's transformation and re-birth under Bettina's wing comes in 'Nobody Sleeps' (3:4). Motherhood is the focus of this episode with Lisa's problematic path towards 'nurturing mother' and Ruth's trajectory out of it. Waking in his marital bed Nate attempts to rouse Lisa. To his horror it is Ruth purring sexually at his side and not his wife. As we have seen with Tony Soprano, the classic Freudian interpretation of this dream is the son's Oedipal desire for the mother – and we soon discover that Nate's nightmare is becoming a reality when Ruth and Lisa are framed together in the kitchen, looking uncannily alike. It would seem that Nate's dream is not simply about his desire for his own mother but hints at how his Oedipal journey is leading him to repeat his father's life and choices.

From the 'Pilot' onwards, Ruth has struggled with split subjectivity – mother to her family and sexual woman to her various lovers. While she has, in some ways, managed to merge these opposing sides of her personality, the introduction of Bettina's unruliness and Lisa's nurturing unleashes a merging of all her past selves showing how the unruly woman's 'rebellion against her proper place not only inverts the hierarchical relation between the sexes but unsettles one of the most fundamental of social distinctions – that between male and female'.[20] Laughingly revealing uncomfortable truths about herself and her sons, Ruth crosses a line and forces them to reveal their repressions. Not only does she cross the line of family secrets laid bare, but she also drunkenly crosses the line between funeral and family home and death and life. 'Burning Down the House' sung by Bonnie Raitt is a fitting soundtrack as Bettina and Ruth enact their own deaths and, accompanied by a now awake Maya and a tipsy Lisa, encroach on the set of the following day's funeral. Ruth's Medusan laugh in 'Life's Too Short' (1:9) has come full circle, found its unruly expression and signals the death of the old Ruth.

It is clear that Ruth still has many mistakes to make despite her liberation by Bettina. Her friend's departure in 'The Trap' (3:5) leaves Ruth once again alone. Impulsively hugging on the stairs, the women observe Arthur Martin, the new apprentice who will provide a focus for Ruth's newly unleashed sexual self. It should be no surprise that Ruth becomes a voyeur over the course of season three, after all she has attained subjectivity, a new symbolic status, and 'her desire sets things in motion'.[21] Pursuing Arthur, she embraces her desire, kissing him unexpectedly on the lips and then doing it again despite his protestations ('Tears, Bones and Desire', 3:8).

Regardless of his six previous marriages, Ruth proposes to George Sibley (James Cromwell) within six weeks of meeting him, proving that she may have completed a journey but, in many ways, is still repeating old patriarchal patterns ('Twilight', 3:12). Marriage may not be made in heaven, but it does fulfil Ruth in many ways; and it is one way of ensuring adult company and a fulfilled sex life. Lisa's death at the end of season three also temporarily returns Ruth to a mothering role, albeit that of surrogate mother to the now motherless Maya. The patriarchal family is not only reconfigured, but also promises to test the limits of her newfound freedom.

Ruth's journey does not end here though. 'Grinding the Corn' (4:9) sees Bettina and Ruth reunited and taking a road trip to Mexico rather than babysitting Maya for yet another afternoon. Drinking Tequila and laughing outrageously on the way to Rosarita, the trip only ends after Ruth's horse dies underneath her. Despite many losses, her liberation is more or less complete. Even though she never really goes back to her old ways, her choice to care for second husband George in his dementia takes Ruth to a completely different level of caring. By the end of the final season, Ruth seems to have truly reconciled her feelings of guilt. She has survived the loss of Nate Sr, weathered the throes of middle-aged passion with her various suitors; survived the death of her eldest son Nate; and has been able let her daughter leave home with her blessing. Ruth's obituary tells us that she opened the Four Paws Pet Retreat in Topanga Canyon and spent the last twenty years of her life caring for animals with her friend Bettina – a truly fitting way to complete a life that, for better or worse, has been spent caring for others.

E. Ann Kaplan suggested as long ago as 1983 that 'the Mother offers a possible way to break through patriarchal discourses since she has not been totally appropriated by dominant culture'.[22] The death of the patriarch in *Six Feet Under* allowed representations of mothering and especially the middle-aged mother to become, for better or worse, reconfigured. Emerging from the sudden and untimely death of her husband, Ruth's journey clearly problematizes many assumptions about maternity and motherhood along the way. Her narrative may not be particularly revolutionary, after all she does marry a man who receives faeces in the post ('In Case of Rapture', 4:2) rather than endure a life of loneliness, but the fact that she has a narrative at all is due to the fact that *Six Feet Under* lifts the lid on repression and exposes numerous liminal spaces for the viewer. Steeping each narrative in the omnipresent threat of death allows traditionally taboo and dangerous areas safe expression. Ruth's narrative may not tell us if mother knows best but at least it gives us a rare and honest glimpse into her world.

Notes

1. Eric Mink, '6 Feet Stiffs Viewers', *Daily News* (New York), 1 June 2001, p. 112.
2. Wendy Lesser, 'Here Lies Hollywood: Falling for *Six Feet Under*', *New York Times*, 22 July 2001, https://tinyurl.com/mpvcpvtk (accessed 8 June 2022).
3. Phil Rosenthal, 'Let Them Blow Your Mind', *Chicago Sunday Times*, 28 February 2002, p. 89.
4. Linda Stasi, 'Esprit de Corpse', *New York Post*, 29 May 2001, p. 83.
5. Robert Deam Tobin, '*Six Feet Under* and Post-Patriarchal Society', *Film and History*, 32:1 (2002): 87.
6. Jacques Lacan, *Ecrits: A Selection* (London: Routledge, 1997).
7. Michelle Boulous Walker, *Philosophy and the Maternal Body: Reading Silence* (London and New York: Routledge, 1998), p. 135.
8. Ibid.
9. Nancy Chodorow, *The Reproduction of Mothering: Psychoanalysis and the Sociology of Gender* (Berkeley, Los Angeles and London: University of California Press, 1978), p. 9.
10. Ron Magid, 'Family Plots', *American Cinematographer*, 83:11 (2002): 76.
11. Ibid.
12. Betty Fairchild and Nancy Hayward, *Now That You Know: A Parent's Guide to Understanding Their Gay and Lesbian Children* (New York: HarperCollins Paperbacks, 1998).
13. E. Ann Kaplan, *Motherhood and Representation: The Mother in Popular Culture and Melodrama* (London and New York: Routledge, 2002), p. 183.
14. Boulous Walker, *Philosophy*, p. 136.
15. Ibid.
16. Julia Kristeva, *Powers of Horror: An Essay on Abjection*, translated by Leon S. Roudiez (New York: Columbia University Press, 1982), p. 72.

17 Hélène Cixous; 'The Laugh of the Medusa', *Signs*, 1:4 (1976): 875–93, translated by Keith Cohen and Pala Cohen.
18 Boulous Walker, *Philosophy*, p. 136
19 Kathleen Rowe, *The Unruly Woman: Gender and the Genres of Laughter* (Austin: University of Texas Press, 1995), p. 43.
20 *Ibid*.
21 Kaplan, *Motherhood*, p. 204.
22 Kaplan, *Motherhood*, p. 11.

7

Deadwood (HBO, 2004–6)

Towards the end of season one of *Deadwood* we are treated to a rare moment of self-disclosure during Al Swearengen's (played by Ian McShane) drunken soliloquy in 'Jewel's Boot is Made for Walking' (1:11). Much has upset Al over the course of this day but the catalyst for this particular outburst is the discovery that Trixie (Paula Malcomson), his number one prostitute[1] and confidante, has visited Sol Star (John Hawkes) for an illicit 'fuck on the house'. Swearengen's jealous revenge is to summon Star to the Gem and, with Trixie as witness, order the bewildered man to pay five dollars for his pleasure. Public humiliation for Trixie is not enough for Al, however, as that night he sends her packing, saying '[T]onight you sleep with your own'. Picking an unnamed prostitute, and in the privacy of his bedroom, his full rage erupts as he demands anonymous, disconnected sex: 'I was fuckin' her and now I'm going to fuck you if you don't piss me off or open your yap at the wrong fuckin' time. The only time you're supposed to open your yap is so I can put my fuckin' prick in it. Otherwise, you shut the fuck up.' As the owner of the Little Gem and all the women in it, Al is clearly someone that can pick whichever woman he wants to share his bed and, yet, his naked contempt for the woman in his bed is shocking as he tells her: '[S]hut the fuck up. You suck my dick and shut the fuck up.'

Swearengen's violent and emotional response to Trixie's infidelity is clearly an overreaction. She may well have dented his sexual prowess and masculinity, but he has had to weather worst storms than this: he has had a price on his head throughout most of season one; his saloon has struggled to survive competition from rival Cy Tolliver's (played by Powers Boothe) up-market Bella Union; and he is only just managing to maintain a hold over his business dealings in Deadwood. The Reverend Smith's (played by Ray McKinnon) gradual descent into madness and the re-emergence of the warrant on Swearengen's head has upset him even more and Trixie's illicit liaison is just the last straw in a long line of upsets. While Trixie's actions may have been the last straw, Swearengen's venomous outpourings are disproportionate and an unnerving moment in the narrative as his outburst reveals much about this paradoxical character and his utter contempt for women. This chapter will argue that, through an application of post-Freudian feminist psychoanalytic theory, much can be understood about this particular man's utter contempt for women. As we shall see, the fictional Al Swearengen, like most of *Deadwood*, is based upon real historical events and characters. Most revealing is that the real Swearengen's backstory is vastly different from the fictional one and, by looking at both of them, we can understand that the negative male attitudes towards motherhood we see in this short scene are not restricted to the nineteenth century.

Psychoanalyst Karen Horney is one of the first women to ever have been allowed to study medicine. Taking her place at the University of Freiburg (one of the first in Germany to allow women to enrol) she transferred to the University of Berlin and received her MD in 1911. Horney's training as an analyst took place after a series of personal tragedies – losing her parents and giving birth to her first child in the space of a year. Horney was a pioneer in feminist psychoanalysis, questioning what she considered 'a male-biased view of the psychology of women in contrast to Freud's views' and arguing that the 'etiology of "female neurosis" was the male-dominated culture that had produced Freudian theory'.[2] This did not endear her to Freud and, after he cooled towards her, Horney left Berlin (where she had been director of training at the Berlin Psychoanalytic Institute) and became the first associate director and head of training at the new Institute for Psychoanalysis in Chicago.[3] Horney moved to New York in 1934 and it was here that her major theories were formulated.[4] Her essays, which had an impact on feminist theory in the 1970s, were collected into the volume, *Feminine Psychology* (1967), and published after her death in 1952.

Horney's work has been largely ignored, except of course by feminists, which may partly be due to her theorizations of motherhood – particularly her idea that men's fear of their mothers is less to do with the Oedipus Complex, as formulated by Freud, than their dread of woman 'as a sexual being'. Arguing that, because 'the male has to entrust his genitals to the female body, that he presents her with his semen and interprets this as a surrender of vital strength to the woman, similar to his experiencing the subsiding of erection after intercourse as evidence of having been weakened by the woman.'[5] Swearengen's extreme reaction to Trixie's infidelity can be partly explained through an application of Horney's theories, particularly if her visit to Star has implied a sexual desire not satisfied by Swearengen's outward virility and sexual swagger. Already made vulnerable by his attachment to Trixie, Al's masculinity certainly seems to have been affected by a 'dread of not being able to satisfy the woman'[6] as well as a more general sense of betrayal. Horney's work here offers a persuasive account of the troubling misogyny at work in *Deadwood*. Unconvinced that Freud's 'controversial postulate of the Oedipus complex' is a stage of development 'that every child has to go through',[7] Horney suggests that much male insecurity stems from an earlier age when he 'felt himself to be a man, but was afraid his masculinity would be ridiculed'. She adds that 'traces of this insecurity will remain more frequently than we are inclined to admit, frequently hidden behind an overemphasis on masculinity as a value in and of itself'.[8] Trixie's liaison with another man reveals a chink in Swearengen's emotional armour, reveals a fragility in his masculinity and, in the light of Horney's thesis, we are offered an insight into the trauma experienced by Swearengen as his sense of masculinity collapses so totally in the light of Trixie's actions.

This peek at Swearengen's unconscious and his character's motivation is nothing compared to the revelations that follow. He may tell the prostitute, 'don't be sorry, don't look fuckin' back because, believe me, no-one gives a fuck', but this is exactly what he does over the course of the next few minutes. Launching into the sorry tale of his early life and setting the pace of the fellatio to match the narrative thrust of his story, Swearengen reveals the source of his misery – that his mother sold him to 'Mrs. fat-ass fucking Anderson' (the same woman that now supplies Al with women for the Little Gem). That this is the root cause of his rampant misogyny is evidenced by Swearengen's rising vitriol and heightened sexual arousal as his story unfolds. It may be the 'seven dollars and sixty-odd fucking cents' that she left him with 'on her way to sucking cock in Georgia' that fuels his outrage towards the prostitute in his bed, but the fantasy he weaves around his mother's life exposes the torment at the heart of his masculinity. Postulating that his mother probably became 'a mayor or some other type of success story unless by some fucking chance she wound up as a ditch for fucking come', Swearengen uses this maternal fantasy to achieve his own orgasm. Telling the woman in his lap 'Now. Fucking. Go. Faster ...' he ejaculates, seemingly adding his own ejaculatory fluid to the 'ditch' that is his mother.[9]

If Horney is to be believed, and men's problems are the result of their early relationship with their mothers, this scene shows how it must 'be very difficult to fully free oneself from these early experiences'.[10] Swearengen's orgasmic rendering of this last memory of his mother – the return of the repressed – perfectly illustrates Horney's hypothesis and serves as a good example of the direct link between the sins of the mother revisited on the son. By abandoning him to the care of 'Mrs. fat-ass fucking Anderson' Swearengen's mother has not only committed one of society's greatest maternal crimes (short of infanticide) but also left her son to negotiate his own upbringing under the protection of an indifferent caretaker and ruthless businesswoman, one that supplies female children to brothels. If it is true that 'at puberty a boy's task is obviously not merely freeing himself from his incestuous attachment to his mother, but more generally, to master his dread of the whole female sex'[11] then Swearengen's path to mature masculinity was clearly marked by abandonment and fraught with difficulty. And it does not take much to equate this drunken, humourless, ejaculating man with the spectre of an abusive childhood.

So far, so damaged. This brief analysis argues that Swearengen is certainly much more of a 'motherfucker' than a 'cocksucker' but is this not a pointless exercise? What does it matter whether Swearengen was abandoned as a child and left to fend for himself? After all, he is a fictional character. It would seem that now is as good a time as any to remind ourselves that Al Swearengen is the brain child of David Milch whose television series, *Deadwood*, was a fictionalization of the real town of Deadwood. What can a look at the real Swearengen tell us about the fictional character and is there any point in investigating the historical record of a person who resided in Deadwood in 1876?

Ellis Alfred Swerengen (sometimes spelled Swearingen, Swearengen or Swerengen) reportedly did 'move to Deadwood in the summer of 1876' and was 'one of the earliest non-mining men in the area'.[12] According to historical records, after owning two establishments – a temporary dance hall and The Cricket Saloon – he opened the Gem Variety Theater on 7 April 1877 offering entertainment for the men of the community by providing comedians, dancers and singers as well as staging boxing prize fights. The Gem Variety Theater was described at the time, by the *Daily Pioneer*, as being 'neat and tastefully arranged as any place of its kind in the west',[13] but, of course, this was just a front for the more serious and lucrative business of selling women for sex. Tempted by the real Swearengen's offers of a stage career, women soon discovered that they would be put into business as prostitutes and, before long, the saloon 'gained a reputation for its debasement of the women who were pressed into service there',[14] with Swearengen and his staff notorious for brutality. According to *The Black Hills Visitor*: 'The Gem had a reputation for the most vile entertainment featuring the debasement of women in a generally violent and wide open town.'[15] Swearengen's callous attitude to women is well documented and creator David Milch obviously researched the background of his character well. What then prompted Milch to divert from Swearengen's 'real' story into yet another tale woven from poetic and dramatic license? What do we make of the fictional character's maternal abandonment issues when it is revealed that the real Swearengen was actually born on 8 July 1845, one of twin brothers, 'the oldest of eight children, and raised by parents Daniel and Keziah Swerengen until they were adults in Iowa'?[16] In the light of a relatively stable upbringing, it appears that the dramatic license taken here may tell us something about the motivations of the writers of this episode, David Milch and Ricky Jay.

Historian G. J. Barker-Benfield tells us that pioneer couples 'have not captured American myth' anything like the lone hunter with 'the promise of total mobility because he was free of women'.[17] It may not actually matter to the development of the series that, in reality, Swearengen was married three times. His first wife, Nettie, divorced him soon after arriving in Deadwood citing spousal abuse.

He married two more times while living in Deadwood, both of his wives leaving him, both also citing spousal abuse.[18] Al's violence towards Trixie in the first episode for killing a customer in self-defence is clearly in keeping with the real Swearengen's backstory, and instigates a narrative arc that culminates in this scene of drunken fellatio. What is most interesting about this particular revelation, however, is that it adds another, more contemporary, layer to the legend of the lone frontiersman that Barker-Benfield suggests 'was largely a creation of the eastern imagination'.[19] The absence of Nettie and Swearengen's other wives removes any threat of the civilizing force traditionally embodied in the frontier wife. It also serves to bolster the already well-established myth of the 'cold, implacable pioneer'[20] that continues to haunt our post-modern imaginations.

Returning to the woman in Swearengen's bed is informative in light of this reasoning. Especially when we consider that the real Swearengen recruited his women from the east and, being a peddler of dreams, promised to make them performers at his theater. Once the women had arrived courtesy of a complementary one-way ticket, they found themselves stranded 'with little choice other than to work for the notorious Swearengen or be thrown into the street. Some of these desperate women took their own lives rather than being forced into a position of virtual slavery'.[21] Compare this to Milch's fictional Swearengen whose women 'are bought at the same orphanage where he was raised, including a cripple who has absolutely no use to him at any pragmatic level. He is constantly presenting himself as a pure pragmatist, yet to insist on getting your whores at one particular orphanage is at once an impulse to take revenge on women, and also to rescue women'.[22] Unsurprisingly it seems that the real Swearengen shared none of our Al's impulses to rescue women and the twist to this tale is as revealing as Swearengen's confession. The contradictory emotional pull that Milch invests in his character is obviously itself a pragmatic decision and there is a certain neatness to the cause-and-effect nature of taking revenge on women while also rescuing them. But the question remains: why does he need to take revenge on them at all? A return to Karen Horney may shed some light on this paradox. Arguing that men 'have never tired of fashioning expressions for the violent force by which man feels himself drawn to the woman, and side by side with his longing, the dread that through her he might die and be undone,'[23] she adds, '[may] not this be one of the principal roots of the whole masculine impulse to creative work – the never-ending conflict between the man's longing for the woman and his dread of her?'[24] This may well be a question to be levelled at the writers of *Deadwood*. Especially in the light of Swearengen's real backstory that reveals no particular motivation for his brutality towards women, just the result of a 'cold' and 'pitiless' attitude towards the push westwards with 'the demands of this struggle [affecting] the attitude of the American male toward his wife and family'.[25]

If *Deadwood*'s portrayal of Swearengen owes more to post-Freudian and postfeminist thinking than a nineteenth-century sensibility, what do we make of our twenty-first-century Swearengen's misogyny? As a media-savvy audience, we are smart enough to know that, among other things, visual fiction often demands the compression of many characters into one, a series of events into a single action-packed day, and the suspension of disbelief in order to allow the drama to work. It should not matter to us that the real Swearengen was, by all accounts, more of a brutal misogynist than the one portrayed in *Deadwood*. As the central character of the series, it is vital that viewers find him sympathetic and engaging enough to care about and yet realistic and compelling enough to watch week after week. In fact, is it not remarkable (fellatio aside) that compared to other portrayals of masculinity in the show, Swearengen is positively agreeable? Cy Tolliver is a good example. Beating Flora (Kristen Bell) and Miles Anderson (Greg Cipes) to near-death in public in order to 'make an example of them' proves his implacable attitude towards women and children (or teenagers). He shows no remorse for forcing his favourite prostitute, Joanie Stubbs (Kim Dickens), to shoot Flora to 'put her out of her misery' after he has shot her brother ('Suffer Little Children', 1:8) and evokes Alexis de Tocqueville's description of the frontier man as someone who is 'a cold and insensible being'.[26] To this extent, Tolliver better embodies the nineteenth-century American frontier male as 'hard, closed off from the feelings regarded ... as "natural to the heart"'[27] than Al Swearengen.

If Tolliver is a more reliable representation of nineteenth-century masculinity (interestingly there is no real Cy Tolliver to compare him to) then it is not surprising that Swearengen is a more agreeable character than his historical predecessor. After all, if a contemporary audience is to identify with a man capable of appalling acts of brutality, there must be sufficient motivation. With an eye to postfeminism and, in order to wreak his revenge on women, what better justification can he be given than a mother that abandoned him to a terrible fate? After all, for Horney, the dread of woman is so powerful that 'the grotesque nature of the anxiety, as we meet with it in the symbolism of dreams and literary productions, points unmistakably to the period of early infantile fantasy'.[28] Not Swearengen's early infantile fantasy of course, especially now that we know the 'true story' behind his character, but the projection of this dread onto a fictional character.

Returning to the scene of Swearengen's fellatio should be instructive in light of the above. The grotesque nature of the dread of woman (or the anxiety surrounding it) seems to be so threatening to the creators of *Deadwood* as to insinuate itself onto Swearengen's drunken climax. Horney may reassure us that, despite man's attitude to motherhood being a 'large and complicated chapter ... [even] the misogynist is obviously willing to respect woman as a mother and to venerate her motherliness under certain conditions',[29] there is little evidence of this within *Deadwood*, and particularly in this scene, as the absence of respect is replaced by degradation and humiliation. In fact, by applying a modern-day cause-and-effect sensibility to the character of Swearengen – as an alibi for his terrible misogyny – an even more sinister dread of woman emerges, one that is evidenced by the sexualization of the mother to achieve climax and one that obviously haunts the creators of *Deadwood*. This terrible dread is usually only alluded to and, further, is one that the male has 'many strategic reasons for keeping ... quiet'.[30] Horney argues that for men the real dread of woman is because, as a boy, his 'penis is too small for his mother's genital'.[31] Thankfully she assures us that this is all an unconscious process, but nevertheless argues that as 'it is the mother from whom we receive not only our earliest experience of warmth, care, and tenderness, but also our earliest prohibitions'[32] the resulting power over her son means that he is hit 'in a second sensitive spot – his sense of genital inadequacy, which has presumably accompanied his libidinal desires from the beginning'.[33] The result of this is, for

Horney at least, 'of vital importance' as the boy's frustration 'by his mother must arouse a twofold fury in him: first through the thrusting back of his libido upon itself, and secondly, through the wounding of his masculine self-regard'. She thus concludes that 'the impulses take on a sadistic tinge'.³⁴ If this scene is a purely fictional twenty-first-century fantasy, then what are we to make of the sadistic tinge contained within?

G. J. Barker-Benfield's investigation into the history of sexual politics proves illuminating here as he suggests that in the nineteenth century 'there was a uniquely extreme distinction between sexual roles in America'.³⁵ His thesis argues that 'white American men's experience of the increasingly democratic society was one of unrelenting pressure, and that their sexual beliefs and their treatment of women were shaped very largely by that pressure'.³⁶ Citing 'westward expansion, the economic pattern of boom and bust, the separation of the sexes associated with industrialization, and increasing democracy'³⁷ he is concerned with how nineteenth-century values are reflected in gender roles, especially the evidence that 'male attitude[s] ... demanded not only that two styles of life, male and female, be separate, but that women should remain subordinate, and in the home'.³⁸ His overriding concern is that 'the pressure these circumstances generated led American men to view their own sexuality and women in a particular and negative way'³⁹ and suggests that we are still suffering the damaging effects of this formulation in American society today. This irony is not lost on him as he describes the political climate emerging from the turmoil of the 1960s with the 'leading edge of reaction ... the Christian Right, with views on sex and on the position of women by no means remote from those described in Horrors'.⁴⁰ It should be noted that he was writing at the time of Bill Clinton's impeachment following his sexual shenanigans with a White House intern and not Trump's 'pussy-grabbing' rise to prominence. Yet, there is a certain echo of contemporary anxieties contained in his statement that of all the repercussions the most 'salient has been the opposition to women's right to abortion'.⁴¹ With the constant battle raging over women's reproductive rights there is not much to choose between the ideologies being discussed here. It also reveals the pertinence of reclaiming nineteenth-century sexual mores in the twenty-first century.

It is not too surprising that *Deadwood*, screened as it was on HBO, the underbelly of the networks and purveyor of the darker side of life, enters into a dialogue with the sex wars raging in America. Surely, and in this age of self-help and therapeutic confession as seen on television, the creators of the series are enlightened enough to realize the impact of a scene like this and something as powerful as Swearengen's re-telling of maternal rejection while climaxing into a prostitute's mouth should not disappear into the ether without comment? Given the sheer audaciousness of the sequence it is surprising that the scene is overlooked in reviews, commentaries and on the HBO website episode guide. Is it possible that the nature of this trauma and the dread it invokes is so terrible that the existence of it has to be totally repressed? Horney again sheds more light on an ever-present resentment towards women that finds its inception in the child's early years. It is worth reminding ourselves that Horney was writing this over a century ago, but I would ask the question, has anything really changed when we hear that men's 'resentment expresses itself, also in our times, in ... distrustful defensive maneuvers against the threat of women's invasion of their domains; hence their tendency to devalue pregnancy and childbirth and to overemphasize male genitality'.[42] That the fellatio performed on Swearengen reveals all this within the space of minutes leads me to echo Karen Horney's words:

> Is it not really remarkable (we ask ourselves in amazement), when one considers the overwhelming mass of [this] transparent material, that so little recognition and attention are paid to the fact of men's secret dread of woman?[43]

Thanks to *Deadwood*, and one audacious scene, Karen Horney needs worry no longer. It may have been remarkable 'that women themselves have so long been able to overlook it',[44] but with such a clear example of the blaming of the mother for the sins of the son, for the overt sexualization of that relationship and for expressing such utter contempt for the poor woman performing fellatio on him, I thank the misogyny and brutality of Al Swearengen. This scene may leave us with a nasty taste in our mouths but Swearengen partly redeems himself by telling the hapless prostitute 'OK, go ahead and spit it out. You don't need to swallow.' What a gent, what a relief, and what a pity he no longer reigns at the heart of *Deadwood*.

Notes

1 I am deliberately using the term prostitute here rather than sex-worker as the latter implies a voluntary status whereas the women in *Deadwood* are sexually exploited.
2 Sander L. Gilman, 'Images in Psychiatry: Karen Horney, M.D., 1885–1952', *American Journal of Psychiatry*, 158:8 (2001), https://tinyurl.com/yp7zjvts (accessed 9 June 2022).
3 *Ibid.*
4 Karen Horney, *The Neurotic Personality of Our Time* (London and New York: Routledge, 2014) and *New Ways in Psychoanalysis* (New York: W.W. Norton & Company, 2000) (first published in 1937 and 1939, respectively).
5 Karen Horney, *Feminine Psychology* (New York: W.W. Norton & Company, 1993), pp. 116–17.
6 Horney, *Feminine Psychology*, p. 126.
7 Horney, *Feminine Psychology*, p. 125.
8 Horney, *Feminine Psychology*, p. 127.
9 For Ina Rae Hark this scene reveals Swearengen's view of his mother as 'alternately with being an excellent role model whose ruthless pragmatism he has emulated to secure his own success and a worthless, debased abdicator of her sacred maternal duty who deserves to be treated as he treats the women who work for him at the Gem'. *Deadwood* (Detroit: Wayne State University Press, 2012), p. 88.
10 Horney, *Feminine Psychology*, p. 126.
11 Horney, *Feminine Psychology*, pp. 140–1.
12 Kathy Weiser, 'Al Swearengen & the Notorious Gem Theater', *Legends of America*, July 2020, https://tinyurl.com/bddazw9h (accessed 9 June 2022).
13 *Ibid.*
14 *Ibid.*
15 Anon, 'Al Swearengen', *The Black Hills Visitor Magazine*, https://tinyurl.com/4enafvjm (accessed 8 June 2022).
16 Weiser, 'Al Swearengen'.
17 G. J. Barker-Benfield, *The Horrors of the Half-Known Life: Male Attitudes toward Women and Sexuality in Nineteenth-Century America* (New York and London: Routledge, 2000), p. 8.
18 Weiser, 'Al Swearengen'.
19 Barker-Benfield, *The Horrors*, p. 8.
20 Barker-Benfield, *The Horrors*, p. 6.
21 Weiser, 'Al Swearengen'.

22 David Milch, quoted in Heather Havrilesky, 'The Man Behind "Deadwood"', *Salon.com*, 5 March 2005, https://tinyurl.com/2p9yckxy (accessed 9 June 2022).
23 Horney, *Feminine Psychology*, p. 134.
24 Horney, *Feminine Psychology*, p. 135.
25 Barker-Benfield, *The Horrors*, p. 5.
26 Barker-Benfield, *The Horrors*, p. 6.
27 Barker-Benfield, *The Horrors*, p. 7.
28 Horney, *Feminine Psychology*, p. 141.
29 Horney, *Feminine Psychology*, p. 114.
30 Horney, *Feminine Psychology*, p. 136.
31 Horney, *Feminine Psychology*, p. 142.
32 Horney, *Feminine Psychology*, p. 126.
33 Horney, *Feminine Psychology*, p. 142.
34 Horney, *Feminine Psychology*, p. 143.
35 Barker-Benfield, *The Horrors*, p. 20.
36 Barker-Benfield, *The Horrors*, p. liv.
37 Barker-Benfield, *The Horrors*, p. xiv.
38 Barker-Benfield, *The Horrors*, pp. 20–1.
39 Barker-Benfield, *The Horrors*, p. xiv.
40 Barker-Benfield, *The Horrors*, p. xxxvi.
41 *Ibid.*
42 Horney, *Feminine Psychology*, p. 115.
43 Horney, *Feminine Psychology*, p. 136.
44 *Ibid.*

Part III

Adaptations

8

The Killing (AMC/Fox/Netflix, 2011–14)

The latest era of 'too much television'[1] has brought many European forms of serial television to audiences, most notably the Nordic Noir drama series. A deal struck by Murdoch's BSkyB in 2010 to have exclusive British screening rights to all HBO series, including their back catalogue, allowed these dramas to make their home on British terrestrial television (BBC 4 at 9pm on Saturday evenings) and turned attention away from the dominance of quality American series with their mainly male showrunners and brooding antiheroes.[2] Dark and stylish (and sporting those trademark Faroe Island jumpers) *Forbrydelsen*'s (DR/ZDF Enterprises, 2007–12) Sarah Lund offered us an alternative version of police work, one not defined by her gender.[3] Produced in Denmark, a country famous for its family-friendly policies and where men and women are encouraged to share childcare equally, *Forbrydelsen* showed audiences an unconventional, complex and flawed side of mothering, one that was totally out of step with its American counterparts. This chapter argues that by analysing the adaptation of *Forbrydelsen* to *The Killing* (AMC/Fox/Netflix, 2011–14), it is possible to understand how narrative functions as a 'fundamental unit of cultural transmission'[4] by exposing a hostility towards mothers in the American version that is absent from the original.

AMC may have been a relatively new kid on the original programming block but the channel had been around since 1984 making its name by showing old films – American Movie Classics – hence its acronym. The success of its made-for-television movie, *Broken Trail*, directed by Walter Hill, which became 2006's highest rated cable movie,[5] paved the way for the channel's incursion into original programming and, like most success stories before, with little to lose, AMC could afford to take risks. Picking up the HBO reject, *Mad Men*, proved fortuitous for AMC and the channel soon shot to global success with Vince Gilligan's story of a cancer-stricken chemistry teacher turned crystal meth cook and dealer. *Breaking Bad* (2008–14), along with the next series, zombie thriller *The Walking Dead* (2010–), confirmed that AMC, although a basic cable channel, could turn out quality television series rivalling its commercial-free predecessor, HBO.

The problem came when AMC had to consolidate its future and, with the end of *Breaking Bad* in sight, the channel found itself looking for new series to continue its record-breaking run. The international trade in adaptations such as ABC's *Ugly Betty* (2006–10) (from Colombia's *Yo Soy, Betty la Fea*, RCN, 1999–2001), Showtime's *Homeland* (2011–20) (from Israel's *Hatufim*, Channel 2, 2010) and HBO's *In Treatment* (2008–) (from Israel's *BeTipul*, HOT3, 2005–8) had confirmed just how successful the television adaptation market could be and, despite the risk associated with imports that had failed to make the grade,[6] the acquisition and adaptation of *Forbrydelsen* to *The Killing* would ensure, AMC hoped, another breakout hit for the channel. Particularly as the Danish version had already been 'exported to an estimated 120 countries' and had set 'a new record for the international penetration and popularity of high-end foreign-language TV drama'.[7] Filming on the show started in 2010 and the series premiered on AMC in the United States on 3 April 2011, only four months after *Forbrydelsen* first hit UK television screens.

The way the narrative of *The Killing* was modified over the course of four seasons reveals much about cultural attitudes towards mothering. For example, Sarah Lund's haphazard parenting style, continually putting the demands of the case before the needs of her teenage son, are never judged in *Forbrydelsen* and yet, in its American iteration, Sarah Linden's mothering is increasingly demonized. This difference may, in part, be explained by Denmark's progressive attitudes to parenting with the country providing one of the most generous parental leave systems in the EU with 'a total of 52 weeks (one year) of leave containing maternity, paternity and parental'. On top of this, once the first year of parental leave is over, Denmark provides daycare facilities for all children from the age of twenty-six weeks to six years, as national municipalities recognize that '[p]roper day care facilities are a necessity for women's full time participation in the labour market on equal terms with men', with the government providing guaranteed daycare facilities with realistic fees linked to income.[8] Compare this to American mothers who suffer the worst maternity benefits in the western world with no paid leave for mothers in any segment of the workforce, only twelve weeks' unpaid leave in companies with fifty or more employees (a voluntary offering) and, with high childcare expenses,[9] it is easy to see which country respects the right of women to work post-childbirth. Little wonder then that a comparison of the attitudes towards mothering in *Forbrydelsen* and *The Killing* reveals a narrative hostility in the US adaptation that is absent from the Danish one.

The location of Seattle (although filmed in Vancouver) provides the perfect backdrop for the dark, brooding re-make in place of *Forbrydelsen*'s Nordic landscape. Resemblances to an earlier police procedural set in Seattle soon became apparent. Whether writer, Veena Sud, deliberately set out to emulate the long-mourned *Twin Peaks* (ABC, 1990–1, Showtime, 2017), is a moot point, but similarities were immediately obvious: The murder by drowning of an outwardly clean-cut and popular teenage heroine, a near seamless switch from 'Who Killed Laura Palmer?' to 'Who Killed Rosie Larsen?' and a soundtrack reminiscent of the Danish series coupled with a *Twin Peaks*-esque dreamy, hypnotic tone, meant that comparisons were inevitable.[10] Fidelity to the original text is not necessary for an adaptation to be successful but, with the 'sentimentalization' of a grief-stricken family,[11] *The Killing* soon descended into an over-blown melodramatic narrative that was compared unfavourably to the original.[12]

Sarah Linden is about to depart for a new life in California with her partner (Rick Felder, played by Callum Keith Rennie) and son, Jack (Liam James), until the discovery of a body on her last day on the job in Seattle presents her with one last case to solve. Teamed with her replacement, Steven Holder (Joel Kinnaman), a jive-talking detective with his own shady past and, reminiscent of the odd-couple pairing of Sarah Lund and Jan Meyer (Søren Malling), the story unfolds in much the same way as *Forbrydelsen*'s. Prevented from leaving, both Lund and Linden are portrayed as women driven by the demands of their jobs, both compelled to solve a murder at the heart of the series, both prioritizing the case over their own lives, including mothering their teenage sons. It soon becomes clear, however, through a gradually revealed backstory, that Linden's drive to solve the case and inability to care for her own child is due to a childhood spent in foster care after being abandoned by her own mother; a backstory not in the Danish version. Replacing Lund's caring mother, Vibeke (Anne Marie Helger), is social worker Regi Darnell (played by Annie Corley), a no-nonsense, straight-talking woman who hints at the emotional and psychological toll of Linden's obsessive work ethic, an obsession that brought her close to mental breakdown and loss of her son, Jack, during her work on a previous case.

Sarah Linden's mothering is not the only focus of criticism in the first two seasons, however, as the narrative repeatedly makes links between bad mothering and troubled teens. Subtle changes to the way Rosie Larsen's parents react to the murder of their daughter tell us much about how this particular adaptation can be understood as 'a barometer for the state of [the] society' at the centre of its narrative.[13] When the prime suspect in her daughter's murder case, Rosie's teacher, Bennet Ahmed (Brandon Jay McLaren) is released, Rosie's mother, Mitch Larsen (Michelle Forbes) instigates his near-death beating by her husband Stan (Brent Sexton). Stan's terrible retribution and resulting incarceration, it is suggested, is her fault, as is his subsequent re-involvement with the Russian mafia. Mitch eventually walks away from her husband and two young boys and, in another change to *Forbrydelsen*'s narrative, takes time away from the family. A move that led to her being named one of the '10 Worst Moms on TV', along with Sarah Linden, who was accused of 'not actively trying to kill her son, but … may end up doing so anyway'.[14]

Due to falling audience figures[15] AMC cancelled *The Killing* but 1.5 million viewers were considered enough for Fox and Netflix to resurrect the series. Season three saw Linden again dragged back into an investigation, this time involving the disappearance of street children in Seattle, a case that brought with it associations of Linden's own troubled childhood. In this third outing Linden's 'bad' mothering is temporarily overshadowed by the appalling parenting of missing teenager Kallie (Cate Sproule). Blamed for her daughter's fate and portrayed as being guilty of putting her boyfriend, Joe Mills' (played by Ryan Robbins) needs above Kallie, Danette Leeds (Amy Selmetz) is the epitome of neglectful maternity. Joe's mother, Mama Dips (Grace Zabriskie), may shield her son's paedophilic activities from the police, but it is Danette that is ultimately held responsible as she slowly realizes that her violent boyfriend may be implicated in the case. As Danette unravels, her 'bad' mothering is compounded by the knowledge that it was she who invited a violent paedophiliac pornographer into their home with tragic consequences.

It is not just neglectful mothers that put their children's and others' lives at risk in season three of *The Killing* but men like Pastor Mike (Ben Cotton) who preys on the homeless teenagers he purports to shelter and death row inmate Alton (James 'Little JJ' Lewis) who hangs himself in his cell after receiving forgiveness from his siblings for the murder of their parents. As Linden becomes increasingly obsessed in her bid to save death row inmate Ray Seward (Peter Sarsgaard), his final moments not only reveal his possible innocence but Linden's maternal guilt towards her own son, Jack ('Six Minutes', 3:10). In this dark world of serial killing, street children and death row, parental responsibility is held to blame for the perils that befall these children – whether murderous or not – and it is the bad choices of mothers that are held ultimately responsible. The revelation that it is Linden's ex-lover, Police Chief James Skinner, Head of Special Investigations Unit, who is the serial killer compounds her guilt. Heavily implied is that Linden is as bad a judge of character as Kallie's mother, Danette, as she rekindles her relationship with Skinner, unaware of his hidden life, before his murderous identity is revealed.

If bad mothering is, over the course of three seasons, held responsible for the fates of teenage victims in *The Killing*, by the time the series had been cancelled and resuscitated for a third time by Netflix, Linden and Holder would venture into even darker territory. In a narrative liberally adapted from seasons three and four of *Forbrydelsen*, Holder and Linden, who are both implicated in the shooting of Skinner, are called to the bloody scene of the murders of the Stansbury family ('Blood in the Water', 4:1). The only survivor, Kyle Stansbury (Tyler Ross) can remember nothing of the incident and this final outing of the series follows the parallel investigations into the murders of Skinner and the Stansbury family. Publicity in advance of the final season assured viewers of the freedom afforded by Netflix, reminiscent of interviews given by David Chase and Alan Ball in the early days of HBO: 'We can curse now', enthused Veena Sud in an interview with *TVline.com*, 'Holder's not the only one who developed a potty mouth over the hiatus. Even Linden gets an F-bomb'.[16] The article goes on to celebrate the joy of the commercial-free environment afforded by Netflix: 'in other words, the show's relatively short six-episode season will actually have a running time closer to eight'.[17] Six one-hour-long episodes that would allow series creator, Veena Sud, the freedom to delve even deeper into the dark world of maternal deprecation without commercial breaks.

If Sarah Linden, Mitch Larsen and Danette Leeds were victims of *The Killing*'s misogyny in seasons one to three, then the freedoms afforded by distribution through Netflix allows an intense hostility towards women who fail to live up to culture's expectations of idealized maternal 'duty'. In this season, it is not only the accusations of bad mothering that Holder repeatedly spits at his partner, but the way the narrative descends into a melodramatic invective against women who fail in their 'natural' maternal role. St. George's naval college, at the centre of the mystery, is populated by male cadets under the care of Colonel Margaret Rayne (Joan Allen), a stern and unsympathetic commanding officer who practices 'tough love' on her charges. Without that nurturing mother, it is suggested, young men descend into an Orwellian dystopia where aggression and bullying are the norm and empathy is scarce. At the heart of the case is the gradual exposé of events leading up to the night of the murders and the revelation that, as suspected, Kyle Stansbury is guilty of the crime. Revealed along the way is the unprofessional nature of his mother Linda Stansbury's (played by Anne Marie DeLuise) tennis coaching and her sexual penchant for young boys, the cruelty of Philip Stansbury (Bruce Dawson) towards his son and the eventual revelation of the true maternal relationship between Rayne and her young charge. While the reputation of fathers does not escape blame, in a world in which parental neglect runs amok, it is the mothers that receive the harshest narrative treatment as is evidenced by the initiation ceremony that leads to Kyle's eventual breakdown and murderous rampage.

The narrative trajectory of this final outing shows us just how engrained some cultural attitudes are and how industrial contexts affect such portrayals. *The Killing*'s season four finale ('Eden', 4:6), freed from the constraints of network and cable television, shows how vilified 'bad' mothers can be, particularly when they commit the ultimate crime of 'maternal neglect' by sending their sons away to boarding school. Forced to witness yet another hazing event in which boys, left to their own devices, could find ever-more inventive ways to humiliate each other, *The Killing* shows just how disturbed these misomaters can be. New recruits, forced to strip and masturbate over a picture of their mothers, with encouragement to 'come over the face of the woman who loved you enough to send you away' is shocking in its naked hatred of motherhood but, in a world in which women are denigrated for their maternal 'shortcomings', it is a sadly inevitable fate. The question remains, however, are such contemptuous attitudes towards mothers and motherhood so acceptable as to go unremarked? A brief survey of the reviews refers to the 'ham-fisted' approach to the family theme contained in season four (no pun intended here) and 'the boarding-school unpleasantness' as 'not new ground in its own right, not even by the longest of long shots'.[18] As in *Deadwood* before it, not one critic refers to the level of hatred directed towards mothers, let alone the way this emotion is sexually expressed.

Created by Veena Sud and enjoying an unusual gender balance behind the scenes with a 'fifty percent female and male, writers' room',[19] it is clear that female showrunners and writers do not necessarily mean better narrative treatment for mothers and *The Killing* is an excellent example of the drawbacks of taking a feminist approach that 'attributes the shaping of female agency mainly to direct female creative control, without adequate consideration of the economic restructuring needed to actualize equal opportunity and rework commonsense assumptions about gender equality'.[20] In an industry still controlled by principally male executives, this is a good example of how the cultural and industrial context of a television series can have a bigger influence than any kind of feminist sensibility the creator may have. For Isabel Pinedo, the differences between the Danish version (which had a male creator) and its US adaptation shows how a society that 'institutionalizes gender equality' also shapes working practices and, regardless of whether the personnel behind the scenes are male or female,[21] leads to the masculinization of quality American television discussed in the introduction to this book.

Despite the dark maternal paths the viewer has been taken down, the final episode of *The Killing* works hard to reach a satisfactory conclusion, a happy-ever-after that ties up loose ends and glosses over the preceding unpleasantness. Skinner's killers walk free from a police department desperate to avoid scandal, the remaining bodies of the street children are recovered, Holder makes peace with Kallie's mother, Kyle Stansbury confesses to the crime of familicide and Linden is reunited with her absent mother as well as finding peace with son Jack. The last scenes find us some years into the future. Holder is separated from the mother of his child and, sober after a long-standing drug habit, running the local Narcotics Anonymous branch. Linden is travelling, unable to settle, still looking for her place in the world. In another departure from the Danish version that saw Lund boarding a plane, flying away from certain incarceration, Holder and Linden, this last scene suggests, will become a romantic couple. Whereas the hazing incident and the heinous attitudes towards mothers escaped the ire of critics, the promise of a happy ending was so shocking that it prompted one critic to remark:

> The idea that the two of them might start a relationship seemed more disgusting than all the blood that was sprayed around the blindingly-white house where the Stansburys were murdered. The thought of the two of them kissing felt weirder than watching your parents hold hands.[22]

What upsets some people does seem strange, particularly when *The Killing* has trodden such a misogynistic and melodramatic path.

Back in 1975, Laura Mulvey's argument that 'the strength of the melodramatic form lies in the amount of dust the story raises along the road, the cloud of overdetermined irreconcilables which put up a resistance to being neatly settled, in the last five minutes, into a happy end'.[23] The world of *The Killing* worked hard to damn the possibility of happy family life, particularly when it involved working mothers, but the movement towards a happy ending for Linden and Holder suggests that, in the melodramatic form, there is still an investment in the family, despite the many maternal failings that have been exposed along the way.

Notes

1 Cynthia Littleton, 'FX Networks Chief John Landgraf: "There Is Simply Too Much Television"', *Variety*, 7 August 2015, https://tinyurl.com/yvhhsh3n (accessed 8 June 2022).
2 James Robinson, 'BskyB Buys Complete HBO Catalogue', *Guardian*, 29 July 2010, https://tinyurl.com/2p8jdrze (accessed 8 June 2022).
3 *Borgen* (DR1, 2010–13) quickly followed, with Sidse Babett Knudsen as Statsminister Birigitte Nyborg proving that mothers could not only solve murders but they could also run a political party, be (for the first season at least) happily married and, with help, juggle childcare and a demanding career.
4 Gary R. Borlotti and Linda Hutcheon, 'On the Origin of Adaptations: Rethinking Fidelity Discourse and "Success" – Biologically', *New Literary History*, 38:3 (2007).
5 Earning it sixteen Emmy nominations, winning four (Deborah Jaramillo, 'AMC: Stumbling Towards a New Television Canon', *Television & New Media*, 14:2 (2013): 177).
6 *Men Behaving Badly* (BBC, 1992–8), *Absolutely Fabulous* (BBC, 1992–2012), *Coupling* (BBC, 2000–4), *Life on Mars* (BBC, 2006–7) and *Gavin and Stacey* (BBC, 2007–19) to name but a few.
7 Ray Weaver, 'A Year on From *The Killing* that Reinvented Noir', *Copenhagen Post*, 18 October 2013. Quoted in Trisha Dunleavy, 'Transnational Television, High-End Drama, and the Case of Denmark's Forbrydelsen', *Semantic Scholar*, 2014, DOI: 10.1177/1527476412442105.
8 European Union report, 'European Platform for Investing in Children', *European Commission*, https://tinyurl.com/mt2mejv2 (accessed 8 June 2022).
9 'The average cost of center-based daycare in the United States is $11,896 per year ($991 a month) for infants and $10,158 per year ($847 a month) for toddlers. Prices for infant daycare can range from $5,760 to $20,880 a year ($480 to $1,740 monthly), according to ChildCare Aware of America.' Jill Ceder, 'Childcare Costs', *verywellfamily*, 22 June 2020, https://tinyurl.com/ydky9eh7 (accessed 8 June 2022).
10 Ed Brubaker, 'The Killing: Comparing the Danish Show to the American Show', *birthmoviesdeath.com*, 21 June 2011, https://tinyurl.com/5n792pec (accessed 7 June 2022) and Mike Hale, 'The Danes do Murder Differently', *New York Times*, 28 March 2012, https://tinyurl.com/58eaxh9c (accessed 9 June 2022).

11 Melanie Kohnen, '"This was just a melodramatic crapfest": American TV Critics' Reception of *The Killing*', *Journal of Popular Television*, 1:2 (2013): 267–72.
12 Janet Staiger, 'Serialization and Genre Expectations: The Case of *The Killing*', *Flowtv.org*, 2 July 2012, https://tinyurl.com/ytw72pcs (accessed 8 June 2022).
13 Andrew K. Nestingen, quoted in Gunhild Agger, 'Nordic Noir on Television: *The Killing I-III*', *Cinema & Cie*, 12:19 (2012): 46.
14 Mitch Larsen ranks fourth and Sarah Linden eleventh out of twelve on this list. *Yahoo.com*, 10 August 2012, https://tinyurl.com/ysc87385 (accessed 9 June 2022).
15 Down from 2.17 million viewers in season one to 1.58 million at the end of season two, *TV Series Finale*, https://tinyurl.com/wyeu7a99 (accessed 8 June 2022).
16 Michael Ausiello, '*The Killing* on Netflix: Longer Episodes and F-Bombs Galore', *TVLine*, 4 July 2014, https://tinyurl.com/jtt3mhne (accessed 8 June 2022).
17 *Ibid*.
18 Noel Kirkpatrick, '*The Killing* Season 4 Review: The Short Goodbye', *tv.com*, 3 August 2014, https://tinyurl.com/3ayze2sp (accessed 29 December 2014).
19 Isabel Pinedo, '*The Killing*: The Gender Politics of the Nordic Noir Crime Drama and its American Remake', *Television and New Media*, 22:3 (2019): 300.
20 Pinedo, '*The Killing*', 309.
21 *Ibid*.
22 Joel Keller, '"The Killing" Goes Out as One of the Most Baffling Shows Ever Made', *IndieWire*, 16 September 2014, https://tinyurl.com/4wsw3vmv (accessed 9 June 2022).
23 Laura Mulvey, *Visual and Other Pleasures* (London: Macmillan, 1989), p. 40.

9

Game of Thrones (HBO, 2011–19)

Much has been written about the adaptation of *A Song of Ice and Fire* to *Game of Thrones* (HBO, 2011–19) – its historical veracity,[1] as an adapted text,[2] audience engagement with the series,[3] the philosophy that informs it,[4] and as part of the wider gendered transmedia universe[5] – and this is only a very brief list that does not include the reams of newspaper, magazine and journal articles devoted to the series. This chapter does not even try to engage with all of these contributions but will return to themes already raised in this book, specifically the chapters on *Deadwood* (historical verisimilitude) and *The Killing* (national attitudes towards the maternal) and, while not principally concerned with theories of adaptation, I will again focus on what is revealed about attitudes towards motherhood through the adaptations of books to television. A central question in this chapter is to discern whether *Game of Thrones* is intrinsically misogynist or whether the series is actually a critical commentary on the overtly sexist nature of a patriarchal fantasy world.

As we have seen, since the mid-1990s HBO led the way in the cable sector by producing quality original series and selling them directly to the audience – a business model that would later be taken up by Netflix and others. In the midst of the increased competition for original series during these years, HBO appeared to falter – *Deadwood*'s surprise cancellation in 2004, *Carnivale*'s (2003–5) a year later and the negative critical reaction to *Rome* (2005–7) – heralded some fallow years for the channel. The 2008 departure of the chief executive officer, Chris Albrecht, who was credited with ushering in this latest golden age of television, compounded HBO's woes, as did the cancellations of David Milch's *John from Cincinnati* (2007) and *Luck* (2011). Amidst rumours that the channel was losing its way, HBO made that now infamous mistake of passing on Matthew Weiner's *Mad Men* (2007–15). AMC's huge global success with both *Mad Men* and *Breaking Bad* (2008–14) led cultural commentators to speculate that HBO had 'finally tumbled from its pedestal'.[6] It certainly seemed that way with insiders calling them 'HB-Over' despite the fact that shows like *Entourage* (2004–11) and *Curb Your Enthusiasm* (2000–) were riding high and *Boardwalk Empire* (2010–14) was already in the works.

It is impossible to tell whether HBO really did read the runes or if it was just coincidence, but they optioned *A Song of Ice and Fire* in the same year that *Mad Men* premiered on AMC (2007). The channel had already enjoyed limited success adapting Israel's *BeTipul* (HOT3, 2005–2008) to *In Treatment* (2008–) as well as witnessing the meteoric success of the adaptation of *Yo Soy, Betty la Fea* (RCN, 1999–2001) to *Ugly Betty* (ABC, 2006–10). Looking back, it certainly seems that HBO saw the future of television moving away from original series and into adaptations as George R. R. Martin's five-part book series, if successful, would ensure longevity and insure against the lack of originals on the market. With AMC hot on their heels, *Game of Thrones* and *The Killing* both began filming in 2010 with both channels hoping that their respective adaptation would be the next breakout hit for the channel. We have already seen how AMC's adaptation of *Forbrydelsen* fared after three cancellations and a move to Netflix, but the success of HBO's adaptation of *Game of Thrones* would be quite a different story, putting HBO back on the map, launching its streaming model and attracting a new wave of subscribers.[7] Certainly not a series for the faint-hearted, first reports were that *Game of Thrones* was unapologetically misogynist, cruel and violent and, with the first episode seeing Bran Stark (Isaac Hempstead Wright) pushed from a tower after witnessing incest between twin brother and sister Jaime and Cersei Lannister (played by Nikolaj Coster-Waldau and Lena Headey), the telvision series promised to live up to expectations.

Critics were initially lukewarm with Ginia Bellafante of the *New York Times* famously asking 'What is "Game of Thrones" doing on HBO?'[8] and, dismissing the series as 'boy fiction', assured readers that ' "Game of Thrones" serves up a lot of confusion in the name of no larger or really relevant idea beyond sketchily fleshed-out notions that war is ugly, families are insidious and power is hot'.[9] Journalists from the *New York Times* certainly seemed to have a problem with the series leading television critic, Martha Nussbaum, to comment that, even though she had initially dismissed the series she soon realized that '[f]antasy – like television itself, really – has long been burdened with audience condescension: the assumption that it's trash, or juvenile, something intrinsically icky and low'.[10] Nussbaum points out that, although superficially just another 'guts-and-corsets melodrama', *Game of Thrones* should be considered on the same level as the classic shows that came before it where the 'undergirding strength of each series is its insight into what it means to be excluded from power: to be a woman, or a bastard, or a "half man"'.[11]

Again it is useful to look at the background, particularly when Martin says that he got his inspiration for the source novels from 'the European medieval age, during which time royal marriages were political and women used as pawns'.[12] While *Game of Thrones* has been said to draw on 'social realism and historical fiction', turning these elements into 'pitch-black fantasy, which holds torture, terror, sexual abuse, murder, and suffering',[13] it is worth looking at the HBO adaptation to see if we can discern anything about the attitudes of the television industry and the way motherhood is regarded in the twenty-first century. We have seen how disingenuous some writers can be with their insistence on the veracity of historical sources and bearing in mind that, even if *A Song of Ice and Fire* is a work based on the War of the Roses,[14] it is still a fantasy fiction, and it may well be worth delving into medieval history to see whether the representation of motherhood in *Game of Thrones* is based on any kind of historical veracity. Nicole M. Mares looks back to medieval times to investigate whether the women in *Game of Thrones* would have actually been as powerful in history as they are in the series. For Mares, the series 'depicts a number of powerful women who exercise remarkable agency in determining their own fates',[15] arguing that, even if 'George R.R. Martin and the producers of the *Game of Thrones* series take liberties in the depiction of female characters in the Seven Kingdoms, the women portrayed in the series do enjoy freedoms that may have been available to certain subsets of medieval women'.[16] For Janice Liedl, the 'parents in Westeros have as many problems as any historical parents in the Middle Ages and

Renaissance – maybe even more, because they were raising families in a world where dragons and magic hold sway'.[17] So far, so inconclusive and if the women in *Game of Thrones* and *A Song of Ice and Fire* do share characteristics with medieval women, 'the power these women command in the series often comes at a high price: it is a consequence of a certain kind of powerlessness'.[18]

With little further to be gained from investigating historical veracity, maybe more insight can be achieved by looking at the differences between mothers in the adaptation from books to television. According to Marta Eidsvåg this is a far more profitable endeavour as, while motherhood 'is an integral theme in George R. R. Martin's *A Song of Ice and Fire*', the HBO adaptation fails its source women. For Eidsvåg the HBO mothers are 'weaker, more traditionally motherly, less provocative and often less central to the narrative than the mother figure in Martin's books'.[19] Eidsvåg bases her analysis on the four archetypes outlined by E. Ann Kaplan in her essay 'The Case of the Missing Mother: Maternal Issues in *Stella Dallas*'. Listed as 'The Good Mother,' 'The Bad Mother or Witch', 'The Heroic Mother' and 'The Silly, Weak, or Vain Mother',[20] Eidsvåg argues that while Martin's origin tale contains 'complex and diverse' mothers that share some characteristics with these archetypes, they do not easily fit into any of the categories while the HBO adaptation 'shows a consistent pattern' of bringing the mothers closer to the archetypes outlined by Kaplan.[21] Eidsvåg's essay is particularly useful in its delineation of Cersei Lannister and Catelyn Stark (Michelle Fairley), showing how their adaptation to screen moderates their motherhood. In this schema, both Cersei and Catelyn emerge as clear maternal archetypes – the Bad Mother and the Silly Mother – while their literary antecedents are drawn with much more complexity. Eidsvåg's analysis argues that the adaptation shies away from subjects like abortion, maternal sexuality as well as the more powerful murderous aspects of both women. Her conclusion? Despite Martin's source novels having 'women and mothers aplenty. They are strong and weak, kind and cruel, often provocative',[22] and while other controversial aspects of the adaptation are amplified and exaggerated, the mothers in the HBO adaptation fall short. For Eidsvåg the result is a 'mainstreaming of the mothers and to some extent the families'[23] where 'their motherhood ends up weakening rather than strengthening them'.[24]

This is where our look at motherhood and its adaptation to television becomes really interesting. If HBO is a place that prides itself on being 'Not TV', where sexuality and violence can become even more provocative and outrageous than on any other channel, why is motherhood treated this way? Particularly as there is no restraint when it comes to female nudity, with 'HBO's staging of women having sex ... while male characters offer information (exposition) ... coined as "sexposition"' and applied retrospectively to other HBO shows and 'its gender politics in general'.[25] In addition, HBO has added female nudity and sex 'into scenes of violence and torture'[26] and, even more revealing, where sex is consensual in the book it has been 'changed into rape' in the television series.[27] It does seem peculiar that while HBO seems to be intent on sexualizing violence and torture, introducing scenes of depravity that do not appear in the book series, mothers are shaped into sanitized and diluted versions that easily fit into Kaplan's maternal archetypes. Could it be that there is another agenda here? One that continues to put mothers in their place even when the source material empowers them? Throughout this book we have seen how revealing an application of feminist psychoanalysis can be in any discussion of television mothers, is it possible that feminist psychoanalytic theory will again be able to shed light on the way women and mothers have been adapted in HBO's series – this time *Game of Thrones*?

Known as 'The French Feminists', Luce Irigaray, Julia Kristeva and Hélène Cixous emerged from Lacanian psychoanalysis to formulate women-centred theories, particularly related to the maternal. Like Karen Horney, Irigaray certainly paid a price for questioning the male bias of both philosophy and psychoanalysis in her 1974 publication, *Speculum of the Other Woman*,[28] in which she criticized the phallocentric nature of both Freudian and Lacanian psychoanalysis. This led to her expulsion from the University of Vincennes on the orders of Jacques Lacan himself, a major interruption to her career but one that ultimately led to her becoming one of the most influential feminists in Europe. Arguing that the phallocentric nature of both Freudian and Lacanian psychoanalysis neglected to address a feminine perspective and could not explain woman's journey towards adulthood, Irigaray began to work towards a theory that could explain women's societal and economic subjugation. In 1977, Irigaray published *This Sex Which is Not One* (*Ce Sexe qui n'est pas un*) which built on *Speculum of the Other Woman*, arguing that, if female sexuality 'has always been conceptualized on the basis of masculine parameters' then this bias 'seems rather too clearly required by the practice of male sexuality'.[29]

While her formulation of the sexuality of women is key to subsequent feminist theories, it is her writing about motherhood and its place within a capitalist patriarchal society that is of most interest here, as she argues that all women throughout history are defined by their potential as 'mother'. Taking a Marxist feminist approach, Irigaray argues that our culture is 'based upon the exchange of women' which is due to the phallocentric nature of a system in which women are always struggling to achieve subjectivity. Quoting anthropologist Claude Lévi-Strauss, whose theories of kinship depend upon the scarcity of women and the incest taboo, Irigaray argues that, as the world of work is inherently male:

> The production of women, signs, and commodities are men's business. The production of women, signs, and commodities is always referred back to men (when a man buys a girl, he 'pays' the father or the brother, not the mother ...) and they always pass from one man to another, from one group of men to another. The work force is thus always assumed to be masculine, and 'products' are objects to be used, objects of transaction among men alone.[30]

Women, then, become defined solely by their value to patriarchy, which is ultimately tied to their reproductive potential and capacity.

In this account it matters not whether *Game of Thrones* is based upon a medieval society or not, as all of these worlds, whether medieval, fantasy, literary or televisual, are patriarchal. As Martha Nussbaum puts it: *Game of Thrones* is 'the latest entry in television's most esteemed category: the sophisticated cable drama about a patriarchal subculture'.[31] That patriarchy is invested in keeping women in their place, in the service of men, defined by their biology, is key to this idea and explains why it makes no difference whether the women in *Game of Thrones* are based on historical fact or not but that they are 'key assets in the struggle for power and the creation of political networks'.[32] Irigaray's work is useful to an analysis of the trade in women in Westeros and, ultimately, how all women are defined by their potential as mothers within patriarchal societies. As Irigaray argues, in society, there are only three kinds of women: the virgin who is valuable for her exchange value; the mother for her use value; and the prostitute who embodies both. Indeed, for Irigaray, 'as commodities, women are thus two things at once: utilitarian objects and bearers of value'.[33]

Putting Irigaray's theories to the test, it is only thirty minutes into the pilot that we witness the exchange value of the virgin. King Robert Baratheon (Mark Addy) tells Ned Stark (Sean Bean) that he will be the new King's Hand and that they will join their families through the marriage of Ned's daughter, Sansa (Sophie Turner), to his son, Prince Joffrey (Jack Gleeson). It may be the mothers that discuss the trade at the king's banquet but the fact remains that they are merely doing the bidding of the king.[34] Cersei summons Sansa to her table, asks her age, whether she 'is still growing' (a sign that she is pre-pubescent) and if she has 'bled yet'. Cersei tells Catelyn 'I hear we might share a grandchild one day' ('Winter is Coming', 1:1). Just as Catelyn was unable to prevent her youngest son from witnessing the beheading of his father, she is powerless to stop the trade in her daughter's womb, and is resigned to Sansa leaving the North in order to provide future heirs for the king.

Sansa's innocent naïveté and excitement at the proposed union between her and Joffrey fast disappears as this first season draws to a close. Her womb maybe worth much to the future king and his mother but Joffrey has no investment in keeping her happy and, once he has ordered the execution of her father ('Baelor', 1:9), Sansa realizes that his cruelty knows no bounds. By the time we get halfway through season two Sansa understands that she is in grave danger and, in 'A Man Without Honor' (2:5), wakes from a violent gangrape nightmare to discover blood-stained sheets. With the horrifying realization that she now has to marry King Joffrey and bear his children, Sansa attempts to conceal the evidence of her menstruation by cutting the blood from her bed. Cersei summons her and tells the frightened child, 'You flowered dear, no more, no less.' The ensuing discussion reveals Cersei's collusion in King Joffrey's cruelty as well as her grasp of Sansa's fate. She observes that the prospect of bearing the king's children was one 'that once delighted you. Bringing little princes and princesses into the world. The greatest honour for a queen'. Yet, her discussion of mothering exposes her true agenda and reveals her understanding of Sansa's feelings towards Joffrey. Despite Sansa's passionate assurance that she loves the king with all her heart, Cersei tells the young girl to never love the king, as 'the more people you love, the weaker you are ... Love no-one except your children. On that front a mother has no choice'.

If there was ever any need for evidence of how disposable the prostitute is in a patriarchal world, we need look no further. To prevent her brother, Tyrion (Peter Dinklage) from sending Joffrey onto the battlefield, Cersei finds the prostitute that she thinks is her brother's lover, holds her captive ('The Prince of Winterfell', 2:8)[35] and tells him: 'The most important thing about whores [is] you don't buy them, you only rent them.' This is especially poignant as Ros (Esmé Bianco) has, so far, been bought by Tyrion, turned down by Jon Snow (Kit Harrington) as well as being bought for sex and then rejected for marriage by Theon Greyjoy (Alfie Allen). Early on in *Game of Thrones* it is made clear that prostitutes can never be mother or wife, and the only value they bear is as 'utilitarian objects' of exchange. Whether she is Petyr 'Littlefinger' Baelish's (played by Aidan Gillen) favourite or not, Ros' value is soon exposed. Caught spying for Lord Varys (Conleth Hill), Littlefinger gives her to Joffrey as a punishment and, after a season of sadistic pleasure for the young king, she is used as a crossbow target (Figure 9.1). Ros' shocking demise proves just how disposable the prostitute is in a world where men can, and will, replace any woman with another for sexual services ('The Climb', 3:6).

Figure 9.1 'The Climb', *Game of Thrones*, season 3, episode 6

There is one woman who escapes the restrictions placed upon the virgin, mother and prostitute. Daenerys Targaryen (Emilia Clarke) is one of the last surviving members of the House of Targaryen, rulers of Westeros for nearly three hundred years, and daughter of the mad king, who was killed by Jaime Lannister. Daenerys' initial source of power is through birth, as daughter of King Aerys II Targaryen, her womb is valuable enough to be traded for a whole army by her brother Viserys (Harry Lloyd), in his determination to seize the iron throne ('Winter is Coming', 1:1). Her marriage to Dothraki horse-lord, Khal Drogo (Jason Momoa), begins with a rape (absent from the book) but, after winning her husband over and making him treat her as his equal ('The Kingsroad', 1:2), Daenerys becomes one of the strongest and most powerful of all the women in *Game of Thrones*. Cursed by the witch, Mirri Maz Duur (Mia Soteriou), Daenerys' only child is hideously deformed and dies along with her husband. It may well be that the death of both child and husband are the making of Daenerys as, in this medieval fantasy world, being widowed endows women with the power usually reserved for men as 'widows demonstrate clearly how household-status could confound gender-status, since as heads of the households left by their husbands, widows enjoyed certain rights and obligations usually reserved for men'.[36] It also helps that, emerging unscathed from her husband's funeral pyre, Daenerys has 'given birth' or 'hatched' three baby dragons that will hold Westeros in fear for the rest of the series ('Fire and Blood', 10:1). From this moment on Daenerys' power is only rivalled by the Red Witch Melisandre (Carice van Houten)[37] and, after Melisandre's death, her arch-rival Cersei. As 'breaker of chains and mother of dragons', Daenerys revels in the power that her association with her all-powerful offspring brings, which is even greater than Cersei's powerful positioning as mother of the king. Her commitment to fairness and her release of enslaved people, particularly those of Yunkai, culminate in the season three finale where, held aloft by freed slaves, she is given the name 'Mhysa' (Figure 9.2) – the old Ghiscari word for mother ('Mhysa', 3:10).

But, of course, nothing is ever that easy, particularly in the world of HBO adaptations and, with George R. R. Martin failing to write the end of the book saga, the channel was forced to go its own way for the final three seasons. Despite the audience's love of Daenerys

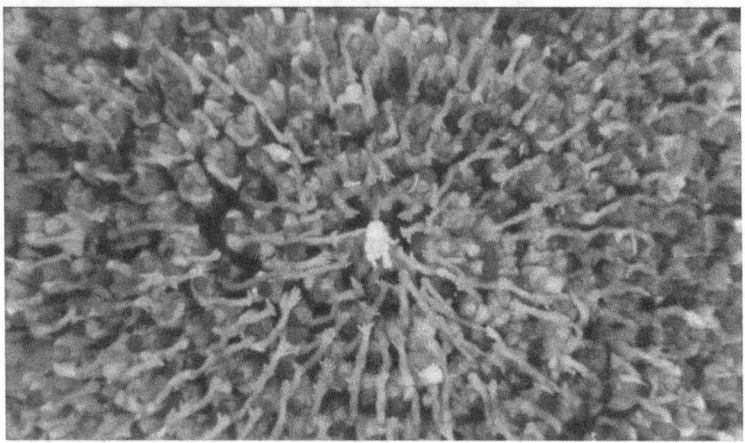

Figure 9.2 'Mhysa', *Game of Thrones*, season 3, episode 10

and her powerful place within the narrative of *Game of Thrones*, the end of her story is predicated on a downfall that should come as no surprise for viewers of HBO. After all, such power threatens the very heart of patriarchy and, as Anne Gjelsvik has argued, 'gender is at the core of the question of whether HBO's production is faithful to Martin's world and its values'.[38] Critics and fans were dismayed at the way the last season of *Game of Thrones* developed. The promise of a relationship between Jon Snow and Daenerys, consummated at the end of season seven ('The Dragon and the Wolf', 7:10), was immediately threatened by the incestuous nature of their relationship – the mirroring of Jon/Daenerys and Cersei/Jaime was now complete. For Callie Ahlgrim, the pitting of 'Mad Queen against Mad Queen' was the final straw in a series that had been demeaning to women throughout. Ahlgrim argues that 'the illustration of Dany's sudden madness played into harmful stereotypes about women and female rulers'. It is not just that Daenerys descended into insanity, after all as daughter of the mad king it had always been a possibility, but that the trigger was so misogynist. After all, she had always been able to overcome her various issues: 'abused by her brother throughout her childhood, sold to a warlord as a political bargaining chip, and being repeatedly raped, enslaved, threatened, and nearly killed'. It does seem a stretch then that 'Daenerys is seemingly pushed over the edge because a man won't return her affection'.[39]

What of the Queen Mother herself? For the creators of *Game of Thrones*, Cersei's villainy is directly linked to her motherhood, as explained by twin brother/lover Jaime: 'All the worst things she's ever done, she's done for her children' ('The Bells', 8:5). In the final scene, abandoned by bodyguard Ser Gregor Clegane (Hafþór Júlíus Björnsson), Cersei finds her way to dying lover Jaime. In the midst of the collapsing Red Keep, atop the huge map of Westeros, Cersei and Jaime are reunited. It seems fitting that the lovers meet their end in the crypts of King's Landing, surrounded by dragon bones, rubble and dust, witnessing the dying embers of the Lannisters' reign together. Cersei's last words, 'I want our baby to live. I want our baby to live', are to no avail. A fierce, protective mother to the end, Cersei dies begging for her life, but more importantly the life of her unborn child.

The way *Game of Thrones* was adapted by HBO reveals the link between biology and reproduction at the heart of this violent and medieval patriarchal world. Over eight seasons, and in a world ruled by primogeniture where heirs are essential and women's only value is their wombs, motherhood is the only power that women can possibly wield. As Karen Horney has suggested, possession of the phallus and the power that it signifies in a patriarchal society is equalled by women's physiological superiority – the capacity to bear children – which is inextricably bound up with the male child's intense envy of motherhood. It is not too big a leap to argue that this envy really does manifest in the depreciation of women in society, particularly mothers, and that men continue to control the representation of motherhood on our television screens to allay those fears.

In *Motherhood Misconceived, Representing the Maternal in US Films*, the authors argue that there is a 'striking consistency in Hollywood's constructions of motherhood' where: 'Mothers reproduce dominant ideology ... yet also become ready targets if they fail to uphold prevailing notions of "good" motherhood.'[40] This would explain why HBO has not only made the mothers in *Game of Thrones* weaker than their literary antecedents but also why the most powerful women in the series have to be literally driven mad and killed rather than take their place on the Iron Throne. In the end it is Bran Stark, the disabled soothsayer, who eventually sits on the throne. Arya continues her journey by sailing West and, after being imprisoned for killing his queen, Jon Snow takes the black and goes back to a lonely existence in The Knight's Watch at The Wall. Sansa is given the North to rule. It is noteworthy that no mothers remain.

Notes

1. Brian A. Pavlac (ed.), *Game of Thrones Versus History: Written in Blood* (Somerset: John Wiley & Sons, 2017).
2. James Lowder (ed.), *Beyond the Wall: Exploring George R.R. Martin's A Song of Ice and Fire* (Dallas: Benbella Books, 2012).
3. Martin Barker, Clarissa Smith and Feona Attwood (eds), *Watching Game of Thrones: How Audiences Engage with Dark Television* (Manchester: Manchester University Press, 2021).
4. Henry Jacoby (ed.), *Game of Thrones and Philosophy: Logic Cuts Deeper Than Swords* (Hoboken: John Wiley & Sons Inc., 2012).
5. Anne Gjelsvik and Rikke Schubart (eds), *Women of Ice and Fire: Gender, Game of Thrones and Multiple Media Engagements* (New York: Bloomsbury, 2016).
6. Bill Carter, 'HBO's Rivals Say It Has Stumbled, Though Catching Up Is Tough', *New York Times*, 23 August 2007, https://tinyurl.com/ay4teaew (accessed 2 June 2022).
7. Joseph Adalian, 'How *Game of Thrones* Helped HBO Break Into the Streaming World', *Vulture*, 16 May 2019, https://tinyurl.com/6fsnuukf (accessed 8 June 2022).
8. Ginia Bellafante, 'A Fantasy World of Strange Feuding Kingdoms', *New York Times*, 14 April 2011, https://tinyurl.com/5n76tw6v (accessed 8 June 2022).
9. *Ibid.*
10. Martha Nussbaum, 'The Aristocrats: The Graphic Arts of "Game of Thrones"', *New Yorker*, 30 April 2012, https://tinyurl.com/3zpt5af6 (accessed 8 June 2022).
11. *Ibid.*
12. Gjelsvik and Schubart, *Women of Ice and Fire*, p. 7.
13. Gjelsvik and Schubart, *Women of Ice and Fire*, p. 6.
14. *Ibid.*

15 Nicole M. Mares, 'Writing the Rules of Their Own Game: Medieval Female Agency and *Game of Thrones*', in Brian A. Pavlac (ed.), *Game of Thrones Versus History: Written in Blood* (Somerset: John Wiley & Sons, 2017), p. 147.
16 *Ibid.*
17 Janice Liedl, 'Rocking Cradles and Hatching Dragons: Parents in *Game of Thrones*', in Brian A. Pavlac (ed.), *Game of Thrones Versus History: Written in Blood* (Somerset: John Wiley & Sons, 2017), p. 134.
18 *Ibid.*
19 Marta Eidsvåg, ' "Maiden, Mother, and Crone": Motherhood in the World of Ice and Fire', in Anne Gjelsvik and Rikke Schubart (eds), *Women of Ice and Fire: Gender, Game of Thrones and Multiple Media Engagements* (New York: Bloomsbury, 2016), p. 151.
20 Quoted in Eidsvåg, 'Maiden, Mother, and Crone', pp. 152–3.
21 Eidsvåg, 'Maiden, Mother, and Crone', p. 153.
22 Eidsvåg, 'Maiden, Mother, and Crone', p. 164.
23 Eidsvåg, 'Maiden, Mother, and Crone', p. 165.
24 Eidsvåg, 'Maiden, Mother, and Crone', p. 166.
25 Gjelsvik and Schubart, *Women of Ice and Fire*, p. 8.
26 *Ibid.*
27 *Ibid.*
28 Luce Irigaray, *Speculum of the Other Woman* (New York: Cornell University Press, 1985) (first published 1974).
29 Luce Irigaray, *This Sex Which is Not One (Ce Sexe qui n,est pas un)* (Ithaca, NY: Cornell University Press, 1981), p. 23 (first published 1977).
30 Irigaray, *This Sex*, p. 171.
31 *Ibid.*
32 Mares, 'Writing the Rules', p. 148.
33 Irigaray, *This Sex*, p. 185.
34 To avoid outcry from viewers all of the younger characters are aged in the television series, for example Joffrey from 11 to 16 and Sansa from 11 to 13.
35 Unbeknownst to Cersei, Tyrion is actually in love with Sansa's handmaiden, Shae (Sibel Kekilli).
36 Judith M. Bennett, *A Medieval Life: Cecilia Penifader of Brigstock c 1295–1344* (Boston: McGraw-Hill College, 1999), p. 124.
37 Who also gave birth to an other-worldly child ('Garden of Bones', 2:4).
38 Anne Gjelsvik, 'Unspeakable Acts of (Sexual) Terror As/In Quality Television', in Anne Gjelsvik and Rikke Schubart (eds), *Women of Ice*

and Fire: Gender, Game of Thrones and Multiple Media Engagements* (New York: Bloomsbury, 2016), p. 58.
39 Callie Ahlgrim, 'Making Daenerys a "Mad Queen" on "Game of Thrones" is the Culmination of Every Demeaning Sexist Trope Over the Show's 8 Seasons', *Insider*, 15 May 2019, https://tinyurl.com/4yz7yfcd (accessed 8 June 2022).
40 Heather Addison, Mary Kate Goodwin-Kelly and Elaine Roth, *Motherhood Misconceived, Representing the Maternal in US Films* (New York: New York State University Press, 2009), p. 4.

10

The Handmaid's Tale (Hulu, 2017–)

We have seen how the Danish series, *Forbrydelsen*, despite having a female showrunner, took motherhood to some very dark places, especially in its final season. Turning to the adaptation of books to television the last chapter looked at *Game of Thrones* and how the strong mothers in George R. R. Martin's source material saw their power significantly diminished in the television series. So far, I have argued that mothers on television are often used to work through unconscious cultural, social and psychological issues and, attempting to follow in the footsteps of film scholar, Laura Mulvey, have used psychoanalytic theory as a 'political weapon' to expose how the 'patriarchal unconscious' structures form, this time, quality American television series.[1] This chapter will turn to Hulu's *The Handmaid's Tale* as yet another example of how a streaming channel has used an adaptation to break into the cluttered television landscape. With its focus on a dystopian America now named Gilead, *The Handmaid's Tale* centres on the oppression and sexual exploitation of women, with the series taking the narrative into even darker and more violent territory than the source novel. In this chapter I will, through an application of some of the work of feminist theorist, Dorothy Dinnerstein, argue that *The Handmaid's Tale* warns of a land where women's oppression has been taken to the extreme. The question remains, however, is it Gilead or America itself that is under scrutiny?

Dorothy Dinnerstein's controversial book, *The Mermaid and the Minotaur: Sexual Arrangements and Human Malaise*,[2] published in 1976, builds upon past feminist psychoanalytic theory to argue that 'all of us are psychologically and socially disadvantaged by being brought up under asymmetrical parenting roles'.[3] Critiquing patriarchal mothering and how these immutably assigned gender roles lead to women's oppression, Dinnerstein takes a complex route which is impossible to adequately summarize here. For the purposes of this chapter, however, I will focus on her proposal that the omnipresence of the mother and her subsequent power over children of both genders causes women to always be 'regarded as dangerous and debased', which will continue 'as long as it is she, and she alone, who first introduces us as infants to the mixed blessing of being human'.[4] As a result of the mother's ubiquity in a child's life, argues Dinnerstein, it is not just men that distrust women but women too as we hold our mothers responsible for 'our discovery as infants that we cannot command the world'.[5] Charlotte Shane makes the point that Dinnerstein herself anticipated 'that her book would "enrage readers"',[6] which may have gone some way towards it being out of print until 1999. Some of the criticisms levelled at her work are that she does not acknowledge racial difference, is utterly heteronormative, does not allow for male caregivers and assumes much about infants that simply cannot be proved.[7] However, Dinnerstein's recognition of how patriarchy forces women into mothering roles reminds us of the theories of Adrienne Rich and Karen Horney and is a 'rigorous analysis of the conditions of motherhood as mutable and in dire need of improvement' and, as such, 'is worth engaging given today's landscape of degraded inquiry on the topic'.[8] Margaret Atwood's *The Handmaid's Tale* was published in 1985 when former B-list actor Ronald Reagan was president. The novel takes place in a world where, due to environmental pollution and the transmission of sexual diseases, fertile women (those that remain) are enslaved. Gilead is an ominous warning of what could happen because of patriarchy's lack of regard for nature and Margaret Atwood's now famous statement that when she 'wrote *The Handmaid's Tale* nothing went into it that had not happened in real life somewhere at some time'[9] becomes ever more chilling with each passing year. Dinnerstein warns of this dystopia in her discussion of the unequal organization of gendered roles within our society, arguing that the world-building project, which in a patriarchal society is assumed to be male, leads to an overvaluation of masculine qualities, including men's 'propensity toward brute "mastery" of external circumstances' and 'apocalyptically exploitative relationship to nature through rampant fetishization of technological enterprise'.[10] A warning that may well have come to fruition as recent newspaper reports tell of 'reproductive health in men and women' declining 'dramatically at least over the past 40 years, [with] a major part of that decline ... linked to everyday exposure to chemicals in the environment that can affect our hormone system'.[11]

It is the collapse of the natural world and reproductive fragility that leads to fertile women being passed from household to household in *The Handmaid's Tale* as the totalitarian theonomic government of Gilead strips them of all their rights in their bid to boost the birth rate. Evocative of Luce Irigaray's theories which tell of a 'new matrix of History' where 'wives, daughters, and sisters have value only in that they serve as the possibility of, and potential benefit in, relations among men',[12] the women in Gilead are brutally subjugated. Coded by the colours they wear, women are reduced to basic functions: Marthas (who cook and look after the Commanders' houses) dress in muted green; Aunts (who train the handmaids) wear brown; Econowives (who are of lower social class and have to fulfil all basic functions) wear grey; and Commanders' wives wear blue or teal. The handmaids, who are known only by their patronymic monikers, denied even the use of their own names, all wear long red dresses and cloaks with white coifs or wings to conceal them from public view. For Offred (June in the television series, played by Elisabeth Moss), the narrator of the book, the handmaid is worth less than concubines, geisha girls or courtesans – they are 'two-legged wombs, that's all, sacred vessels, ambulatory chalices' valuable only 'for breeding purposes'.[13]

Optioned by Hulu as a ten-episode straight-to-series adaptation, *The Handmaid's Tale* was announced in April 2016, four months before the streaming channel revealed that it was planning to discontinue its free video-on-demand service. For many this move was inevitable as, even if it had been 'a revelatory user experience: leagues better than pirated content, and a boon for audiences and networks alike',[14] with the competition from other subscription services, the cessation of the free streaming service was the next logical step for the channel. For senior vice president, Ben Smith, Hulu had already begun 'emphasizing its subscription offering over its free service' by improving its subscription model as well as 'creating the best experience possible and delivering the best content'.[15] It is this need to attract new, premium subscribers and deliver quality content that gave Hulu the impetus to sign *The Handmaid's Tale* and, much like AMC before it, the channel used the adaptation to attract audiences to the higher priced ad-free service that it had launched the year before.

It is easy to see how the series would resonate with viewers, particularly after the November 2016 election of former reality television star Donald Trump when sales of the novel had already 'spiked 200 percent'.[16] The television adaptation not only boosted Hulu's subscription service but also spoke directly to a populace horrified by the election of the Republican president. With no credentials for the role, other than a stint in *The Apprentice* (NBC, 2004–17), Trump's election, like Reagan's before him, threatened women's rights, particularly those related to reproduction and abortion. Even though the first season of the television series had already been scripted and had begun filming at the time of the presidential election in 2016, it is hard not to view it as an 'allegorical response to the dystopian moment that Americans' had stumbled into: 'After all, the country had just elected a president who, among other things, had bragged of his own acts of sexual assault and was doing his best to eliminate reproductive rights for women, both nationally and internationally.'[17]

The difficulties inherent in adapting the feminist novel to television were not lost on Bruce Miller, the series' creator, who reportedly said: 'One of the big aspects of "Handmaid's" was that Offred (Elisabeth Moss) was victimized by a society that was institutionally misogynist ... There are aspects of that you just can't understand being a boy.'[18] Whether 'boy' or 'man', Miller certainly knew that employing women would help overcome this particular hurdle, and it was cinematographer Reed Morano's commitment to the vision of the series that got her the job as she presented him with 'a 60-page lookbook for the show, capturing the exact tone and emotional state they were aiming for'.[19] Although worried about being accused of 'positive discrimination' in an industry that is so overwhelmingly male, Miller confirms that they got 'the best person for the job and part of that job was to represent a female and a male sensibility accurately and compassionately'.[20] Employing women to bring the novel to life was clearly a positive step for the series and, working as a team on the show's aesthetic was important to Morano, as '[t]he look of Gilead needed to convey tension; to convey segregation and strictness of the new world',[21] which 'inspired her to opt for a very symmetrical composition in establishing shots',[22] including the overhead shot focusing on 'dozens of crimson-clad handmaids gathered on a green field'.[23] The feeling of claustrophobia was compounded by Morano's tight, close-up, camerawork, forcing us to get into Offred's head 'so the audience felt as though they were hearing Offred's thoughts and seeing the world through her eyes'.[24] This feeling was enhanced by Ane Crabtree's costume design which, although feeling 'karmically wrong', forced her 'into the mind set of a man tasked with remaking the world'.[25]

The first season of *The Handmaid's Tale* won eight Emmy Awards (out of thirteen nominations) including the Award for Outstanding Drama Series – the first time that a series produced by a streaming site had won the award.[26] Reed Morano won awards for Outstanding Directing of a Drama Series and Outstanding Cinematography for a Single-Camera Series (One Hour) for the pilot episode 'Offred', not bad for a woman whose previous cinematography experience was limited to Beyoncé's *Lemonade* (HBO, 2016) and *Vinyl* (HBO, 2016). Initial reviews of *The Handmaid's Tale* were overwhelmingly positive. Sophie Gilbert, for example, claimed that '[t]he Hulu show has created a world that's visually and psychologically unlike anything in film or television', adding that the 'cult status of the novel' has 'transcended the realm of fiction to become a kind of cultural shorthand for female oppression'.[27] Gilbert cites the 2017 Women's March on Washington as evidence that Hulu's television series was truly touching a nerve as protestors carried signs that read 'Make Margaret Atwood Fiction Again'. In addition, women in Texas in March in the same year 'dressed as handmaiden's to protest bills undermining abortion rights in the state'.[28] Gilbert adds: 'That so many women feel so keenly attuned to it now demonstrates an acute awareness that the impulse to police women's behaviour and reproductive systems is as old as history itself.'[29]

Despite these accolades, the second season of *The Handmaid's Tale* did not deliver on the feminist promise of season one as the tone became increasingly darker. The book finishes with Offred unsure whether she is leaving 'into the darkness or the light' as she is bundled into a van by 'Eyes', who may or may not be members of the rebel group Mayday. The second season, with no source novel to guide it, opens with a gagged Offred who, along with other handmaids, are man-handled out of vans and herded into a vast stadium ('June', 2:1). Nooses are already in place and, as the rope is placed around each of their necks, we witness their abject terror as the execution order is given. Even though the trapdoors do not open, allowing the rebellious handmaids a last-minute reprieve, the opening minutes of season two are truly shocking. Aunt Lydia (Ann Dowd) is, of course, instrumental in their punishment as she emerges from the darkness quoting scriptures. That this was their lesson for refusing the order to stone Ofwarren (Janine Lindo played by Madeline Brewer) to death in season one is met with Offred's incredulous voiceover: 'Our father who art in heaven ... seriously? ... what the actual fuck?'

It is not just the harsh treatment meted out in Gilead that comes under scrutiny in season two as, in flashback, we witness June and Luke's (O-T Fagbenle) daughter, Hannah (Jordana Blake), sent to hospital with a fever. Although clearly a loving mother, June is treated with disdain for working and, in a scene reminiscent of the 1990s 'mommy wars', is treated as an unfit mother by the hospital aide. Implied here is that whether women live in Gilead or a 'free' America, mothers who do not stay at home and devote themselves to childcare are considered selfish and negligent. In this iteration, *The Handmaid's Tale* becomes much more than a 'feminist horror'[30] story and 'reveals how visionary television can feel when it immerses itself in the experiences of women'.[31] Being written after the 2016 election, for many commentators, season two directly commented on Trump's America. No one could ever have imagined, however, how the first episode would foretell future events when the news, which is told in flashback, tells of a Washington under siege with 'twenty or thirty guys with machine guns shooting from the gallery' of the Capitol Building. Although Margaret Atwood had included this insurrection in her book,[32] it would have been impossible for either Atwood or the series creators to foresee a future where Washington, DC and the Capitol Building really were under attack and yet, on 6 January 2021, after Trump failed in his re-election bid, that is exactly what happened. Edited alongside June's escape in a refrigerated meat wagon, the parallels between Gilead and 'free' America could not be clearer. It is fair to say that, even though these events were fictionalized thirty-five years earlier, nobody could have envisaged an America where right-wing religious fanatics and conspiracy theorists would attempt to overturn the capital. Sometimes truth really is stranger than fiction.

Over the course of season two, *The Handmaid's Tale* slowly reveals ever-more inventive ways to control the handmaids, June (Offred) in particular. The season two episode, 'The Last Ceremony' (2:10) opens with the ritualized rape of Emily (Ofroy, played by Alex Biedel) who has been returned from the Colonies because a bomb killed thirty-one handmaids ('First Blood', 2:6). The voice-over tells how the monthly ritual becomes 'normal', just another 'job to be gotten through as fast as possible'. 'An act of copulation, fertilization perhaps, no more to you than a bee is to a flower.' Compare this to the scene halfway through this episode as, after June's false labour has led to Serena Joy's humiliation in front of the Commanders' wives, she decides (on the advice of Aunt Lydia) that the birth of June's baby must be 'helped along'. As if the monthly rape ritual is not bad enough, this scene is remarkable even in a series that is built upon the sexual violation of women. Despite their past differences, Serena Joy unites with her husband to 'get the baby out' of June quickly so that she can be sent to another household as far away as possible. As Serena holds June down, her husband forces himself on her and, rather than quiet acceptance of her fate, June fights back.

There can be few that missed the furore over this episode of *The Handmaid's Tale* as, coupled with the scenes of sexual assault on series like *Game of Thrones*, the media accused the series of featuring this scene 'just to rile up viewers'[33] and HBO was strongly criticized by the press and viewers alike. Yet, some commentators suggested that June's violent rape, while rightly criticized, was worthy of inclusion as 'it drives home how horrific this society is at its core'.[34] A similar defence had been given by the actress Sophie Turner over Sansa Stark's rape in *Game of Thrones* when 'Unbowed, Unbent, Unbroken' (5:6) aired to immense media criticism. Following the rape of her character by new husband Theon Greyjoy (Iwan Rheon) she said: 'The more we talk about sexual assault the better, and screw the people who are saying we shouldn't be putting this on TV and screw the people who are saying they're going to boycott the show because of it.'[35] There is clearly a fine line between rape as entertainment and the fact that in the United States 'RAINN estimates that an American is assaulted every 98 seconds',[36] and, while we can accept that at least the resulting media storms did air the issue of rape in society, there are still problems with the way it is routinely represented on television screens.

Later in the same episode, June is briefly reunited with Hannah, the daughter she has been searching for over the course of nearly two seasons. Far from being a joyful reunion, this lengthy scene caused critics to comment on how unbearably true to life the series was 'with some pretty shocking direct parallels to an actual ongoing national crisis – that of the forced separation between parents and children'.[37] *Vulture*'s Hillary Kelly was moved to comment:

> [I]t's a strange thing knowing that your democratic nation is committing atrocities that we once only imagined took place in distant lands or in the pages of history books, and that our Attorney General is using the same faulty and delusional thinking as the officials running Gilead – that the Bible sanctions such behavior.[38]

However true this statement is, it does reveal an ignorance of the history of enforced separation of children, as '[t]he violence imposed on women's bodies in Atwood's dystopia has already been visited upon the bodies of black and Indigenous women many times over'.[39] This season of *The Handmaid's Tale*, quite apart from being 'meticulously directed, [and] disturbingly reflective of current events',[40] proves how patriarchal rules, both in Gilead and the United States, do not take into account the wishes of the mother or the needs of the child and, for Hamad at least, shows how white motherhood is privileged over any other. She asks: 'Does misogynistic violence really not count until it is inflicted on the body of a white woman?'[41] A question that the critical commentary may well ask itself.

Season three shows it is not only the Aunts and Commanders' wives that oppress and control the handmaids. For Dinnerstein, the entire system of male dominance in patriarchy 'is based on a conspiracy by both men and women'.[42] While 'the complicity of many wealthy women in the tyranny of Gilead is another aspect of the show that sharpens its topical relevance, particularly after an election in which a majority of white women voted against a female president',[43] it is excruciating for viewers to see June join the legion of women who oppress each other, particularly as 'the most memorable villains in ... *Handmaid's Tale* are women: Strahovski's enigmatic Serena, Ann Dowd's vicious Aunt Lydia'.[44] Midway through the season June, who is by this time openly rebellious, informs on a fellow handmaiden, Ofmatthew or Natalie (Ashleigh LaThrop), for confessing that she does not want to carry another child to term ('Unfit', 3:8). Even though Ofmatthew has been spying on June, the chain of events that are instigated by June's actions are shocking as the pregnant handmaid is shot by a Guardian and taken to hospital to carry the baby to term. While there have been other atrocities committed on the handmaids (as if monthly rape, torture and sexual slavery were not enough) the most disturbing aspect of this narrative is how, in her desperation, June has turned against her fellow handmaid. Forced to pray until Ofmatthew's baby is born, June comes to terms with her actions but, later in this season, we witness just how ruthless and desperate she has become as she fails to save Eleanor Lawrence's (played by Julie Dretzin) life after a suicide attempt ('Sacrifice', 3:12). Despite their mutual fondness, June worries that Eleanor will reveal her plan to smuggle the daughters out of Gilead and fails to raise the alarm when she finds her unconscious. It seems that June's assimilation into the legions of mutually oppressive women is complete.

If the attack on Washington foretold a future event, the finale of season three, 'Mayday' (3:13), evokes one of the most heinous periods of global history as the opening scenes are reminiscent of Nazi Germany with women forced into buses and cages in the same way as Jewish people were herded into trains and gas chambers. Naked women are glimpsed in the background and there is no need to explain that these past scenes of June's capture link the Nazi death camps and their ruthless experimentation on women and children with Gilead and its own peculiar form of population control. June's open revolt against Commander Lawrence confirms this mirroring as she tells him that the thought of fourteen-year-old children being married and raped and maimed 'in this insane fucking world' is just too much and that even a Commander's daughter is not protected from having 'her clit cut off when she falls in love'. Despite everything that has gone before, this final episode closes on the power of the collective as Marthas and handmaids all rally together to save the young girls of Gilead. The final scene, where a wounded June is carried off by the handmaids, recalls so many of the overhead shots of the series – this time, rather than conveying segregation and the strictness of the regime, the shot works to emphasize movement of the handmaids as one. This powerful ending hints at how the collective strength of women can overcome patriarchal oppression, but only by working as a team.

The *New York Times* declared that season two was 'dutifully brutal, complete with ample torture, rapes, executions and murders', adding: 'It gave in to every one of the show's most tedious instincts … every inch of existence is awful.'[45] For *Time*, at the end of season three, 'a series that began as a revelation has … become a chore'[46] with the second season merely rehashing 'the misery of the previous season: Women got raped, families got torn apart, lawbreakers got executed, the hypocrisy of powerful men get a free pass'.[47] Many critics remarked on the fact that the 'ordinary' Offred was turned into an exceptional woman: 'Instead of being a person, this woman who's spent the last few years in sexual servitude is now a quippy unstoppable Feminist Badass.'[48] More than one commentator talked about the continued political relevance of the series, particularly 'the flurry of abortion bans making their way through various state legislatures [which] has made it seem like our society is only a "Praise be" or two away from turning into Gilead right now'.[49] While it is difficult to disagree with the criticism that *The Handmaid's Tale* is a relentless round of misery inflicted on women, it is possible to see that Gilead and Trump's America were not a million miles apart.

According to author Margaret Atwood, even though the book is an allegory of a fictionalized world, contemporary America does acutely resonate. For example, 'the witch and demon imagery' that was 'applied to Hillary Clinton' coupled with the fact that former Vice President Mike Pence refused to have dinner with any woman that is not his wife. Just these two examples smack 'of the same kind of Puritanism that saw women condemned as witches and harlots'.[50] We could quite easily add the treatment of working mothers to this list, the infertility issues, the way the women of Gilead are oppressed by each other, and the way mothers and children continue to have their babies ripped from their arms – all to suit a patriarchal agenda. Even while President Biden moves to make America a more equitable society, there are many that would keep it in the dark ages – a country not unlike the fictional Gilead.

Notes

1 Laura Mulvey, *Visual and Other Pleasures* (London and New York: Palgrave Macmillan, 1989), p. 14.
2 Dorothy Dinnerstein, *The Mermaid and the Minotaur: Sexual Arrangements and Human Malaise* (New York: Harper & Row, 2021) (original publication date 1976).
3 Charlotte Shane, 'Mommy Issues: Reconsidering *The Mermaid and the Minotaur*', *Dissent*, 65:3 (2018): 93.
4 Ann Snitow, 'Thinking About *The Mermaid and the Minotaur*', *Feminist Studies*, 4:2 (1978): 190
5 *Ibid.*
6 Shane, 'Mommy Issues', 93.
7 Jane Flax, 'Reentering the Labyrinth: Revisiting Dorothy Dinnerstein's *The Mermaid and the Minotaur*', *Signs: Journal of Women in Culture and Society*, 27:4 (2002): 1037–57, https://tinyurl.com/57us42rm (accessed 9 June 2022).
8 Shane, 'Mommy Issues', 97.
9 Becca Longmire, 'Handmaid's Tale Author Margaret Atwood Insists Everything in the Book "Happened in Real Life"', *ETCanada*, 11 July 2018, https://tinyurl.com/2p8vmcd3 (accessed 9 June 2022).
10 Shane, 'Mommy Issues', 93.
11 Matthew Rozsa, 'How Plastics Are Making Us Infertile – and Can Even Lead to Human Extinction', *Salon.com*, 4 April 2021, https://tinyurl.com/bdfhc4tz (accessed 9 June 2022).
12 Luce Irigaray, *This Sex Which is Not One (Ce Sexe qui n,est pas un)* (Ithaca, NY: Cornell University Press, 1981), p. 170 (first published 1977).
13 Margaret Atwood, *The Handmaid's Tale* (New York: Houghton Mifflin Harcourt, 1986), p. 136.
14 Emily Jane Fox, 'Hulu's Streaming Service is No Longer Free', *Vanity Fair*, 8 August 2016, https://tinyurl.com/ynurtpnr (accessed 9 June 2022).
15 Shalini Ramachandran and Deepa Seetharaman, 'Hulu Bids Goodbye to Its Free Service', *Wall Street Journal*, 8 August 2016, https://tinyurl.com/y8wcbvy7 (accessed 9 June 2022).
16 Heather Hendershot, '*The Handmaid's Tale* as Ustopian Allegory: "Stars and Stripes Forever, Baby"', *Film Quarterly*, 72:1 (2018): 13.
17 *Ibid.*
18 Libby Hill, 'Meet the Women Who Brought the Misogynist World of "The Handmaid's Tale" to Life', *Los Angeles Times*, 3 May 2017, https://tinyurl.com/2p99z7by (accessed 9 June 2022).

19 Sophie Gilbert, 'The Visceral, Woman-Centric Horror of *The Handmaid's Tale*', *Atlantic*, 25 April 2017, https://tinyurl.com/2ascjx34 (accessed 9 June 2022).
20 Hill, 'Meet the Women'.
21 *Ibid.*
22 *Ibid.*
23 *Ibid.*
24 *Ibid.*
25 *Ibid.*
26 Lanre Bakare, 'Emmys 2017: The Handmaids Tale Makes History on Politically Charged Night', *Guardian*, 18 September 2017, https://tinyurl.com/2p8dy3cy (accessed 8 June 2022).
27 Gilbert, 'The Visceral'.
28 *Ibid.*
29 *Ibid.*
30 *Ibid.*
31 *Ibid.*
32 'It was after the catastrophe when they shot the president and machine gunned the Congress and the army declared a state of emergency.' Atwood, *Handmaid's Tale*, p. 174.
33 Hillary Kelly, '*The Handmaid's Tale* Recap: Brief Encounter', *Vulture*, 20 June 2018, https://tinyurl.com/bdhuabmr (accessed 9 June 2022).
34 Taylor Maple, 'Why That Horrifying "Handmaid's Tale" Scene Was Actually Necessary', *bustle.com*, 20 June 2018, https://tinyurl.com/j6n7253y (accessed 9 June 2022).
35 Quoted in Nina Bahadur, 'The Complicated Politics of Sansa's "Game of Thrones" Rape Scene', *self.com*, 7 July 2017, https://tinyurl.com/y9cm9m7p (accessed 8 June 2022).
36 *Ibid.*
37 David Canfield, '*The Handmaid's Tale* Recap: Can This Show Get Any Darker?', *ew.com*, 20 June 2018, https://tinyurl.com/bdhuabmr (accessed 9 June 2022).
38 Kelly, '*The Handmaid's Tale* Recap'.
39 Ruby Hamad, *White Tears, Brown Scars* (New York: Catapult, 2020), p. 170.
40 Jen Chaney, 'The Handmaid's Tale Wraps Up a Good But Frustrating Season', *Vulture*, 11 July 2018, https://tinyurl.com/3awkdn3c (accessed 9 June 2022).
41 Hamad, *White Tears*, p. 170.
42 Miriam M. Johnson, 'Women's Mothering and Male Misogyny', in Andrea O'Reilly (ed.), *Maternal Theory: Essential Readings* (Toronto: Demeter Press, 2007), p. 204.

43 Gilbert, 'The Visceral'.
44 *Ibid.*
45 Margaret Lyons, ' "The Handmaid's Tale" Season 2 is Brutal and Not Much Else', *The New York Times*, 11 July 2018, https://tinyurl.com/4jmf4chm (accessed 9 June 2022).
46 Judy Berman, '*The Handmaid's Tale* Could Be So Much Better. But First It Has to Leave Its Star Behind', *Time*, 27 June 2019, https://tinyurl.com/59a7cjxz (accessed 9 June 2022).
47 *Ibid.*
48 *Ibid.*
49 Jen Chaney, 'In *The Handmaid's Tale* Season 3, Gilead's Still Gonna Gilead', *Vulture*, 4 June 2019, https://tinyurl.com/5b2jem4y (accessed 9 June 2022).
50 Gilbert, 'The Visceral'.

11

Big Little Lies (HBO, 2017–19)

As a result of the rise in women-centred series, much attention has been given to the idea that the twenty-first century is a golden era for women and television. The recent rise in streaming sites and subsequent demand for content to fill them has indeed had a positive impact on female employment. Even so, as Martha Lauzen's annual 'Boxed In' report reveals, there are still 'a startlingly high' percentage of programmes that employ 'no women in behind-the-scenes roles'.[1] In fact, there were still only 33 per cent of women in key behind-the-scenes positions on broadcast networks in 2020–1,[2] a figure that has declined by 2 per cent from 2019–20.[3] Remembering that programmes substantially benefit from having at least one female in behind-the-scenes creative roles as they feature 'more female characters than programs with exclusively male creators',[4] it should be no surprise that gendered inequality in representational terms is still an issue for US cable and network television.

At the same time, there has been a critical shift in the profiling of women's television work. Even if most of the recognition of women's agency is largely centred on US television, the resulting discourse constructs 'a perception of the current cultural moment as a golden age of television for women'[5] which runs counter to the privileging of male antiheroes in drama with their 'sexist and abusive treatment of women'.[6] More women working in television in creative roles has been equated with the rise of 'feminist' television, although, as Claire Perkins and Michele Schreiber point out, this idea pivots on the idea of the female auteur where 'these figures are popular *because* they are visible, and the more visible they become the more self-evident the feminist content of their work is made to appear' (emphasis in original).[7] Warning against the notion of a feminist genre of television, the authors argue that, due to the number of female filmmakers moving across to television, the medium is being understood 'as a new site of independent production for women, with amplified connotations of freedom and authorial control'.[8] A suggestion that could quite easily be applied to the involvement of Reese Witherspoon and Nicole Kidman and their respective production companies in the creation of *Big Little Lies* (HBO, 2017–19).[9]

In this final chapter, I will look at what happens to mothers on television when more women are employed behind the scenes of a production. How do female producers, directors and writers make sense of maternity? Does it necessarily follow that more women behind the camera make for a more nuanced and sympathetic onscreen interpretation of motherhood? It may be that the rise of streaming services has allowed women to 'exercise more control and singularity of vision than has historically been offered in television production',[10] but does this necessarily mean that there will be a fairer treatment of mothers in television narratives or will these 'post-feminist' productions still become mired in the same old archetypes? This chapter will argue that, even with big stars (mothers themselves) at the helm, and with mothers front and centre of the narrative, Dorothy Dinnerstein's suggestion that women also 'suffer from the overbearing power of the mother' which leads to them distrust 'the mother in themselves'[11] must be correct. On the evidence of *Big Little Lies* it seems that women behind the scenes sadly have no more power over the depiction of motherhood than the male showrunners that have come before them.

The first season of HBO's *Big Little Lies* (2017–19) screened to much anticipation. Advance publicity told how both Reese Witherspoon and Nicole Kidman's production companies wanted to option Liane Moriarty's book less than a month after its publication in 2014. With a female-centred cast including Kidman and Witherspoon, Zoë Kravitz, Laura Dern and Shailene Woodley, adapted for television by veteran writer David E. Kelley, and directed by Jean-Marc Vallée, the show looked promising. Set in Monterey, California, the pilot episode opens to idyllic ocean views, a parade of beautiful children and stylish women, all set to the strains of Michael Kiwanuka's 'Cold Little Heart'.[12] Although glossy and welcoming, a darker undercurrent is evident: fish under water, a hand points a gun, hands encircle a throat, sharks swim, but these shadows do nothing to disrupt the sunny atmosphere of the opening credits. Until the first scenes of blue and red lights flashing over an Elvis poster hint at trouble ahead. Police are investigating an accident at a school trivia night. We hear the dialogue between two investigators, the camera edits between a point-of-view shot, with the sound of rapid and heavy breathing, back to the detectives' reaction to a dead body. We then immediately switch to a series of 'talking heads' where various witnesses tell us that, underneath this glossy exterior, things are not quite as they seem at Otterbay Elementary School ('Somebody's Dead', 1:1). So far, so enigmatic.

Big Little Lies garnered rave reviews and was nominated for sixteen Primetime Emmy Awards in its first season, winning eight, including Outstanding Limited Series, Directing (Jean-Marc Vallée), Supporting Actress (Laura Dern) and Supporting Actor (Alexander Skarsgård).[13] Reese Witherspoon was beaten to the Award for Lead Actress by Nicole Kidman, which immediately led to rumours that the stars were feuding. For some it was clearly too much to believe that successful women could work together as an anonymous source reported: 'The success of *Big Little Lies* has gone to both of their heads and there's now a power struggle between the two stars. Behind closed doors, their egos are clashing and they bicker over the smallest thing.' The evidence for this? The Emmy Awards in September where, having won Outstanding Limited Series, 'Reese grabbed the statue and refused to let it go – even when Nicole tried to have a turn holding it'.[14] Rumours again surfaced in 2020 when the two women were reported as being at loggerheads over Nicole Kidman's adaptation *9 Perfect Strangers* (Hulu, 2021) which was 'apparently the catalyst tearing these women apart'[15] and again when it was reported that the friends had fallen out over *Big Little Lies* season three.[16] The point is not whether Kidman and Witherspoon are friends or not, but the way the media positions them in furious competition, as if it is impossible for women to be anything but rivals.

This is significant to a reading of the television series as, like the press reports about Kidman and Witherspoon, the first episode 'sets up all the cliches of female rivalry, maternal hypercompetitiveness and marital fidelity (or lack thereof) and then sets about investigating and deconstructing them'.[17] If we cast our minds back to the mommy wars that raged in the American press back in the mid-1990s, they certainly seem to have reared their ugly heads again in Monterey, California as Madeline (Reese Witherspoon) tells new arrival Jane Chapman (Shailene Woodley): 'I'm a stay-at-home mom myself so I'm happy to welcome another full-time mom to the ring. You know sometimes I think it's like us against them. You know the career mommies, them and all their various board meetings that are so important … I think they spend more time on those board meetings than they do actually parenting.' Jane's response, that she actually has a part-time job, prompts Madeline to tell her 'So do I. But it doesn't really count. The over and under in this town is actually about one hundred and fifty thousand dollars, I work in community theatre, twenty hours a week so, I'm definitely an under.' Within the first seven minutes of the series, the battle-lines are drawn and, as *Vulture*'s Hillary Kelly tells us: 'In no time at all, *Big Little Lies* will make you squirm with discomfort and schadenfreude as you watch beautiful, complicated women build each other up and rip each other to shreds. Rejoice, for the Mommy Wars are back!'[18]

Of course, it is not only the mommy wars that are the focus of *Big Little Lies* as, underneath the outwardly privileged lives of the women, lurks the murky undercurrent of Jane Chapman's rape and the domestic abuse taking place in the outwardly perfect marriage of uber mom Celeste Wright (Nicole Kidman) and her good-looking husband, Perry (Alexander Skarsgård), whose violence against his wife is explosive and often leads to sado-masochistic 'make-up' sex between them. For the *Guardian*'s Lucy Mangan, 'its portrait of domestic violence … is masterly',[19] a tour-de-force performance from Nicole Kidman that not only won her a sheaf of awards but, quite rightly, brought attention to the fact that spousal abuse can impact anyone – even rich and powerful couples.[20] Moriarty tells us that she drew inspiration from real life for Celeste and Perry's story from a woman 'who reverted to a childhood instinct of hiding under her bed when she saw her elderly abusive father repeat the violent behaviour toward her mother that he had exhibited while she was growing up'.[21] She also reveals that Perry is based on 'a really horrible ex-boyfriend ... who I took great pleasure in killing off'.[22] Also revealed in the moments before the final episode's fateful push is that Jane's rapist is Perry and that the assault took place while he was married to Celeste ('You Get What You Need', 1:7).

Despite the positive reviews received by *Big Little Lies* in its first season, there were rumblings about the way the series had dealt with race. Its source novel, originally set in Australia, had been completely devoid of racial diversity, so the fact that bi-racial lead Bonnie Carlson (Zoë Kravitz) was included in the adaptation was certainly a step in the right direction. By making Bonnie, Nathan Carlson's (played by James Tupper) new wife, a mixed-race woman, the creators must have thought that the racial diversity box, missing from the source novel, had been ticked. What a pity that Bonnie's portrayal, as a benign, make-up free, Alpaca-cardigan wearing yoga teacher, was less well developed than the other leads. For many this decision smacked of rote casting or tokenism, after all, what other way to read a character who exists only to pour oil on troubled waters and is largely excluded from the community of white privileged women? What are we to make of the fact that Bonnie's race is never mentioned? Should we understand her portrayal as a good example of 'how black people, black women especially, have to exist in predominantly white spaces' or, could it be, because 'the writers themselves were unable or unwilling to deal with race?'[23] This all makes the decision to have Bonnie run out of the crowd to push Perry to his death puzzling and totally out of character.

It is in season two that the trouble really started for *Big Little Lies*. Clearly the grumblings about race were taken seriously by producers and, yet, the inclusion of more black characters did nothing to alleviate criticisms. True, a more racially diverse cast including second-grade teacher Michael Perkins (Mo McRae), Celeste's lawyer, Katie Richmond (Poorma Jagannathan) and Detective Adrienne Quinlan (Merrin Dungey) did assuage the whiteness of the cast but, lacking backstories, the characters do nothing to lessen the way 'the show approaches ethnicity in a post-racial, color-is-not-an-issue way'.[24] But, this is not even the biggest issue at stake in *Big Little Lies*' racial casting. The biggest problem is the inclusion of Bonnie's mother, Elizabeth Howard (Crystal Fox), who is invited by her son-in-law, Nathan, in his attempt to '[g]et to the bottom of what is bothering Bonnie' ('Tell-Tale Hearts', 2:2).

We have seen how, when a source story is exhausted, writers of adaptations often make wrong turns, but the decision to switch Bonnie's abusive parent from her father to her mother is more than a little puzzling. The book tells us that Bonnie has been victim and witness to her father's abuse, which gives her motivation for the sudden, and unexpected, attack on Perry at the end of season one. This also chimes in with Moriarty's explanations of the domestic abuse storyline. What makes no sense, however, is the substitution of an abusive white father with an abusive black mother. Unless, of course, there is a desire to stir up some of the angry black woman tropes that continue to circulate in a racially troubled society. Add to this Elizabeth's psychic abilities and the way she leaves voodoo totems in her daughter's bedroom, and she has turned into a textbook racialized stereotype to which no series should ever give airtime, particularly in a country where race 'remains one of the country's most heated and divisive issues'.[25] For *Atlantic* writer, Sophie Gilbert, the idea to make Bonnie's mother the abusive parent was 'a fascinating one. Far more women I know were damaged by the mothers than their fathers, and *Big Little Lies*' steps in this direction broadened its exploration of the harm that children can suffer'.[26] There is much to disagree with here, particularly Gilbert's colourblind assessment of Elizabeth. In a series that has already failed the only lead black character, to then blame her mother for everything that has gone wrong in her life is misguided at best and looks like a deliberate attack on older mothers whether black or white ('The Bad Mother', 2:6).

If season one focused on male violence, season two deals with its aftermath and, in a series desperately working against closure, the inclusion of yet another older mother, Mary Louise Wright (Meryl Streep), is a bitter pill to swallow. Grieving her son's death, Mary Louse's investigation into what really happened to Perry is the driving force behind the second season and, yet again, we are treated to an example of the older woman so spitefully described in Philip Wylie's *Generation of Vipers*. Like Livia Soprano before her, Mary Louise is a bitter woman who views everyone with distrust. She uses the same double-register as Ruth Fisher but, unlike Ruth, wields her barbs knowingly, regularly and with spite. Mary Louise's avowed intent is to get to the bottom of what happened to her son who, in her eyes at least, is a saint. Again, for Gilbert, who seems totally unaware of the venom behind these portrayals of older women, '[i]n Streep's hands, Mary Louise was the most subversive of female characters: an elderly woman with opinions'.[27] Yet, in television terms at least, Mary Louise is not the first elderly woman to be narratively punished for holding opinions and, sadly, it seems like she won't be the last.

Mary Louise wreaks havoc on the women in Monterey as her passive aggressivity is honed to perfection. Remarking on how short Madeline is, she adds, 'I don't mean it in a negative way. Maybe I do. I find little people to be untrustworthy' ('What Have They Done', 2:1). Later, when Madeline meets Mary Louise at the realtor, she confronts the older woman. Mary Louise agrees that Madeline did not deserve her rudeness and tells her that she reminds her of her best friend from boarding school who 'was just an itty bitty thing with a big bubby personality to hide that she was utterly bad inside. ... I suppose I punish you for that'. The backhanded apology is a reminder that Mary Louise is anything but sorry and is single-minded in her mission to uncover who killed her son. For Shirley Li, Mary Louise 'embraces her role as the grieving mother and dutiful grandmother – and she uses it as a Trojan horse for her villainy'. Li continues, 'underneath that soft-spoken demeanor is a woman capable of exploiting the insecurities and underlying guilt of the women her son knew. It's an insidious form of cruelty packaged inside a well-meaning, maternal façade'.[28] But why do we need to have yet another older harridan on our television screens?

It is not just the older mother that is so badly served in this second season of *Big Little Lies* as the breakdown of Renata Klein's (played by Laura Dern) marriage to Gordon (Jeffrey Nordling) reveals a narrative hostility towards the working mother. The only career woman in the group, season one saw her and Madeline at loggerheads, only coming together because of the death of Perry, and in season two her husband loses all of their money through securities fraud ('Tell-Tale Hearts', 2:2). Renata's reaction to Gordon's arrest by the FBI precipitates a character assassination that is not restricted to her pitiful husband but she is narratively annihilated as, learning her husband has lost their money, she visits him in jail and angrily spits at him: 'I will not not be rich.' Gordon is portrayed as an uncaring, foolhardy and childish man and Renata's invective is only a shadow of what is to come over the course of the season as she totally loses control at the overwhelming terror of being poor. Treating every man within her radius with searing sarcasm and contempt, as a portrait of a woman breaking down, Laura Dern gives an outstanding performance. Renata is clearly motivated by the terror of coming from a poor childhood but is it a coincidence that the sole career woman in *Big Little Lies* is so unsympathetically drawn?

It is, of course, Mary Louise that gives voice to what Renata fears all the other mothers are saying about her. At this point Mary Louise has victim-blamed both Celeste and Jane, tried to get custody of her grandsons, given evidence that her daughter-in-law is an unfit mother and, in keeping with the 'bad' mother of the soap opera, is one of the most unlikeable characters in the series. On the way to the final day in court, she bumps into Renata in a coffee shop. By this time the bankruptcy court has revealed that Gordon and Renata's nanny is suing them for $160,000 for the special 'services' she has provided for Gordon. Renata is at breaking point. She gives the barista short shrift and Mary Louise's barbed comment about Celeste refusing a nanny for being 'more trouble than they are worth' causes Renata to explode, telling her: 'This is exactly what you did the last time you were at my house. Stay-at-home moms who make me feel that I should be locked up for neglect because I have a fucking career? I have spent every day of my goddamn life putting my family and my child first. So don't go there judgy judger' ('I Want to Know', 2:7). This is not the end of Renata's revenge, however, as, later, she discovers Gordon playing with his train set. His cocksure demeanour as he tells her that having sold it for $410,000, the new owner has allowed him to keep it and, now the nanny is gone, 'I need something to play with' sends Renata into a blind rage and, grabbing a baseball bat, she destroys the only property left from their marriage, screaming 'maybe you should have showed a woman a bit of respect. No more bullshit. No more lies', before storming out of the house.

Big Little Lies concludes with the women joining together again as, differences aside, they support Bonnie into the police station. It is not only Renata that refuses to live with lies. And yet, the narrative rewards the women that toe the line. Madeline and Ed have renewed their vows, Celeste has retained custody of the twins and Jane has overcome the trauma of her rape and, in a relationship with work colleague Corey Brockfield (Douglas Smith), has the first consensual sex of her young life. On the other hand, some women are not so lucky: Bonnie's mother Elizabeth dies, Mary Louise is revealed, in court, to be an unfit mother herself, Bonnie leaves Nathan and surrenders herself to the police, and Renata, penniless and alone, has to confront her own past and rebuild her life after bankruptcy.

The conclusion and narrative punishment for the women of *Big Little Lies* is compounded by media stories surrounding season two director, Andrea Arnold, OBE. As if to undermine the 'connotations of freedom and authorial control'[29] afforded by the employment of independent filmmakers, Arnold, known best for Cannes Jury Prize winning films *Fish Tank* (2009) and *American Honey* (2016) was brought on to direct *Big Little Lies* while Jean-Marc Vallée directed HBO's *Sharp Objects* (2017).[30] Media reports tell how she was the perfect choice for the series, with sources describing how the dailies were filled with 'Arnold's trademark restless camera searching for grace notes – those gestures, movements, and poetic frames of natural light that added another layer to what is not being said'.[31] It seems that Arnold was initially given free rein with the series, Kidman and Witherspoon loved working with her, and she had been told that they wanted 'an Andrea Arnold version of the show and all that entailed'.[32] If there seems to be a choppy, not-so-feminist take on the second season, complete with the puzzling insertion of a parade of men that Celeste is supposed to have had one-night-stands with, it may be explained by the fact that in late 2018 'creative control was handed over to executive producer and season one director Jean-Marc Vallée',[33] who re-edited the series and did his best to unify the look of season two with his style from season one.

Of course, it is impossible to know the truth at the bottom of these rumours. Nicole Kidman and Reese Witherspoon, themselves at the heart of a number of stories, denied that creative control was taken away from Arnold and she is still credited as director on all seven episodes of season two. According to Casey Bloys, HBO's president of programming, 'We're indebted to Andrea. But as anybody who works in TV knows, a director does not have final creative control',[34] adding that 'it is not unusual in television for an executive producer like Vallée to come on board and "hone" episodes' and that 'director's cuts of television episodes are rarely what end up being released'.[35] This idea, that an executive producer and erstwhile director (male) and screenwriter (also male) and the (mainly male) executives at HBO have ultimate power over the finished product, should answer the question of whether we can view contemporary women's television as feminist. Even the joint powerhouse of Reese Witherspoon, Nicole Kidman and Andrea Arnold are subsumed under the men behind the scenes and, rather depressingly, as Bloys tells us, for 'anyone who understands television and how it works, this is business as usual'.[36]

Notes

1 Martha Lauzen, 'Boxed In: Women On Screen and Behind the Scenes on Broadcast and Streaming Television in 2020–21', 2021, https://tinyurl.com/4f2brdjz (accessed 27 April 2023).
2 Lauzen, 'Boxed In, 2020–21', p. 2.
3 *Ibid.*
4 Lauzen, 'Boxed In, 2020–21', p. 6.
5 Claire Perkins and Michele Schreiber, 'Independent Women: From Film to Television', *Feminist Media Studies*, 19:7 (2019): 919.
6 Perkins and Schreiber, 'Independent Women', 920.
7 *Ibid.*
8 *Ibid.*
9 Hello Sunshine (Witherspoon) and Blossom Films (Kidman).
10 Perkins and Schreiber, 'Independent Women', 920.
11 Ann Snitow, 'Thinking About *The Mermaid and the Minotaur*', *Feminist Studies*, 4:2 (1978): 190.
12 Polydor, 2016.
13 In total, the series received nineteen major nominations in 2018, winning thirteen awards including Golden Globes, Screen Actors Guild and Empire Awards, among others. Anon, 'Big Little Lies', *Los Angeles Times*, https://tinyurl.com/bdh3f726 (accessed 9 June 2020).
14 Patricia Smails, 'Nicole and Reese: They Can't Stand Each Other', *New Idea*, 7 December 2017, https://tinyurl.com/32fy7mfj (accessed 9 June 2022).
15 Brianna Morton, 'Nicole Kidman, Reese Witherspoon Friendship Ending Over "9 Perfect Strangers"?', *Gossip Cop*, 28 July 2020, https://tinyurl.com/yck6tzh3 (accessed 9 June 2022).

16 Griffin Matis, 'Report: Nicole Kidman, Reese Witherspoon Feuding Over Season 3 of "Big Little Lies"', *GossipCop*, 17 February 2021, https://tinyurl.com/2p9dynmd (accessed 9 June 2022).
17 Lucy Mangan, '*Big Little Lies*: Kidman and Witherspoon Shine in Masterly Twist on *Desperate Housewives*', *Guardian*, 17 February 2017, https://tinyurl.com/5n984e36 (accessed 9 June 2022).
18 Hillary Kelly, '*Big Little Lies* Season-Premiere Recap: Murder, Mean Girls, and Monterey', *Vulture*, 19 February 2017, https://tinyurl.com/2p86cuz8 (accessed 9 June 2022).
19 Mangan, '*Big Little Lies*'.
20 2017 Emmy, Gold Derby Award, Online Film & Television Association, 2018 Screen Actors Guild Award, UK Empire Award, GALECA Award, Golden Globe, Satellite Award, and Broadcast Film Critics Association Award for Best Actress.
21 Mahita Gajanan, '*Big Little Lies* Author Liane Moriarty on Why Her Story is Universal', *Time*, 17 February 2017, https://tinyurl.com/4whwdfbs (accessed 9 June 2022).
22 Antonia Blyth, 'Liane Moriarty Reveals the Horrifying True Story Behind *Big Little Lies*', *Elle*, 18 September 2017, https://tinyurl.com/bdfs94ne (accessed 9 June 2022).
23 Zeba Blay, 'Bonnie and the Brilliant Racial Tension of "Big Little Lies"', *Huffpost*, 6 April 2017, https://tinyurl.com/2p9x73xv (accessed 9 June 2022).
24 Reshmi Hebbar, 'The HBO Hit has Expanded its Cast, but it's Struggling to Diversify its Stories', *Slate.com*, 11 July 2019, https://tinyurl.com/2zdca9pt (accessed 9 June 2022).
25 Greg Braxton, 'Commentary: "Big Little Lies" is Less White this Season. That Doesn't Mean it's Smart about Race', *Los Angeles Times*, 16 June 2019, https://tinyurl.com/36xxmthd (accessed 9 June 2022).
26 Sophie Gilbert, 'In Defense of *Big Little Lies*' Second Season: Could any Show Meet the Expectations that the HBO Series Set?', *The Atlantic*, 22 July 2019, https://tinyurl.com/mtnwe2pb (accessed 9 June 2022).
27 *Ibid*.
28 Shirley Li, 'Why Meryl Streep's Sly Matriarch Works So Well on *Big Little Lies*', *The Atlantic*, 11 June 2019, https://tinyurl.com/m5fty87w (accessed 9 June 2022).
29 Perkins and Schreiber, 'Independent Women', 920.
30 Another series featuring a monstrous mother.
31 Chris O'Falt, '"Big Little Lies" Season 2 Turmoil: Inside Andrea Arnold's Loss of Creative Control', *IndieWire*, 12 July 2019, https://tinyurl.com/k2ened93 (accessed 9 June 2022).

32 *Ibid.*
33 *Ibid.*
34 Quoted in Zack Sharf, 'HBO's Casey Bloys: Andrea Arnold Was "Never Promised" Creative Control on "Big Little Lies" Season 2', *IndieWire*, 24 July 2019, https://tinyurl.com/4eevbycx (accessed 9 June 2022).
35 *Ibid.*
36 *Ibid.*

Conclusion

As I argued in the introduction to this book, the study of mothers and their portrayal on American television is a woefully neglected area. Informed by cultural studies and feminist theory, I hope that my work has gone partway towards addressing that issue. As we endure the legacy of a Trumpian presidency with the continued attack on reproductive and abortion rights, a pandemic that has seen more mothers than ever losing their jobs, the impact of the war in Ukraine and climate change, it is clear that motherhood has never been regarded so poorly in society. In order to contextualize this claim, the first chapter offered an historical overview of the positioning of women and mothers within patriarchal society. Looking back to the eighteenth century, I argued that the positioning of mothers can be traced back to pre-industrial revolution when men's labour moved into cities and mothers were confined to the home – forever tied to their biology. This chapter looked at how this biological determinism has led to maternal inequalities in the modern workplace before turning to gendered employment within the television industry. Taking my lead from feminist theory, particularly the work of Nancy Fraser, I argued that a study of representation needs to take all of this into account in order to understand society's treatment of mothers.

The next two chapters worked through a history of mothers on network television since the late 1940s. This was a very broad sweep and my aim was to contextualize a version of motherhood familiar to anyone who grew up watching network television (whether on British or American screens). Chapter 2 looked at the idealized and ever-smiling mother at the heart of the home and argued that this version of motherhood only ever existed in the hearts and minds of television executives and overlooked how many mothers actually worked outside the home. Nevertheless, this version of mothering was held as an ideal against which mothers are still judged. Chapter 3 brought the television mom up to date, finishing with an extended look at one of the most popular sitcoms of all time, *Friends*, with its references to a wide variety of extraordinary mothers that are rare on network television.

Chapter 4 moved on to look at one of the most famous and well-loved sitcoms from the late 1990s. HBO's *Sex and the City* was mired in discussions about its feminist credentials from the start: Were 'our girls' feminist or not? Did their love of shoes, sex and shopping betray a distinctly anti-feminist conservative agenda? While everyone was obsessed with the four single Manhattanites' designer clothes, lifestyles and their attempts to have sex like men, a much more revolutionary agenda passed most people by. Miranda Hobbes' surprise pregnancy revealed many of the truths behind the myths of motherhood that continue to be peddled to this day. As I argued in this chapter, one of the most remarkable things about Miranda's pregnancy storyline is how few commented on its revolutionary potential. This chapter concluded with an analysis of the mother in both films as well as a discussion of the revival *And Just Like That ...*

Moving onto the drama series that made HBO its name, the radical potential of Miranda's mothering in *Sex and the City* is instantly overshadowed by the first of many 'bad' mothers that would become a feature of many of the series that followed. In Chapter 5 I argued that *The Sopranos*' Livia is a damning portrayal of the older mother. Ostensibly based on David Chase's own mother, she was not only represented as a bitter and vindictive woman but is blamed for her son's anxiety attacks as well as the attempt on his life. What stands out is that the possible damage inflicted on Tony by his father's line of work is glossed over by Tony and everyone else. In their rush to condemn the ageing matriarch of the Soprano family, most critical commentators overlooked the way Tony's therapist, Dr Melfi, was instrumental in judging Livia. Symptomatic of a woman with no societal role, Livia Soprano serves as a timely warning of negative attitudes towards mothers once their childbearing and childrearing years are over.

Chapters 5, 6 and 7, having previously been published, all allowed me to re-visit the mothers at the centre of those narratives.

Six Feet Under was the least commercially successful of these as coming hot on the heels of *Sex and the City* and *The Sopranos*, a series about a funeral home was always going to be an awkward fit. Eager to dismiss Ruth, media commentators pushed her into the same mould as Livia Soprano, unfairly comparing to *The Sopranos'* matriarch. While Ruth is not the most popular HBO character, she is one of the most poignant, as her journey towards subjectivity is one that faces all mothers. Whether chosen, or forced, stay-at-home or go to work, the mothering role is one with a time span that often abandons women to a lonely fate once their children have left home. Ruth's narrative, as I argued in this chapter, is a timely reminder of what awaits all mothers once their children have fled the nest.

Chapter 6's *Deadwood* gave us a portrait of motherhood unlike any other. Re-visiting this character some sixteen years later, I found myself still shocked at the sexual violence of the scene I wrote about so long ago. Al Swearengen's tale of his mother's abandonment is overtly sexualized – receiving fellatio from an unnamed prostitute while recounting the tale of his maternal abandonment was, for me, a clear projection of male Oedipal issues. In addition, I argued that this scene showed how the mother is held to blame for the subsequent mistreatment of women. It also allowed an in-depth investigation into creative poetic license as I looked into the veracity of the historical Swearengen's tale, his upbringing and why David Milch was compelled to change his narrative in this way.

Deadwood also served as an ideal introduction to the next series, Chapter 7's *The Killing*. The adaptation market is a rich area to consider as, unlike originals, differing cultural attitudes towards motherhood can be discerned in the adaptation of stories. Chapter 7 was another re-working of an article that had been published in the past but, this time, I could focus on the way the television market had adapted to the rise of streaming channels. Re-making *Forbrydelsen* as *The Killing* is a useful case in point as Denmark and the Nordic countries support working mothers with generous family leave and subsidized childcare whereas American mothers receive no such help. My analysis of this series focuses on the hostility towards mothers that choose to work outside the home and how the climactic scene (in more ways than one) reveals a violent misogyny towards mothers that fail to live up to culturally sanctioned expectations.

Conclusion

The adaptation of George R. R. Martin's books to *Game of Thrones* rescued HBO from a series of setbacks, launched it into the streaming wars and turned out to be one of its most successful series to date. There were many column inches devoted to the show, how it was adapted, how historical it was and how it exposed gender relations within the fantasy world. While the ageing of the characters, the sexualization of the torture scenes and the addition of the rape of Daenerys, Sansa and Cersei was openly discussed, the way the mothers were treated was largely ignored. By looking at the differences in the source novels and the television series this chapter argued that Luce Irigaray's theory of the commodification of women in a patriarchal society is particularly revealing when it is applied to HBO's adaptation. By stripping the mothers of their agency I argued that this was a good example of the power of the mother on television and how she is so threatening that her representation has to be weakened.

Chapter 10 looked to another non-HBO adaptation, this time Hulu's *The Handmaid's Tale*, arguing that the channel optioned this series as a way of breaking into an already saturated streaming landscape. Reading the show through the theories of Dorothy Dinnerstein, I argued that the series shows how damaged both men and women are by patriarchal parenting. Dinnerstein's warnings that asymmetrical parenting roles and the fetishization of technology will lead to the eventual breakdown of nature sadly seem to be coming true. Gilead is held up as a dire warning of a world where the depletion of natural resources has led to a decrease in fertility and, as a result, women have lost all of their freedoms. In this chapter, I suggested that the series is as critical of modern America as it is of the fictional Gilead and that we are quite possibly headed towards the natural disasters warned of in Atwood's book.

I was really looking forward to writing the final chapter. *Big Little Lies* would, I naïvely thought, prove how women behind the scenes could produce a female-friendly television series. I, and so many of my female friends, enjoyed *Big Little Lies* on first viewing but, on re-viewing the series, I was bitterly disappointed. This final chapter returned us to the mommy wars of the 1990s, but, if *Sex and the City* revealed the truth of working motherhood, *Big Little Lies* focused on competitive mothering in a regressive step that did the representation of mothers few favours. In addition, even in a series created by women and centered on motherhood, career and older mothers continue to be vilified. On the surface *Big Little Lies* promised to be female-friendly, but the series is mired in the same hostility towards older mothers that we saw in *The Sopranos*. This time, however, there is an additional layer of racialized stereotyping. Along with other feminist television academics, I had hoped that evidence of women working behind the scenes would lead to a more 'feminist television'. Of course, this could not be true as, whether we like it or not, the television industry remains dominated by white, middle-class men. Even as we can hope for a better future, it is going to take more than Reese Witherspoon and Nicole Kidman to give us a sympathetic treatment of motherhood on television.

Unfortunately, the only real conclusion I can come to after a decade of research is that there exists a deep cultural antipathy towards motherhood. Through an application of (mainly) feminist psychoanalytic theory, the mothers I have discussed in these pages are fairly representative of the way motherhood is regarded more widely. Either idealized or demonized, mothers rarely find subjectivity past their basic biological function. In addition, for cable and streaming channels especially, the debasement of motherhood and women is regularly used as a way of breaking into a cluttered telvision universe. As much as society depends upon women to have children, it fails to support them and yet we depend upon mothers to replenish the next generation. While bearing this burden of regeneration, women still get pushed into mommy-track jobs, are demonized for not living up to society's standards, suffer a lifelong motherhood penalty and, once their childbearing years are over, are pushed to one side. With this in mind, I cannot help but wonder (said, of course, in my best Carrie-like voice), why on earth would anyone volunteer for this job?

In answer to this, and in order to lighten the mood, I am going to conclude this book with some reference to some of the more positive representations of mothers that have been on our screens recently. *Mare of Easttown* (HBO, 2021) proved to me that men can create excellent maternal characters if they just put their minds to it. Thank goodness for Brad Inglesby, Kate Winslet and Jean Smart who all showed us a genuine side of mothering rarely seen on American television. It wasn't just *Mare of Easttown* that has given me joy. *Lovecraft Country* (HBO, 2020) was a wonderful example of how just a few tweaks to casting and emphasis could result in a much more female-friendly adaptation. Misha Green's adaptation, juxtaposing male characters with females, resulted in a series in which generations of women were guardians of the Book of Names, instead of the men of the novel. In a powerful episode set in the Tulsa Riots ('Rewind 1921', 1:9) not only was a hidden history brought to life but the celebration of maternal power was embedded right in the heart of the episode. *Lovecraft Country* features a woman, a mother no less, who refuses to feel guilty for following her heart's desire and it is her daughter who delivers the final crushing blow that releases the family from evil. Showrunner Misha Green's adaptation ensured the spirit of female power imbued the narrative of this series from the start.[1]

Of course, the sitcom was prominent in my viewing over the past pandemic years. The breakaway (and unexpected) success of Canadian series, *Schitt's Creek* (CBC, 2015–20), starred Catherine O'Hara as the indomitable Moira. A mother like no other who truly broke the mould of 'bad mothers' by showing that you don't have to be selfless and domesticated in order to love and be loved by your family. In many ways Moira paved the way for Jean Smart's Deborah Vance in HBO's *Hacks* (2021–). A sharp-tongued comedienne who, once again, proves that mother and daughter relationships do not have to cloy, are often acerbic, and yet despite the barbs, like Dorothy (Bea Arthur) and Sophia (Estelle Getty) in *The Golden Girls* (NBC, 1985–92), can be loving and forgiving.

The biggest lesson to learn is that we should never take representation for granted as it is linked, for better or worse, to our economic and political positioning. Nothing that we watch is 'just' television, as characters are created by and for people that have been influenced by past television series and exist within a culture with its own ideological tropes. As American television is traded across the globe, it is foolhardy not to look at these globally popular series as part of the ideological mesh of carriers that create meaning, especially if we are to understand how a small but 'powerfully dominant, ruling class'[2] maintains power over us.

The fact that reproduction reduces wages, career prospects and, inevitably, pension benefits does not only impact women. The series that I have discussed show how mothering practices impact everyone, male, female, young and old, and it is to the benefit of everyone that mothers are treated equally. The inevitable conclusion that I have come to is that, if women are to eventually achieve equality with men, society needs to first address the inequalities associated with mothering. As the great Ruth Bader Ginsburg once said: 'Women will have achieved true equality when men share with them the responsibility of bringing up the next generation.'[3] You can be sure that our future depends upon it.

Notes

1 *Watchmen* (HBO, 2019) embeds the Tulsa Riots right into the heart of its series from the opening scene of the pilot.
2 Stuart Hall, 'Culture, the Media, and the "Ideological Effect"', in Stuart Hall and David Morley (eds), *Essential Essays, Volume 1* (Durham, NC: Duke University Press, 2019), p. 318.
3 Lynn Sherr, 'A Conversation with Justice Ruth Bader Ginsburg', *The Record*, 56:1 (2001): 18.

Select bibliography

Adalian, Joseph, 'How *Game of Thrones* Helped HBO Break Into the Streaming World', *Vulture*, 16 May 2019.

Addison, Heather, Mary Kate Goodwin-Kelly and Elaine Roth, *Motherhood Misconceived, Representing the Maternal in US Films* (New York: New York State University Press, 2009).

Agger, Gunhild, 'Nordic Noir on Television: *The Killing I-III*', *Cinema & Cie*, 12:19 (2012): 39–50.

Ahlgrim, Callie, 'Making Daenerys a "Mad Queen" on "Game of Thrones" is the Culmination of Every Demeaning Sexist Trope Over the Show's 8 Seasons', *Insider*, 15 May 2019.

Akass, Kim, 'Mother Knows Best: Ruth and Representations of Mothering in *Six Feet Under*', in Kim Akass and Janet McCabe (eds), *Reading Six Feet Under: TV to Die For* (London: I.B. Tauris, 2005), pp. 110–20.

Akass, Kim, 'You Motherfucker: Al Swearengen's Oedipal Dilemma', in David Lavery (ed.), *Reading Deadwood: A Western to Swear By* (London: I.B. Tauris, 2006), pp. 23–32.

Akass, Kim, 'The Show that Refused to Die: The Rise and Fall of AMC's *The Killing*', *Continuum: Journal of Media and Cultural Studies*, 29:5 (2015): 743–54.

Akass, Kim and Janet McCabe, 'Beyond the Bada Bing! Negotiating Female Narrative Authority in *The Sopranos*', in David Lavery (ed.), *This Thing of Ours: Investigating the Sopranos* (New York: Columbia University Press; London: Wallflower Press, 2002), pp. 146–61.

Akass, Kim and Janet McCabe (eds), *Reading Sex and the City* (London: I.B. Tauris, 2004).

Akass, Kim and Janet McCabe, '"Blabbermouth Cunts"; or Speaking in Tongues: Narrative Crises for Women in *The Sopranos*', in David Lavery, Douglas L. Howard and Paul Levinson (eds), *The Essential Sopranos Reader* (Lexington: The University Press of Kentucky, 2011), pp. 93–104.

Alakeson, Vidhya, 'The Price of Motherhood: Women and Part-time Work', *The Resolution Foundation*, 9 February 2012.
Allen, Leigh, 'Filming the *I Love Lucy* Show', *American Cinematographer*, 1 April 2020.
Ang, Ian, *Watching Dallas: Soap Opera and the Melodramatic Imagination* (London: Routledge, 1985).
Anon, 'Dan Quayle vs Murphy Brown: The Vice-President Takes on a TV Character Over Family Walues', *Time*, 1 June 1992.
Anon, *Hello!* 758, 1 April 2003, p. 82.
Anon, 'CSI Show "Most Popular in World" ', *BBC News*, 31 July 2006.
Anon, 'UK Gender Pay Gap Widens After Childbirth, Study Finds', *Irish Times*, 23 August 2016.
Anon, 'Women Showrunners Who Are Breaking the Glass Ceiling', *WMC News & Features*, 24 September 2020.
Anon, 'Al Swearengen', *The Black Hills Visitor Magazine*, n.d.
Anon, 'Big Little Lies', *Los Angeles Times*, n.d.
Armstrong, Mark, 'First Look: The News in Brief, July 11, 2002', *eonline*, 11 July 2002.
Atwood, Margaret, *The Handmaid's Tale* (New York: Houghton Mifflin Harcourt, 1986).
Ausiello, Michael, '*The Killing* on Netflix: Longer Episodes and F-Bombs Galore', *TVLine*, 4 July 2014.
Bakare, Lanre, 'Emmys 2017: The Handmaids Tale Makes History on Politically Charged Night', *Guardian*, 18 September 2017.
Barker, Martin, Clarissa Smith and Feona Attwood (eds), *Watching Game of Thrones: How Audiences Engage with Dark Television* (Manchester: Manchester University Press, 2021).
Barker-Benfield, G. J., *The Horrors of the Half-Known Life: Male Attitudes toward Women and Sexuality in Nineteenth-Century America* (New York and London: Routledge, 2000).
Barreca, Regina, 'Why I Like the Women in *The Sopranos* Even Though I'm Supposed Not To', in Regina Barreca (ed.), *A Sitdown with The Sopranos: Watching Italian American Culture on T.V.'s Most Talked-About Series* (London: Palgrave Macmillan, 2002), pp. 27–46.
Beauvoir, Simone de, *The Second Sex* (London: Vintage Books, 2011).
Belkin, Lisa, 'The Opt-Out Revolution', *New York Times Magazine*, 26 October 2003.
Bellafante, Ginia, 'A Fantasy World of Strange Feuding Kingdoms', *New York Times*, 14 April 2011.
Berman, Judy, '*The Handmaid's Tale* Could Be So Much Better. But First It Has to Leave Its Star Behind', *Time*, 27 June 2019.
Blay, Zeba, 'How Feminist TV Became the New Normal', *HuffPost US*, 18 June 2015.

Blay, Zeba, 'Bonnie and the Brilliant Racial Tension of "Big Little Lies"', *Huffpost*, 6 April 2017.
Blyth, Antonia, 'Liane Moriarty Reveals the Horrifying True Story Behind *Big Little Lies*', *Elle*, 18 September 2017.
Bodroghkozy, Aniko, '"Is This What You Mean by Color TV?": Race, Gender, and Contested Meanings in *Julia*', in Joanne Morreale (ed.), *Critiquing the Sitcom: A Reader* (Syracuse: Syracuse University Press, 2002) pp. 129–49.
Borlotti, Gary R. and Linda Hutcheon, 'On the Origin of Adaptations: Rethinking Fidelity Discourse and "Success" – Biologically', *New Literary History*, 38:3 (2007): 443–58.
Boulous Walker, Michelle, *Philosophy and the Maternal Body: Reading Silence* (London and New York: Routledge, 1998).
Bradford Wilcox, W., 'The Evolution of Divorce', *National Affairs*, 51 (2009).
Branigan, Tania, 'Friends and Buffy Slayed in Parents' Hate-list', *Guardian*, 24 August 2002.
Braxton, Greg, 'Commentary: "Big Little Lies" is Less White this Season. That Doesn't Mean it's Smart About Race', *Los Angeles Times*, 16 June 2019.
Bridge, Gavin, 'Netflix Released More Originals in 2019 than the Entire TV Industry did in 2005: 371 Series, Movies Represents Over 50% Increase in Streaming Service's Content Volume vs. 2018', *Variety*, 17 December 2019.
Brubaker, Ed, 'The Killing: Comparing the Danish Show to the American Show', *birthmoviesdeath.com*, 21 June 2011.
Brunsdon, Charlotte, *Screen Tastes: Soap Opera to Satellite Dishes* (London: Routledge, 1997).
Brunsdon, Charlotte, *The Feminist, the Housewife and the Soap Opera* (Oxford: Clarendon Press, 2000).
Brunsdon, Charlotte, Julie D'Acci and Lynn Spigel, 'Introduction', in Charlotte Brunsdon, Julie D'Acci and Lynn Spigel (eds), *Feminist Television Criticism: A Reader* (Oxford: Clarendon Press, 1997), pp. 1–16.
Bryant, Miranda, 'Maternity Leave: US Policy is Worst on List of the World's Richest Countries', *Guardian*, 27 January 2020.
Bukszpan, Daniel, 'America's Most Destructive Riots of All Time', *cnbc.com*, 13 September 2013.
Bursztynsky, Jessica and Sarah Alessandrini, 'Netflix Closes Down 35% Wiping More than $50 Billion Off Market Cap', *cnbc.com*, 20 April 2022.
Bushnell, Candace, *Sex and the City* (New York: Warner Trade Books, 1996).

Canfield, David, 'The Handmaid's Tale Recap: Can This Show Get Any Darker?', *ew.com*, 20 June 2018.
Capretto, Lisa, '"The Cosby Show" and Race: Phylicia Rashad Weighs In On Sitcom's Portrayal of a Black Family', *Huffpost*, 9 July 2013.
Carter, Bill, 'HBO's Rivals Say It Has Stumbled, Though Catching Up Is Tough', *New York Times*, 23 August 2007.
Cavendish, Lucy, 'Motherhood: Stay-at-Home or Back-to-Work? The Battle Continues', *Observer*, 28 March 2010.
Ceder, Jill, 'Childcare Costs', *verywellfamily.com*, 22 June 2020.
Chaney, Jen, 'The Handmaid's Tale Wraps Up a Good But Frustrating Season', *Vulture*, 11 July 2018.
Chaney, Jen, 'In The Handmaid's Tale Season 3, Gilead's Still Gonna Gilead', *Vulture*, 4 June 2019.
Chodorow, Nancy, *The Reproduction of Mothering: Psychoanalysis and the Sociology of Gender* (Berkeley, Los Angeles and London: University of California Press, 1978).
Conley, Christine, Working Title Films, personal communication, 25 November 2014.
Coontz, Stephanie, *The Way We Never Were: American Families and the Nostalgia Trap* (New York: HarperCollins/Basic Books, 1992).
Coontz, Stephanie, 'What "Killed" the Institution of Marriage? L-O-V-E', *History News Network*, 5 January 2005.
Correll, Shelley J., Stephen Benard and In Paik, 'Getting a Job: Is There a Motherhood Penalty?', *American Journal of Sociology*, 112:5 (2007): 1297–339.
Del Rosario, Alexandra and Mellie Andreeva, '"And Just Like That …" Delivers HBO Max's Strongest Series Debut; "The Sex Lives of College Girls" Peaks in Viewers with Finale', *Deadline*, 10 December 2021, https://tinyurl.com/5dvjzhnt (accessed 2 June 2022).
Dickler, Jessica, 'First Time Moms See a 30% Drop in Pay. For Dads, There's a Bump Up,' *cnbc.com*, 30 April 2019.
Dinnerstein, Dorothy, *The Mermaid and the Minotaur: Sexual Arrangements and Human Malaise* (New York: Harper & Row, 2021).
Doane, Mary Ann, *The Desire to Desire: The Woman's Film of the 1940s* (Bloomington: Indiana University Press, 1987).
Dominiczak, Peter, 'Nigel Farage: Mothers are Worth Less to Finance Firms than Men', *Telegraph*, 20 January 2014.
Douglas, Susan J. and Meredith W. Michaels, *The Mommy Myth: The Idealization of Motherhood and How It Has Undermined Women* (New York: Free Press, 2005).
Dow, Bonnie J., *Prime-Time Feminism: Television, Media Culture, and the Women's Movement Since 1970* (Philadelphia: University of Pennsylvania Press, 1996).

Select bibliography

Dunleavy, Trisha, 'Transnational Television, High-End Drama, and the Case of Denmark's *Forbrydelsen*', *Semantic Scholar*, 2014.

Eidsvåg, Marta, '"Maiden, Mother, and Crone": Motherhood in the World of Ice and Fire', in Anne Gjelsvik and Rikke Schubart (eds), *Women of Ice and Fire: Gender, Game of Thrones and Multiple Media Engagements* (London: Bloomsbury Academic, 2016), pp. 151–70.

Ellmann, Nora and Jocelyn Frye, 'Efforts to Combat Pregnancy Discrimination', *Center for American Progress*, 2 November 2018.

European Union report, 'European Platform for Investing in Children', *European Commission*, December 2021, https://tinyurl.com/5k8tx53b (accessed 27 April 2023).

Faludi, Susan, *Backlash: The Undeclared War Against Women* (London: Chatto & Windus/Vintage, 1992).

Farber, Stephen, 'Sex and the City 2: Film Review', *Hollywood Reporter*, 14 October 2010.

Federal Communications Commission (FCC), 'The Telecommunications Act of 1996', para. 1.

Feuer, Jane, Paul Kerr and Tise Vahimagi (eds), *MTM Quality Television* (London: BFI, 1985).

Feuer, Jane, *Seeing Through the Eighties: Television and Reaganism* (London: bfi publishing/NC: Durham: Duke University Press, 1995).

Flax, Jane, 'Reentering the Labyrinth: Revisiting Dorothy Dinnerstein's *The Mermaid and the Minotaur*', *Signs: Journal of Women in Culture and Society*, 27:4 (2002): 1037–57.

Flint, Joe, '"Sex and the City" Finale Scores Series' Highest Ratings Ever', *Wall Street Journal*, 25 February 2004.

Fox, Emily Jane, 'Hulu's Streaming Service is No Longer Free', *Vanity Fair*, 8 August 2016.

Fraser, Nancy, *Fortunes of Feminism: From State-Managed Capitalism to Neoliberal Crisis* (London and New York: Verso, 2015).

Friedan, Betty, *The Feminine Mystique* (New York: W.W. Norton, 1963).

Gajanan, Mahita, '*Big Little Lies* Author Liane Moriarty on Why Her Story is Universal', *Time*, 17 February 2017.

Gallagher, James, 'Fertility Rate: "Jaw-dropping" Global Crash in Children Being Born', *BBC.com*, 15 July 2020.

Genzlinger, Neil, 'They Just Can't Wait to Be King', *New York Times*, 29 March 2012.

Geraghty, Christine, *Women and Soap Opera: A Study of Prime Time Soaps* (Cambridge: Polity Press, 1991).

Gilbert, Sophie, 'The Visceral, Woman-Centric Horror of *The Handmaid's Tale*', *Atlantic*, 25 April 2017.

Gilbert, Sophie, 'In Defense of *Big Little Lies* Second Season: Could Any Show Meet the Expectations that the HBO Series Set?', *Atlantic*, 22 July 2019.

Gilman, Sander L., 'Images in Psychiatry: Karen Horney, M.D., 1885–1952', *American Journal of Psychiatry*, 158:8 (August 2001), https://tinyurl.com/553ryued (accessed 27 April 2023).

Gjelsvik, Anne, 'Unspeakable Acts of (Sexual) Terror As/In Quality Television', in Anne Gjelsvik and Rikke Schubart (eds), *Women of Ice and Fire: Gender, Game of Thrones and Multiple Media Engagements* (New York: Bloomsbury, 2016), pp. 57–78.

Gjelsvik, Anne and Rikke Schubart (eds), *Women of Ice and Fire: Gender, Game of Thrones and Multiple Media Engagements* (New York: Bloomsbury, 2016).

Grimes, Christopher and Harriet Clarfelt, 'Netflix Shares Fall Almost 40% After Subscribers Warning', *Financial Times*, 20 April 2022.

Grose, Jessica, 'America's Mothers are in Crisis: Is Anyone Listening to Them?', *New York Times*, 4 February 2021.

Haglund, David, 'Reagans's Favorite Sitcom', *Slate*, 2 March 2007.

Hale, Mike, 'The Danes do Murder Differently', *New York Times*, 28 March 2012.

Hall, Stuart, 'Culture, Media, and the "Ideological Effect"', in Stuart Hall and David Morley (eds), *Essential Essays, Volume 1* (Durham, NC: Duke University Press, 2019), pp. 298–336.

Hamad, Ruby, *White Tears, Brown Scars* (New York: Catapult, 2020).

Hammad, Hannah, 'The One with the Feminist Critique: Revisiting Millennial Postfeminism with Friends', *Television & New Media*, 19:8 (2018): 692–707.

Hark, Ina Rae, *Deadwood* (Detroit: Wayne State University Press, 2012).

Havens, Timothy, '"The biggest show in the world": Race and the Global Popularity of *The Cosby Show*', *Media Culture & Society*, 22 (2000): 371–91.

Hebbar, Reshmi, 'The HBO Hit has Expanded its Cast, but it's Struggling to Diversify its Stories', *Slate.com*, 11 July 2019.

Hendershot, Heather, '*The Handmaid's Tale* as Ustopian Allegory: "Stars and Stripes Forever, Baby"', *Film Quarterly*, 72:1 (2018): 13–25.

Hersey Nickel, Eleanor, '"I'm the Worst Mother Ever": Motherhood, Comedy and the Challenges of Bearing and Raising Children in "Friends"', *Studies in Popular Culture*, 35:1 (2012): 25–45.

Hill, Libby, 'Meet the Women Who Brought the Misogynist World of "The Handmaid's Tale" to Life', *Los Angeles Times*, 3 May 2017.

Hinsliff, Gaby, 'I Had It All, But I Didn't Have a Life', *Observer*, 1 November 2009.

Hobson, Dorothy, *Crossroads: The Drama of a Soap Opera* (London: Methuen, 1982).

Hobson, Dorothy, *Soap Opera* (London: Wiley, 2003).

Hodson, Heather, 'The Sex and the City Girls are Back in Town', *Daily Telegraph*, 17 May 2008.
Holden, Stephen, 'Sympathetic Brutes in a Pop Masterpiece', *New York Times*, 6 June 1999.
Holloway, Daniel, 'Number of Scripted TV Shows Declines in 2020, FX Says', *Variety*, 29 January 2021, https://tinyurl.com/25bmkr59 (accessed 27 May 2022).
Horney, Karen, *Feminine Psychology* (New York: W.W. Norton & Company, 1993).
Horney, Karen, *New Ways in Psychoanalysis* (New York: W.W. Norton & Company, 2000).
Horney, Karen, *The Neurotic Personality of Our Time* (London and New York: Routledge, 2014).
Howard, Douglas L., '"Soprano-Speak": Language and Silence in HBO's *The Sopranos*', in David Lavery (ed.), *This Thing of Ours: Investigating The Sopranos* (New York: Columbia University Press; London: Wallflower Press, 2002), pp. 195–202.
Irigaray, Luce, *This Sex Which is Not One (Ce Sexe qui n'en est pas un)* (Ithaca, NY: Cornell University Press, 1981).
Jacobs, Jason, 'Violence and Therapy in *The Sopranos*', in Michael Hammond and Lucy Mazdon (eds), *The Contemporary Television Series* (Edinburgh: Edinburgh University Press, 2005), pp. 139–58.
Jacoby, Henry (ed.), *Game of Thrones and Philosophy: Logic Cuts Deeper Than Swords* (Hoboken: John Wiley & Sons Inc., 2012).
James, Caryn, 'TV Weekend: "Sopranos": Blood, Bullets and Proust', *New York Times*, 2 March 2001.
Jaramillo, Deborah, 'AMC: Stumbling Towards a New Television Canon', *Television & New Media*, 14:2 (2012): 167–83.
Johnson, Catherine, 'Tele-branding in TVIII: The Network as Brand and the Programme as Brand', *New Review of Film and Television Studies*, 5:1 (2007): 5–24.
Johnson, Miriam M., 'Women's Mothering and Male Misogyny', in Andrea O'Reilly (ed.), *Maternal Theory: Essential Readings* (Ontario: Demeter Press, 2007), pp. 201–23.
Johnson, Ted, 'Risks and Rewards', *Variety*, 25–31 August 2003.
Kaplan, E. Ann, *Motherhood and Representation: The Mother in Popular Culture and Melodrama* (London and New York: Routledge, 2002).
Keller, Joel, '"The Killing" Goes Out as One of the Most Baffling Shows Ever Made', *IndieWire*, 16 September 2014.
Kelly, Hillary, '*Big Little Lies* Season-Premiere Recap: Murder, Mean Girls, and Monterey', *Vulture*, 19 February 2017.

Kelly, Hillary, '*The Handmaid's Tale* Recap: Brief Encounter', *Vulture*, 20 June 2018.
Kinser, Amber E., *Motherhood and Feminism* (Cypress: Seal Press, 2010).
Kitroeff, Natalie and Jessica Silver-Greenberg, 'Pregnancy Discrimination Is Rampant Inside America's Biggest Companies', *New York Times*, 8 February 2019.
Kleiman, Dena, 'Many Young Women Now Say They'd Pick Family Over Career', *New York Times*, 28 December 1980.
Knox, Simone and Kai Hanno Schwind, *Friends: A Reading of the Sitcom* (New York: Palgrave Macmillan, 2019).
Kohnen, Melanie, ' "This was just a melodramatic crapfest": American TV Critics' Reception of *The Killing*', *Journal of Popular Television*, 1:2 (2013): 267–72.
Kristeva, Julia, *Powers of Horror: An Essay on Abjection*, translated by Leon S. Roudiez (New York: Columbia University Press, 1982).
Lauzen, Martha, 'Boxed In: Women On Screen and Behind the Scenes in Television in 2019–20', 2020, https://tinyurl.com/5n7c2eac (accessed 20 April 2022).
Lauzen, Martha, 'Boxed In: Women On Screen and Behind the Scenes on Broadcast and Streaming Television in 2020–21', 2021, https://tinyurl.com/4f2brdjz (accessed 27 April 2023).
Lawson, Mark, 'Mark Lawson Talks to David Chase', in Janet McCabe and Kim Akass (eds), *Quality TV: Contemporary American Television and Beyond* (London: I.B. Tauris, 2007), pp. 185–220.
Lesser, Wendy, 'Here Lies Hollywood: Falling for *Six Feet Under*', *New York Times*, 22 July 2001.
Levine, Elana, *Her Stories: Daytime Soap Opera and US Television History* (Durham, NC: Duke University Press, 2020).
Li, Shirley, 'Why Meryl Streep's Sly Matriarch Works So Well on *Big Little Lies*', *Atlantic*, 11 June 2019.
Liedl, Janice, 'Rocking Cradles and Hatching Dragons: Parents in *Game of Thrones*', in Brian A. Pavlac (ed.), *Game of Thrones versus History: Written in Blood* (London: John Wiley & Sons, 2017), pp. 125–36.
Littleton, Cynthia, 'FX Networks Chief John Landgraf: "There Is Simply Too Much Television" ', *Variety*, 7 August 2015.
Longmire, Becca, 'Handmaid's Tale Author Margaret Atwood Insists Everything in the Book "Happened in Real Life" ', *ETCanada*, 11 July 2018.
Lowder, James (ed.), *Beyond the Wall: Exploring George R.R. Martin's A Song of Ice and Fire* (Dallas: Benbella Books, 2012).

Select bibliography

Lull, James, *Media, Communication, Culture: A Global Approach* (Columbia: Columbia University Press, 1995).

Lyons, Margaret, '"The Handmaid's Tale" Season 2 is Brutal and Not Much Else', *The New York Times*, 11 July 2018.

Magid, Ron, 'Family Plots', *American Cinematographer*, 83:11 (2002): 70–9.

Malanga, Steven, 'Our Vanishing Ultimate Resource', *City Journal*, 20:1 (2010), https://tinyurl.com/rhctefs5 (accessed 10 June 2022).

Mangan, Lucy, '*Big Little Lies*: Kidman and Witherspoon Shine in Masterly Twist on *Desperate Housewives*', *Guardian*, 17 February 2017.

Mares, Nicole M., 'Writing the Rules of Their Own Game: Medieval Female Agency and *Game of Thrones*', in Brian A. Pavlac (ed.), *Game of Thrones versus History: Written in Blood* (Hoboken: John Wiley & Sons, 2017), pp. 147–60.

Matis, Griffin, 'Report: Nicole Kidman, Reese Witherspoon Feuding Over Season 3 of "Big Little Lies"', *GossipCop*, 17 February 2021.

Mazziota, Julie, 'Breastfeeding in Public is FINALLY Legal in All 50 States', *People*, 25 July 2018.

McCabe, Janet and Kim Akass, 'Feminist Television Criticism: Notes and Queries', *Critical Studies in Television*, 1:1 (2006): 108–20.

McCann, Carly and Donald Tomaskovic-Devey, 'Pregnancy Discrimination at Work: An Analysis of Pregnancy Discrimination Charges Filed with the US Equal Employment Opportunity Commission', 26 May 2021, https://tinyurl.com/yrm7vc4m (accessed 28 April 2023).

McCarroll, Christina, 'A "Family" Sitcom for Gen X: "Friends" Cast a New TV Mold', *Christian Science Monitor*, 6 May 2004.

Millea, Holly, 'Oh Baby!', *Elle*, September 2002, p. 338.

Mink, Eric, '6 Feet Stiffs Viewers', *Daily News* (New York), 1 June 2001, p. 112.

Modleski, Tania, 'The Search for Tomorrow in Today's Soap Operas', *Film Quarterly*, 33:1 (1979): 13–21.

Morreale, Joanne (ed.), 'Introduction', in *Critiquing the Sitcom: A Reader* (Syracuse: Syracuse University Press, 2002), pp. xi–xix.

Morris, Chris, 'Netflix Will Spend Over $17 Billion on Content in 2020: Analyst', *Fortune*, 16 January 2020.

Morton, Brianna, 'Nicole Kidman, Reese Witherspoon Friendship Ending Over "9 Perfect Strangers"?', *Gossip Cop*, 28 July 2020.

Mulvey, Laura, *Visual and Other Pleasures* (London and New York: Palgrave Macmillan, 1989).

National Partnership for Women and Families, Fact Sheet, 'America's Women and the Wage Gap', March 2021.

Nussbaum, Martha, '"The Aristocrats": The Graphic Arts of "Game of Thrones"', *The New Yorker*, 30 April 2021.

O'Falt, Chris, '"Big Little Lies" Season 2 Turmoil: Inside Andrea Arnold's Loss of Creative Control', *IndieWire*, 12 July 2019.

O'Hagan, Andrew, 'Sex and the City 2 is Ugly on the Inside', *London Evening Standard*, 28 May 2010.

O'Reilly, Andrea, *Feminist Mothering* (New York: State University of New York Press, 2008).

Otterson, Joe, '487 Scripted Series Aired in 2017, FX Chief John Landgraf Says', *Variety*, 5 January 2018.

Parker, Claire, 'Japan Records its Largest Natural Population Decline as Births Fall', *Washington Post*, 3 June 2022, https://tinyurl.com/yp22we6t (accessed 10 June 2022).

Pattie, David, '"Whatever Happened to Stop and Smell the Roses?": *The Sopranos* as Anti-therapeutic Narrative', in David Lavery, Douglas L. Howard and Paul Levinson (eds), *The Essential Sopranos Reader* (Lexington: The University Press of Kentucky, 2011), pp. 166–79.

Pavlac, Brian A. (ed.), *Game of Thrones Versus History: Written in Blood* (Somerset: John Wiley & Sons, 2017).

Peers, Ellie, 'Introduction', in Alexis Kreager with Stephen Follows, *Gender Inequality and Screenwriters: A Study of the Impact of Gender on Equality of Opportunity for Screenwriters and Key Creatives in the UK Film and Television Industries*, May 2018, https://tinyurl.com/4z6makxb (accessed 28 April 2023).

Pell, Roxie, 'Friends Reunion Nearly Matches Wonder Woman 1984 Views on HBO Max', *ScreenRant*, 29 May 2021.

Perkins, Claire and Michele Schreiber, 'Independent Women: From Film to Television', *Feminist Media Studies*, 19:7 (2019): 919–27.

Peskowitz, Miriam, *The Truth Behind the Mommy Wars: Who Decides What Makes a Good Mother?* (New York: Seal Press, 2005).

Peyser, Thomas, 'Father-On Dude', *Style Weekly*, 6 June 2007, https://tinyurl.com/36xecx2z (accessed 10 June 2022).

Pinedo, Isabel, '*The Killing*: The Gender Politics of the Nordic Noir Crime Drama and its American Remake', *Television and New Media*, 22:3 (2019): 299–316.

Porter, Rick, 'TV Long View: Five Years of Network Ratings Declines in Context', *Hollywood Reporter*, 21 September 2019.

Prange, Stephanie, 'Study: Nearly 80% of US Households Subscribe to Netflix, Amazon Prime and/or Hulu', *mediaplaynews.com*, 28 August 2020.

Press, Andrea, *Women Watching Television: Class, Gender, and Generation in the American Television Experience* (Philadelphia: University of Philadelphia Press, 1991).

Press, Andrea, 'Gender and Family in Television's Golden Age and Beyond', *Annals of the American Academy of Political and Social Science* (September 2009): 139–50.

Psaski, Jen, 'Fact Sheet: The American Families Plan', The White House, 27 April 2021, https://tinyurl.com/2p8b94bh (accessed 8 June 2022).

Quayle, Dan, 'Address to the Commonwealth Club of California', 19 May 1992.

Ramachandran, Shalini and Deepa Seetharaman, 'Hulu Bids Goodbye to Its Free Service', *Wall Street Journal*, 8 August 2016.

Raven, Charlotte, 'All Men are Bastards. Discuss', *Guardian*, 9 February 1999.

Read, Simon, 'Pregnant Women to Get More Job Protection', *BBC News*, 24 January 2019.

Reeves, Jimmie L., Mark C. Rogers and Michael M. Epstein, 'Quality Control: *The Daily Show*, the Peabody and Brand Discipline', in Janet McCabe and Kim Akass (eds), *Quality TV: Contemporary American Television and Beyond* (London: I.B. Tauris, 2007), pp. 79–97.

Rich, Adrienne, *Of Woman Born: Motherhood as Experience and Institution* (New York, London: W.W. Norton & Company, 1986).

Robinson, James, 'BskyB Buys Complete HBO Catalogue', *Guardian*, 29 July 2010.

Rogers, Mark C., Michael M. Epstein and Jimmie L. Reeves, '*The Sopranos* as HBO Brand Equity: The Art of Commerce in the Age of Digital Reproduction', in David Lavery (ed.), *This Thing of Ours: Investigating The Sopranos* (New York: Columbia University Press; London: Wallflower Press, 2002), pp. 42–59.

Romanchick, Shane, 'Here's Why You Can't Keep Up With TV Anymore: 550 Original Series Aired in 2021', *collider.com*, 15 January 2022.

Rosenthal, Phil, 'Let Them Blow Your Mind', *Chicago Sunday Times*, 28 February 2002.

Rosett, Claudia, 'TV: Much More Than a Mob Story', *Wall Street Journal*, 28 January 2002.

Rousseau, Jean-Jacques, *Emile* (Las Vegas: IAP, 2009).

Rowe, Kathleen, *The Unruly Woman: Gender and the Genres of Laughter* (Austin: University of Texas Press, 1995).

Rozsa, Matthew, 'How Plastics Are Making Us Infertile – and Can Even Lead to Human Extinction', *Salon.com*, 4 April 2021.

Sandhu, Sukhdev, 'Sex and the City 2, a Review', *Telegraph*, 28 May 2010.

Sayeau, Ashley, 'As Seen on TV: Women's Rights and Quality Television', in Janet McCabe and Kim Akass (eds), *Quality TV: Contemporary American Television and Beyond* (London: I.B. Tauris, 2007), pp. 52–61.

Schubert, Rikke and Anne Gjelsvik (eds), 'Introduction', in *Women of Ice and Fire: Gender, 'Game of Thrones' and Multiple Media Engagements* (London: Bloomsbury Academic, 2016) pp. 1–16.

Scott, Joan W., 'Experience', in Judith Butler and Joan W. Scott (eds), *Feminists Theorize the Political* (New York: Routledge, 1992), pp. 22–40.

Seiter, Ellen and Gabriele Kreutzner, 'Resisting the Place of the "Ideal Mother"', in E. Seiter, H. Borchers, G. Kreutzner and E. Warth (eds), *Remote Control: Television, Audiences, and Cultural Power* (Abingdon: Taylor & Francis Group, 2013), pp. 237–47.

Setoodeh, Ramin, 'Criticism of "Sex and the City" is Mostly Sexist', *Newsweek*, 2 June 2008.

Shane, Charlotte, 'Mommy Issues: Reconsidering *The Mermaid and the Minotaur*', *Dissent*, 65:3 (2018): 93–100.

Shannon Miller, Liz, ' "Sharp Objects": Why Amy Adams Seemed Destined for the Role, and the Writing Choice that Freaked Out Jean-Marc Vallée', *IndieWire*, 9 July 2018.

Sharf, Zack, 'HBO's Casey Bloys: Andrea Arnold Was "Never Promised" Creative Control on "Big Little Lies" Season 2', *IndieWire*, 24 July 2019.

Sherr, Lynn, 'A Conversation with Justice Ruth Bader Ginsburg', *The Record*, 56:1 (2001): 8–21.

Smails, Patricia, 'Nicole and Reese: They Can't Stand Each Other', *New Idea*, 7 December 2021.

Snitow, Ann, 'Thinking About *The Mermaid and the Minotaur*', *Feminist Studies*, 4:2 (1978): 190–8.

Solsman, Joan E., 'Amazon Buys MGM, Setting up Prime Video for James Bond, Rocky to Move in', *cnet*, 28 May 2021.

Southern, Lucinda, 'As Subscriptions Growth Falters, Netflix Turns to International Growth', *Digiday*, 18 July 2018.

Spangler, Todd, ' "Friends", "Grey's Anatomy" Were Most Binge-Watched TV Shows of 2018, Study Finds', *Variety*, 20 December 2018.

Spangler, Todd, 'Netflix Plans to Raise $2 Billion New Debt to Fund Content Spending', *Variety*, 22 October 2018.

Staiger, Janet, 'Serialization and Genre Expectations: The Case of *The Killing*', *Flowtv.org*, 2 July 2012.

Stasi, Linda, 'Esprit de Corpse', *New York Post*, 29 May 2001.

Statista.com, 'Consumer Spending on Digital Home Entertainment in the United States from 2012 to 2020 by Type', https://tinyurl.com/2ajer23z (accessed 28 April 2023).

Sweney, Mark, 'Netflix and Amazon "will overtake UK cinema box office spending by 2020"', *Guardian*, 14 June 2017.
Sweney, Mark, 'AT&T Agrees Deal to Combine WarnerMedia with Discovery', *Guardian*, 17 May 2021.
Thompson, Tracy, 'A War Inside Your Head', *Washington Post*, 15 February 1998.
THR Staff, 'Hollywood's 100 Favorite TV Shows', *Hollywood Reporter*, 16 September 2015.
Tobin, Robert, '*Six Feet Under* and Post-Patriarchal Society', *Film and History*, 32:1 (2002): 87–8.
Travers, Ben, 'The 18 Netflix Original Series to be Excited about in 2018', *IndieWire*, 28 December 2017.
Travers, Ben, '20 HBO Original Programs to be Excited about in 2020 – "The Outsider," "Perry Mason," and More', *Indiewire*, 2 January 2020.
Tucker, Jasmine, 'The Wage Gap Has Robbed Women of Their Ability to Weather CoVid-19', *National Women's Law Center*, March 2021.
TVSA Team, 'Desperate Housewives On SABC3 Confirmed', *TVSA*, 3 April 2007.
Vasquez, Lane, 'The Truth About Bernadette's Voice on "The Big Bang Theory"', *theThings*, 17 May 2021.
Visram, Talib, 'Netflix Spent an Estimated $15 Billion on Original Content in 2019, Ahead of Disney+ and Apple TV+'s Launches', *Fast Company*, 8 November 2019.
Von Doviak, Scott, 'The Sopranos', *CultureVulture*, n.d.
Walker, Joseph S., '"Cunnilingus and Psychiatry Have Brought Us to This": Livia and the Logic of Falsehoods in the First Season of *The Sopranos*', in David Lavery (ed.), *This Thing of Ours: Investigating the Sopranos* (New York: Columbia University Press; London: Wallflower Press, 2002), pp. 109–23.
Warner, Judith, *Perfect Madness: Motherhood in the Age of Anxiety* (New York: Riverhead Books, 2005).
Weaver, Ray, 'A Year on from *The Killing* that Reinvented Noir', *Copenhagen Post*, 18 October 2013.
Webb, Kevin and Mara Leighton, '17 Critically Acclaimed Amazon Prime Video Original Shows to Add to Your Streaming Queue', *Business Insider*, 21 May 2020.
Weiser, Kathy, 'Al Swearengen & the Notorious Gem Theater', *Legends of America*, July 2020.
Weissmann, Elke, 'Provocation II: Not Another Article on the *Wire*: How Hierarchies of Gender Undermine TV Scholarship and Lead to Abuse', *Critical Studies in Television*, 15:4 (2020): 399–408.

West, Lindy, 'Burkas and Bikinis: I Watched 146 Minutes of *Sex and the City 2* and All I Got Was This Religious Fundamentalism', *Stranger*, 27 May 2010.

The White House, 'Fact Sheet: The American Families Plan', 28 April 2021.

The White House, 'Proclamation on National Equal Pay Day', 24 March 2021.

Williams, Joan, *Unbending Gender: Why Work and Family Conflict and What to Do About It* (Oxford: Oxford University Press, 1999).

Wollstonecraft, Mary, *A Vindication of the Rights of Women* (California: CreateSpace Independent Publishing Platform, 2014).

Woodward, Kathryn (ed.), 'Motherhood: Identities, Meanings and Myths', in *Identity and Difference* (London, Thousand Oaks and New Delhi: SAGE, 1997), pp. 239–98.

WSJ Staff, 'Barbara Billingsley, June Cleaver on "Leave It To Beaver", Dies at 94', *Wall Street Journal*, 16 October 2010.

Wylie, Philip, *Generation of Vipers* (Illinois: Dalkey Archive Press, 1996).

Youngs, Ian, 'Friends is the UK's Most Popular Subscription Streaming Show', *BBC.com*, 9 August 2018.

Index

2 *Broke Girls* 50
9 *Perfect Strangers* 156

ABC 34, 51
abortion 39, 62, 110, 130, 144–5, 150, 166
adaptation 10, 11, 118, 119, 120, 123, 127, 129, 130, 141, 143–4, 168, 171
Addams Family, The 34
African American families 40
Ahlgrim, Callie 136
Albrecht, Chris 127
All in the Family 30, 38–9
Amazon 1, 10, 12
AMC 117–18, 120, 128, 144
America xi, 12, 22, 110, 141, 146, 150, 169
American
 Families Plan, The 24
 family 87
 mothers 25, 119
 myth 106
 popular television 10, 40, 166
And Just Like That ... 73, 167
anti-hero 4, 117, 154
Arnold, Andrea 162
AT&T 10
Atwood, Margaret 11, 142, 145–6, 150, 169
Aunt Lydia 146–7, 149

backlash 61
 against feminism 31
 'bad' mother 5, 50, 61, 120–2, 161, 171
Bader Ginsburg, Ruth 172
Ball, Alan 9, 92, 121
Ball, Lucille 32–3, 62
Baratheon, Joffrey 133–4
Barker-Benfield, G. J. 106–7, 110
Barreca, Regina 86
Belkin, Linda 66
Bettina 97–9
Bewitched 34, 51
Biden, President 23–4, 150
Big Bang Theory, The 50
Big Little Lies 12, 154, 169
biological determinism 166
birth 22, 47
Bloys, Casey 162
Boardwalk Empire 128
'Boxed In' 154
Bradshaw, Carrie 59–62, 65, 73, 170
Brady Bunch, The 35
branding 10, 53, 77
Breaking Bad 118, 128
breastfeeding 64, 72, 79, 91
British television 32
broadcast television 26
BSkyB 117
Buffy the Vampire Slayer 51
Bushnell, Candace 60

cable 10, 25, 52–3, 118, 154, 170
Carlson, Bonnie 158, 161–2
Carnivale 127
Cartesian dualism 19
Cassidy, David 36–7
'castrating' mother 51
castration 78
  complex 91
Cattrall, Kim 74
CBS 30, 32, 34–5, 38, 43, 50
celebrity mom 67, 72
Centre for Contemporary Cultural Studies 2
Chapman, Jane 157, 161
Charmed 51
Chase, David 9, 81, 84, 87, 122, 167
Cheers 50
childbirth x–xi, 24, 111, 119
childcare xi, 22–5, 40, 44–6, 65, 69, 118, 168
children xi, 6, 11, 20, 22, 40, 93–4, 134, 137, 150
Cixous, Hélène 131
class 2–3, 6, 21, 35, 37, 40, 46, 60, 170
Clinton, Bill 110
Clinton, Hillary 150
Coontz, Stephanie 8, 32, 46
Cosby Show, The 40
Crabtree, Ane 145
critical
  commentary 127
  community 8, 78, 86
cult of motherhood 71
cultural
  antipathy 170
  hegemony 2
culture wars 46, 111
Curb Your Enthusiasm 128

de Beauvoir, Simone 86
Deadwood 9, 53, 102, 127, 168
demonization of the mother 12
Dern, Laura 155, 160–1
Descartes, René 19–20
Designing Women 43–4
Desilu 32
Desperate Housewives x, 51
Deutsch, Helene 78
Dick Van Dyke Show, The 34, 37
Dinnerstein, Dorothy 141–2, 148, 155, 169
Discovery 10
Disney ix
divorce 35, 37, 45–6, 106
domestic abuse 157
domestication of motherhood 92
Douglas, Susan 31, 61, 65, 67
Dow, Bonnie J. 43
dragons 135
dread of woman 104–5, 108, 109
DuMont 31

Eidsvåg, Marta 130
Emmy 47, 51, 145, 156
Entourage 128
essentialism 21–2

Faludi, Susan 31, 44
family 5–6, 8, 19–23, 33, 35–6, 38, 46, 48, 66
  values 49
Family Ties 39
FBI 84, 160
fellatio 104, 107–9, 111, 168
female employment 23
Feminine Mystique, The 31, 52
feminism 6, 8, 19, 21–2, 50, 59, 61
feminist 2–3, 6–7, 12, 19–21, 26, 30, 34, 36, 39, 43, 46, 70–1, 91, 123, 131, 141, 144–6, 150, 154, 166–7, 170
  psychoanalytic theory 141, 170
fertility xi, 11, 169
Feuer, Jane 3

Index

Fisher, Claire 93–4
Fisher, David 92–6
Fisher, Nate 93–6, 98–9
Fisher, Nathaniel 9, 92, 95, 99
Fisher, Ruth 9, 87, 159, 168
Forbrydelsen 10, 117–18, 120–1, 128, 141, 168
Fox, Crystal 158
Fraser, Nancy 6, 166
Frasier 50
Freud, Sigmund 78–9, 91, 103
Freudian
  psychoanalysis 131
  theory 78, 103
Friedan, Betty 31, 33, 52
Friends 47, 167

Game of Thrones 11, 127, 141, 147, 169
Geena Davis Institute 26
gender 3, 6, 20, 30, 110, 117, 123, 127, 131, 136, 142, 166, 169
  expectations 33
  inequality 25–6, 154
  wage gap 66
Geraghty, Christine 3
Gilbert, Sophie 145, 159
Gilead 11, 141–3, 145–6, 148–50, 169
Gilmore Girls, The 51
Gjelsvik, Anne 136
global television 8
Goldbergs, The 31
golden age of television 1, 127, 154
Golden Girls, The 43, 171
'good' mother 5, 19, 21, 50
Grace Under Fire 46
Green, Misha 171
Guardian 157
Gunderson, Hiram 93–5

Hacks 171
Hall, Stuart 2
handmaid 143, 145–7, 149
Handmaid's Tale, The 11–12, 141, 169
'have-it-all' mother 40
HBO 1, 4, 8, 10–12, 30, 46, 52–3, 59–60, 75, 77–8, 87, 90, 111, 117–18, 122, 127–31, 135, 137, 147, 155, 162, 167–70
  Max 73
heteronormative 142
history 2, 7–9, 19, 26, 30, 77, 106, 109, 127, 129–30, 132, 166, 169, 171
Hobbes, Miranda 59, 167
Holder, Steven 119, 121–2, 124
Home Improvement 46
Homeland 118
homophobia 49
Horney, Karen 131, 137, 142
How I Met Your Mother 50
Howard, Douglas L. 85
Howard, Elizabeth 158, 162
Huffington Post 12
Hulu 11, 141, 143–5, 169

I Love Lucy 30, 32
ideal mother 5–6, 61, 72
idealized
  maternal duty 122
  maternity 97
  motherhood 68, 72, 78, 95
In Treatment 118, 128
industrial revolution 20
inequality xi, 1
infertility 74, 150
interfering mother 12
Irigaray, Luce 131–2, 143, 169

Jean-Jacques Rousseau 2
John from Cincinnatti 127

Johnson, Miriam M. 77
Jones, Samantha 8, 60, 70
Julia 35

Kaplan, E. Ann 93, 99, 130–1
Kate and Allie 43
Kelley, David E. 155
Kidman, Nicole 155–6, 162, 170
Killing, The 10, 115, 127–8, 168
Kinser, Amber E. 19
kitchen 91–2, 94
Klein, Gordon 160–1
Klein, Renata 160–2
Knocked Up x
Kravitz, Zoë 155, 158
Kreutzner, Gabriele 6
Kristeva, Julia 131

Lacan, Jacques 91, 131
Lacanian psychoanalysis 131
Lannister, Cersei 128, 130, 133–5, 137, 169
'Laugh of the Medusa' 95, 98
Lauzen, Martha 154
'Law of the Father, The' 91
Lear, Norman 30, 37
Leave it to Beaver 30
lesbian mothering 48
Li, Shirley 160
Liedl, Janice 129
liminal 100
Linden, Sarah 118–22, 124
Lovecraft Country 171
Luck 128
Lucy Show, The 33
Lund, Sarah 117, 119, 124

Mackenzie, Madeline Martha 157, 160–1
Mad Men x, 118, 128
male executives 123
Mama 31

Mare of Easttown 170
Mares, Nicole M. 129
Martin, George R. R. 11, 128, 130, 135, 141
Marxist 2, 3
    feminist 132
Mary Kay and Johnny 31
masculinity 3–4, 104, 105, 108, 124
maternal xi, 9, 19, 31–2, 60, 87, 96, 122, 127, 131, 157, 160
    abandonment 105–6, 120, 168
    archetypes 130–1
    care ix
    employment 24
    figures ix
    guilt 68, 72, 121
    instinct 19, 21, 62, 72
    neglect 123
    power 171
    rejection 111
    representation 2, 92
    sexuality 130
    shortcomings 123
    wall 2, 22
maternity ix, 2, 21, 23, 49, 118, 155
    benefits 119
    leave 24, 32
    pay 25
    rights 22
Maude 30, 38–9, 62
McCabe, Janet 81, 85
Melfi, Dr Jennifer 9, 77, 80–5, 96, 167
melodrama 119, 122, 124, 129
menopause 70
menstruation 133
MGM 10
Michaels, Meredith 31, 61, 65, 67
middle-aged mother 9, 38, 93, 99
Milch, David 9, 105–7, 127, 168
Miller, Bruce 144

Index

'Mirror Phase' 91
misogynist 11, 22, 38, 69, 108–9, 127–8, 136, 144, 148
misogyny x, 49, 77, 79, 86, 104, 108–9, 122, 168
Modleski, Tania 4–6
Mommy Myth, The 61
'mommy track' 22, 66, 170
'mommy wars' 8, 66, 146, 157, 169
monstrous mother 50, 81, 86
Morano, Reed 144
Moriarty, Liane 155, 157, 159
mother xi, xv, 2, 4–9, 11, 33–5, 38–40, 44, 47–8, 51, 63, 68, 71–2, 79–80, 82, 86–7, 93–4, 96–7, 104–5, 109, 111, 133–5, 142, 148, 159, 166–7
motherhood x–xii, xv, 2, 6–10, 12, 19, 21–2, 26, 35–6, 40, 43, 46, 48–51, 60–1, 63–5, 67–9, 71, 74, 77, 91, 97, 104, 123, 127, 129–32, 137, 141–2, 148, 155, 166, 168, 170
    culture and society 1
    Misconceived, Representing the Maternal in US Films 137
    on network television 30, 43
    penalty 22, 170
    in US films 230
mothering xi, xv, 2, 8–9, 19, 21, 46, 48–9, 68, 72, 91, 97, 99, 117–18, 120, 142, 168, 170, 172
    on television 27
mother-in-law 69, 97
mothers x–xii, 2, 12, 19–20, 22–3, 25, 30, 33, 46–8, 50–2, 65–6, 78–9, 104–5, 123, 132, 137, 150, 155, 166, 168–9
    on television 7, 17, 141

MTM 37
Mulvey, Laura ix, 2, 4, 124, 141
Murphy Brown 45–6, 62
My Mother the Car 34
myths of motherhood 167

Nazi 149
NBC 34–5, 39, 43, 47, 50
neglectful maternity 121
neoliberal xi, 2, 6–7, 67
    job market 22
Netflix 1, 10–11, 47, 49, 117, 120–2, 127–8
network television 7–8, 10, 30, 32, 35, 37, 39–40, 43, 46, 123, 166
new momism 68, 72
New York Times 23, 43, 66, 90, 128, 150
non-traditional families 46
Nordic 12
    Noir 117
Noxon, Marti 12
Nurse Jackie x
nurturing mother 96, 98, 122
Nussbaum, Martha 11, 129, 132

O'Hara, Catherine 171
O'Reilly, Andrea, 49
Oedipal 81, 85, 98, 168
Oedipus complex 78, 80, 104
Offred 12, 143–7, 150
older mother 5, 12, 90, 159–60, 167, 170
'Opt-Out Revolution, The' 66
Orenstein, Peggy 62
Osborne, June 146, 148–9
overbearing mother 51
Oz 52, 60

paedophile 121
pandemic xi, 1, 23, 166, 171

parental
  leave 118
  neglect 122
parenthood 30
Parker, Sarah Jessica 67, 70
Partridge Family, The 36–7
patriarchal xi, 2, 7, 10–12, 19, 21, 71, 77–8, 81, 86, 97, 99, 127, 132, 137, 142, 150
  institution of motherhood 21
  mothering 142
  unconscious ix, 2, 9, 141
patriarchy 6, 19, 91, 95, 132, 136, 142, 148, 166, 169
pay gap 24
Pence, Mike 150
penis 78
Perkins, Claire 154
Peskowitz, Miriam 66–7
phallocentric 131–2
Pinedo, Isabel 123
'Plan, The' 95–6
postfeminist 2, 50, 59, 108–9, 155
post-Freudian 108
  feminist psychoanalytic theory 103
post-menopausal 9, 79, 93
postpartum 67
  depression 52
pregnancy x, 8, 23–4, 31–2, 47–8, 60, 63, 74, 111, 167
  discrimination 23
Pregnancy Discrimination Act 77
primetime
  series 51
  soap x, 3, 5
  television 35
prostitute 102, 104, 106, 111, 133–4, 168
psychoanalysis 77, 81, 91, 94
psychoanalytic theory 2, 141

quality
  American television x, 2, 5–6, 141
  sitcom, 8
  television 4–5, 91, 118
Quayle, Dan 45

race 6, 12, 34, 36, 40, 44, 46, 142, 148, 158–9, 170
rape 11, 131, 133, 135, 147–9, 157, 169
Reagan, Ronald 142, 144
representation x, 2, 7–8, 11, 19, 22, 25, 27, 40, 50, 59, 77–8, 87, 129, 137, 154, 166, 170–1
reproduction 11–12, 137, 144
rhetoric of choice 66
Rich, Adrienne 21, 68, 142
Roe vs *Wade* xi, 12, 39
Rome 127
Roseanne 46
Rousseau, Jean-Jacques 20
Rowe, Kathleen 97

Sabrina, the Teenage Witch 51
Schitt's Creek 171
Schreiber, Michele 154
second wave feminism 36–7, 45, 66
Second World War 31, 78–9
Seiter, Ellen 6
Serena Joy 147, 149
Sex and the City 1, 4, 8, 30, 46, 52, 57, 77, 90, 167–9
Sex and the City 2 69
sexposition 131
sexuality 95, 132
Shane, Charlotte 142
Sharp Objects 162
Sheinfeld, Amram 79
showrunner 4, 11–12, 117, 123, 141, 155

Index

Sibley, George 93, 99
single
    mothers 45, 48, 51
    parent 65, 67, 94
    sitcom x, 7, 30, 34, 36–9, 43, 45–6, 48, 50–1, 59, 171
    mothers 35, 46
Six Feet Under 9, 53, 87, 90, 168
Skarsgård, Alexander 156
Smart, Jean 171
Smith, Ben 143
Snow, Jon 134, 136
soap opera x, 3–7, 51, 87, 94
Song of Ice and Fire, A 127–9
sonogram 62
Soprano
    Carmela x, 80, 82–3
    Livia 9, 90, 159, 167–8
    Tony 8, 77, 80, 82–6, 98, 167
Sopranos, The 8, 52, 90, 168, 170
spectator 4–5
spousal abuse 106
Stansbury, Kyle 121–2, 124
Stark, Catelyn 130, 133
Stark, Sansa 133, 169
stay-at-home mother 69, 72, 74, 96, 157, 161
streaming 1, 10, 25, 73, 141, 143, 155, 168–70
Strecker, Edward A. 79
Streep, Meryl 159
Sud, Veena 11, 122–3
surrogate 48–50, 69, 99
Swearengen, Al 9, 102, 168
Sweringen, Ellis Alfred 106

Tandem/TAT 37
Targaryen, Daenerys 135–6, 169
television x, xii, xv, 1, 3–4, 6, 12, 19, 22, 32, 46, 49, 111, 129, 144, 154, 160, 168–71
    history 7, 32, 40, 47
    industry 8, 11, 25
    mothers 32, 167
terrible mother 8
therapy 84
'Third Golden Age of TV' 4
This Sex Which is Not One (Ce Sexe qui n'est pas un) 132
Time 45, 150
Time Warner 52
Tolliver, Cy 102, 108
traditional family 32, 35
transphobia 49
trend reporting 44
Trump, Donald 110, 144, 146, 150, 166
Turner, Sophie 147
Twin Peaks 119
Tyler Moore, Mary 34, 37, 90
    Show, The 15, 183

Ugly Betty 118, 128
Uncle Junior 80, 82–4, 87
unfit mother 146, 162
unruly woman 97–8

Vallée, Jean-Marc 155–6, 162
vasectomy 39, 69
Vietnam war 35, 94
villainess 5–6, 12, 74, 87
virgin 133

wage gap 24
Walker, Joseph S. 80, 86
Walking Dead, The 197
Wall Street Journal 30
Warner, Judith 31
WarnerMedia 10
Washington 146, 149
WB, The 51
Weeds x
Westeros 129, 132, 135, 137

widow 135
Williams, Joan 66
Witherspoon, Reese 155–6, 162, 170
Wollstonecraft, Mary 21
womanhood 33
womb 11, 133, 135, 137, 143
women's
 equality 36
 rights xi
Woodley, Shailene 155, 157
Woodward, Kathryn 26

working
 mothers 11, 23–4, 45, 74, 124, 150, 168
 women 24
workplace 31
 pregnancy 23
Wright, Celeste 157, 161–2
Wright, Mary Louise 159–62
Wright, Perry 157–9
Wylie, Philip 9, 79, 86, 96, 159

Yorke, Charlotte 61, 69, 71–2, 74

EU authorised representative for GPSR:
Easy Access System Europe, Mustamäe tee 50,
10621 Tallinn, Estonia
gpsr.requests@easproject.com

www.ingramcontent.com/pod-product-compliance
Lightning Source LLC
Chambersburg PA
CBHW051612230426
43668CB00013B/2084